REINFORCEMENT LEARNING
for
CYBER-PHYSICAL SYSTEMS

with Cybersecurity Case Studies

REINFORCEMENT LEARNING for CYBER-PHYSICAL SYSTEMS

with Cybersecurity Case Studies

Chong Li

Meikang Qiu

CRC Press
Taylor & Francis Group
Boca Raton London New York

CRC Press is an imprint of the
Taylor & Francis Group, an **informa** business

CRC Press
Taylor & Francis Group
6000 Broken Sound Parkway NW, Suite 300
Boca Raton, FL 33487-2742

Printed on acid-free paper
Version Date: 20190122

International Standard Book Number-13: 978-1-138-54353-9 (Hardback)

Library of Congress Cataloging-in-Publication Data

Names: Li, Chong, 1985- author. | Qiu, Meikang, author.
Title: Reinforcement learning for cyber-physical systems with cybersecurity
case studies / Chong Li, Meikang Qiu.
Description: Boca Raton, Florida : CRC Press, [2019] | Includes
bibliographical references and index.
Identifiers: LCCN 2018050901| ISBN 9781138543539 (hardback : acid-free
paper) | ISBN 9781351006620 (ebook)
Subjects: LCSH: Reinforcement learning. | Cooperating objects (Computer
systems) | Computer security.
Classification: LCC Q325.6 .L53 2019 | DDC 006.3/1--dc23
LC record available at https://lccn.loc.gov/2018050901

Visit the Taylor & Francis Web site at
http://www.taylorandfrancis.com

and the CRC Press Web site at
http://www.crcpress.com

To our beloved families

Contents

SECTION II **Reinforcement Learning for Cyber-Physical Systems**

CHAPTER 3 ▪ Reinforcement Learning Problems 43

Preface

As an academic discipline founded in 1956, artificial intelligence (AI) has experienced several spurts of research breakthrough, but each time followed by a long winter of stagnation, a.k.a., AI winter. This is because of the constraints of the computing capability, the costly technology of hardware, the lack of research funds, etc. Instead, other technologies including wireless technologies, information technology and integrated circuit (IC) have significantly advanced and become the mainstream during this period. Starting from 2010, however, advanced computing technologies, big data obtained from people's daily activities, and the integration of subfields in AI research, such as machine learning, neural networks, etc., have shifted the mainstream of social wind to AI research and its wide range of applications. For instance, the recent AI Go-player *AlphaGo Zero*, created by Google DeepMind, can achieve superhuman-level performance with zero human input. In other words, the machine started without any knowledge of the game *Go* and then became its own teacher by playing games against itself. The groundbreaking success of AlphaGo indicates that AI could start off as a new-born human baby, learn to grow up by itself, and eventually perform at a superhuman level to help us solve the most challenging tasks that we are facing now and in the future.

The writing of this book was prompted by the recent development in the domains of *reinforcement learning* (RL) and *cyber-physical systems* (CPSs). Inspired by the behavioral psychology, RL is one of the main areas of machine learning. Different from other machine learning algorithms, such as supervised learning and unsupervised learning, the feature of RL is its unique paradigm of learning, i.e., trial-and-error. Combined with the deep neural network, deep RL becomes so powerful that many complicated systems can be automatically managed by AI agents at a superhuman level. On the other hand, CPSs are envisioned to revolutionize our society in the near future. Such examples include the emerging smart buildings, intelligent transportation and electric grids. However, the conventional hand-programming controller in CPSs could neither handle the increasing complexity of the system, nor automatically adapt itself to new situations that it has never encountered before. The problem of how to apply the existing deep RL algorithms or develop new RL algorithms to enable real-time adaptive CPSs remains open. This book aims to establish such a linkage between the two domains by systematically introducing the RL foundations and algorithms, each supported by one or a few state-of-the-art CPS examples to help readers understand the intuition and usefulness of RL techniques. We believe that the enormous number of in-book CPS examples of RL algorithms will be very beneficial for everyone who uses or will use RL tools to resolve real-world problems.

In the book, we provide a systematic account of key ideas and algorithms of RL and deep RL, and a comprehensive introduction to CPS and cybersecurity. The goal is to have our presentation be easily accessible to readers in either the machine learning or CPS discipline, or in other related disciplines. As a result, this book is not a text that is focused on the rigorous mathematics of RL and CPS theories. In addition, this book is not an up-to-date survey of the available RL algorithms (as the literature is vast and rapidly expanding). Instead, only a few typical RL algorithms are chosen for education.

In Part I, we present a high-level introduction to RL, cyber-physical systems and cybersecurity. One chapter is devoted to introducing the RL concept and history. The other chapter is given to introduce the concept and framework of cyber-physical systems and cybersecurity. In Part II, we formally introduce the framework and define the problem of RL, and then provide two categories of solution methods: model-based solutions and model-free solutions. To have the book self-contained, so that readers without prior exposure to RL can easily follow every argument and discussion, we leverage and re-iterate quite a few materials from Sutton and Barto's classic RL book (1998) rather than providing pointers to the pieces of algorithms or discussions throughout their book. In the end, we use one chapter to introduce deep RL, which is an emerging research area and growing extremely fast in recent years. In Part III, we shift our attention to cybersecurity by reviewing the existing cybersecurity technologies and describing the emerging cyber threats, which cannot be directly handled by the traditional cybersecurity methods. Then we present two case studies of using (deep) RL to solve these emerging cybersecurity problems, which are the original work from our graduate students at Columbia University. This part is intended to illustrate how RL knowledge can be applied to formulate and solve CPS-related problems.

The book is meant for graduate students or junior/senior undergraduate students in the fields of science and engineering, including computer science/engineering, electrical engineering, mechanical engineering, applied mathematics, economics, etc. The target readers also include researchers and engineers in the fields related to RL, CPS, and cybersecurity. The only background required of the reader is a basic knowledge of calculus and probability theory.

In some sense we have been developing the material toward this book for quite a while. Over the past year, we have benefited a lot from the feedback of our graduate students and our colleagues at Columbia University. Many of them have significantly contributed to the book/chapters. In particular, many thanks to: Tashrif Billah for Chapter 1, Longfei Qiu, Yi Zhang, and Xiao-Yang Liu for Chapter 2, Andrew Atkinson Stirn for Chapter 3, Tingyu Mao for Chapter 4, Lingyu Zhang for Chapter 5, Chen-yu Yen for Chapter 6, Longfei Qiu and Xiao-Yang Liu for Chapter 7, Mehmet Necip Kurt and Oyetunji Enoch Ogundijo whose research led to Chapter 8, and Xiaotian Hu and Yang Hu whose research contributed to Chapter 9. We also thank Urs Niesen, Jon Krohn, Peng Zhang, Zhendong Wang, and Yueming Liu for their careful review and constructive feedback on the manuscript. Zhendong Wang and Lei Zhang contributed exercises to Chapter 3, 4&5. Some book exercises and examples are taken or modified from university courses (available online), including Stanford CS221 & CS234, Berkeley CS294–129, Carnegie Mellon University 10–701, University College London GI13/4C60, University of Utah CS6300 and University of Washington CSE 573.

Finally, Dr. Chong Li would like to thank his PhD advisor Nicola Elia. Professor Elia's rigorous attitude and approach to scientific research, and particularly his impressive insight in optimal feedback control and information theory have greatly impacted the way of writing this book. In fact, optimal feedback control has been treated as one of the two main threads in RL history. The other thread arises from the psychology of animal learning. This book is a direct consequence of long-term understanding and in-depth research on the feedback control theory and feedback information theory. Professor Meikang Qiu appreciates the research insight and dedication from his research group members, Professor Keke Gai and Mr. Longfei Qiu, on applying RL to

cybersecurity. The emerging areas of AI for CPS and cybersecurity will
fundamentally change the world, humankind, and the universe.

Author Bios

Chong Li is a co-founder of Nakamoto & Turing Labs Inc. He is Chief Architect and Head of Research at Canonchain Network. He is also an adjunct assistant professor at Columbia University. Dr. Li was a staff research engineer in the department of corporate R&D at Qualcomm Technologies. He received a B.E. in Electronic Engineering and Information Science from Harbin Institute of Technology and a Ph.D in Electrical and Computer Engineering from Iowa State University.

Dr. Lis research interests include information theory, machine learning, blockchain, networked control and communications, coding theory, PHY/MAC design for 5G technology and beyond. Dr. Li has published many technical papers in top-ranked journals, including *Proceedings of the IEEE, IEEE Transactions on Information Theory, IEEE Communications Magazine, Automatica,* etc. He has served as session chairs and technical program committees for a number of international conferences. He has also served as reviewer for many prestigious journals and international conferences, including *IEEE Transactions on Information Theory, IEEE Transactions on Wireless Communication, ISIT, CDC, ICC, WCNC, Globecom,* etc. He holds 200+ international and U.S. patents (granted and pending) and received several academic awards including the MediaTek Inc. and Wu Ta You Scholar Award, the Rosenfeld International Scholarship and Iowa State Research Excellent Award. At Qualcomm, Dr. Li significantly contributed to the systems design and the standardization of several emerging key technologies, including LTE-D, LTE-controlled WiFi and 5G. At Columbia University, he has been instructing graduate-level courses, such as reinforcement learning, blockchain technology and convex optimization, and actively conducting research in the related field. Recently, Dr. Li has been driving the research and development of blockchain-based geo-distributed shared computing, and managing the patent-related business at Canonchain.

Meikang Qiu received B.E. and M.E. degrees from Shanghai Jiao Tong University and received a Ph.D. in Computer Science from the University of Texas at Dallas. Currently, he is a faculty member at Columbia University. He is an IEEE Senior member and ACM Senior member. He is the Chair of the IEEE Smart Computing Technical Committee. His research interests include cyber security, big data analysis, cloud computing, smart computing, intelligent data, embedded systems, etc. A lot of novel results have been produced and most of them have already been reported to the research community through high-quality journal and conference papers. He has published four books, 400 peer-reviewed journal and conference papers (including 200+ journal articles, 200+ conference papers, 70+ IEEE/ACM Transactions papers). His paper published in *IEEE Transactions on Computers* about privacy protection for smartphones has been selected as a Highly Cited Paper in 2017. His papers about embedded system security published in the *Journal of Computer and System Science* (Elsevier) have been recognized as Highly Cited Papers in both 2016 and 2017. His paper about data allocation for hybrid memory published in *IEEE Transactions on Computers* has been selected as a hot paper (1 in 1000 papers) in 2017. His paper on tele-health systems has won the IEEE System Journal 2018 Best Paper Award. He also won *ACM Transactions on Design Automation of Electrical Systems* (TODAES) 2011 Best Paper Award. He has won over ten more conference best paper awards in recent years. Currently he is an associate editor of more than ten international journals, including *IEEE Transactions on Computers* and *IEEE Transactions on Cloud Computing*. He has served as leading guest editor for *IEEE Transactions on Dependable and Secure Computing (TDSC), special issue on Social Network Security*. He is the General Chair/Program Chair of a dozen IEEE/ACM international conferences, such as IEEE TrustCom, IEEE BigDataSecurity, IEEE CSCloud, and IEEE HPCC. He won the Navy Summer Faculty Award in 2012 and the Air Force Summer Faculty Award in 2009. His research is supported by US government entities such as the NSF, NSA, Air Force, Navy and companies such as GE, Nokia, TCL, and Cavium.

I

Introduction

Overview of Reinforcement Learning

CONTENTS

"We are not that far away from developing AIs that can function at a human level in the world."

Richard S. Sutton
University of Alberta, Canada

REINFORCEMENT LEARNING refers to learning through interaction and experience. This natural learning process is prevalent among living beings. An animal learns to behave, walk, or even hunt by learning as it interacts with its surrounding environment. This behavioral psychology has inspired a promising area of research in the field of computer science, which is known as *reinforcement learning*

(RL). In this chapter, the reader will be introduced to the realm of reinforcement learning first. Then we will give a couple of widespread reinforcement learning examples. Finally, we will shed light on the development of reinforcement learning algorithms.

1.1 OVERVIEW OF REINFORCEMENT LEARNING

1.1.1 Introduction

The word *reinforcement* reminds us of some sort of incentive (reward) or disincentive (penalty). Incentive is given to an effort for achieving an end goal while disincentive does otherwise. When a child grows up, he develops his personality receiving feedback from his surroundings. If he does something good, e.g., achieves a good grade in an exam, he is admired and that admiration motivates him to continue the success. On the other hand, if a child tends to side talk in class, he is given some kind of punishment that discourages him to repeat that in the future. Thus, a child learns through his activities, reward, and penalty, the right thing to do. In other words, his or her personality is developed through reinforcement.

In the realm of artificial intelligence, reinforcement also has meaning. There is an agent who wants to achieve a goal. Examples include a robot navigating through a mine field without being blown up, automatic adjustment of a stock price for achieving the optimal profit, and of course the autonomous car. The agent is given some reward for making a good move while it is given a penalty for making an adverse move. Through making mistakes, the autonomous agent learns what decision to make given a scenario that will help him achieve a goal. That is why it is called reinforcement learning of an agent.

Reinforcement learning is a process through which an agent learns from its own experience. The agent has some states, actions, and rewards. There is an initial state and a goal for the agent. After it learns through mistakes, given a state, it can make an optimal move that guides it toward the end goal. We note below the main elements of reinforcement learning and Fig. 1.1 demonstrates their relationships pictorially.

1. *State*: State means a particular condition of the space where the reinforcement learning agent is being trained. It can be a box in a board game, an image frame of a video sequence, or the price

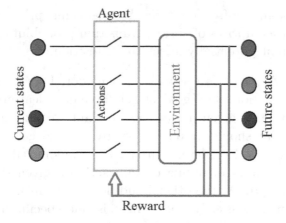

Figure 1.1: A reinforcement learning setting illustrated using electrical circuit components: nodes, switches, and feedback.

of a share in the stock market. In the book, it is always denoted by s for current state and s' for the state immediately after.

2. *Action*: Given a state s, the reinforcement learning agent learns what action a to take. Depending on the action it takes, the current state transitions into a future state s'. After adequate learning, the agent can take an optimal action given a state. For the board game example, actions can be movement in up/down or right/left contiguous boxes.

3. *Reward*: This is the primary element of reinforcement learning that distinguishes the genre of problems from those of machine learning. The notion of reward allows the agent to learn on its own rather than having a supervisor. Every state transition is associated with a reward, either positive or negative, depending on the utility of the action and nature of the problem. In the book, the reward due to the transition from state s to s' after taking action a is denoted by $r(s, a, s')$. It can be the revenue earned when you sell a product, or the storage fee you pay when you fail to sell off a certain quantity of products.

4. *Environment*: A reinforcement learning problem can be model-based or model-free. If it is model-based, then we know the state and reward transition probabilities $p(s', r|s, a)$. On the other hand, if the transition probabilities are not known, then it is

called a model-free reinforcement learning problem. The environment comprises of states, transition probabilities, and factors that might potentially affect the transition.

5. *Policy*: A policy is the agent's behavior. It is a mapping from state to action. The goal of reinforcement learning is to learn a policy, e.g., given a state s, we want to take an optimal action a that should guide us toward the end goal. A policy can be randomized or deterministic. For randomized policies, there is a probability of taking certain action a given the state s denoted $\pi(a|s)$. On the other hand, for deterministic policies (e.g., $\pi(s)$) such as greedy ones, there is one specific action to take given a particular state. There are various algorithms for learning the optimal policy ($\pi^*(s)$ or $\pi^*(a|s)$) specific to model-based or model-free reinforcement learning problems. To name a few, policy iteration, dynamic programming, Q-learning, temporal difference learning, and eligibility traces are some of the well-known methods for finding the optimal policy in a reinforcement learning environment.

6. *Value functions*: In a reinforcement learning problem, each state or state-action pair is associated with a value function that serves as the input argument for finding policy for each state. A value function is the accumulated rewards in a long run. Two kinds of value functions are usually used in reinforcement learning: *state-value function* $V(s)$ and *action-value function* $Q(s, a)$. $V(s)$ is defined as the total amount of rewards an agent will accumulate over the future if starting from that state. Similarly, $Q(s, a)$ is defined as the total amount of rewards an agent will accumulate over the future if starting from that state and taking that particular action.

1.1.2 Comparison with Other Machine Learning Methods

Reinforcement learning is synonymous with self-learning. The reinforcement learning agent does not have a teacher or supervisor, but its environment has the notion of reward. An agent trains itself in the environment exploiting the virtue of positive and negative reward so it can maximize the reward over the long run.

Reinforcement learning is different from the traditional machine

Machine Learning

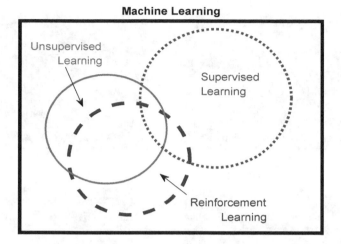

Figure 1.2: Venn diagram describing the relationship among various forms of machine learning.

learning methods; The former has the notion of reward and the latter does not. Traditional machine learning methods include supervised and unsupervised learning. The following are the key points to consider in analyzing their relationship and discrepancies.

1. *Supervised learning:* Input and output data are required. Examples include regression, classification, neural network, etc. These forms of learning occur more in nature than unsupervised ones. Hence, the support of supervised learning in learning is larger than that of unsupervised learning, as shown in Fig. 1.2.

2. *Unsupervised learning:* Only input data is required. Examples include clustering, density estimation, etc. It is a very useful tool in data mining and Knowledge Discovery in Databases (KDD). It is usually used as a data pre-processing tool in supervised learning. Because of this reason, in Fig. 1.2, unsupervised learning has a non-zero support with supervised learning.

3. *Reinforcement learning:* Input data and reward are required. The notion of reward validates the predicted output. In some sense, the reward can also be viewed as output. Thus, *reinforcement learning* is a combination of supervised and unsupervised learning, as shown in Fig. 1.2. Their comparative area of intersection will be justified in later text.

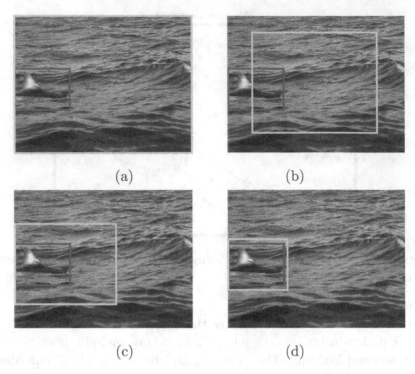

Figure 1.3: Localizing a shark using a reinforcement learning algorithm (high-level description), light gray is the agent, dark gray is the ground truth: (a) initial bounding box; (b) zoom in; (c) shift left; (d) shift left and zoom in. *Image source: Google image.*

In the *reinforcement learning* realm, there is not any knowledgeable supervisor. In its training phase, the agent is not given any clue about the right action. In fact, when the problem is interactive, it is often impractical to obtain examples of desired actions that are both correct and representative of all the situations in the environment where the agent has to act. In an unknown world, where one would expect learning to be most desired, an agent must learn through its own experience. Therefore, the agent learns the right action through a *trial-and-error* approach.

In what follows, we give one example to justify the Venn diagram as shown in Fig. 1.2. Let's say a surveillance camera is facing the sea at Galveston Beach, Texas, which has a high shark sighting rate. We would like to warn the beach goers if there is a shark sighting in the vicinity of the shore and we want to do it autonomously. So, we have to train a reinforcement learning agent by showing him several shark images swimming in the blue Gulf of Mexico. To be more specific, we shall give the ground truth bounding boxes, i.e., *terminal state*, where the shark is located in a video frame, as shown in Fig. 1.3. The agent will take the whole image as the initial bounding box, and then transform the box in a way that it can localize the shark. Hence, in the training, we give the ground truth of bounding box coordinates. The ground truth is minimal supervision. But, we do not tell the agent how it should transform (*actions*) the initial bounding box for detecting the shark in the video frame. The transformation is learned by the agent itself looking at the reward it gets in every transformation, i.e., zooming in/out, shifting left/right, etc. Thus, it is an unsupervised algorithm as well. In summary, since the agent receives nominal supervision, in Fig. 1.2 reinforcement learning has a non-zero intersection with the support of supervised learning. For example, as shown in Fig. 1.3, the ground truth bounding box is given to the reinforcement learning agent for training purposes, i.e., the agent receives nominal supervision. On the other hand, the agent autonomously determines the bounding box deformation—shifting, zooming in/out, etc., exploiting a reward function. Thereby the agent learns bounding box deformation in an unsupervised way. Based on the above discussion, it should be apparent in Fig. 1.2 why reinforcement learning has a larger intersection with unsupervised learning than with supervised learning.

1.1.3   An Example of Reinforcement Learning

Let's consider a robot who wants to navigate through the walls of a maze from a starting position to the terminal position. The positions are defined as *states* in this reinforcement learning problem. In the maze shown in Fig. 1.4 (a), there are 31 states, i.e., boxes. In particular, the starting state is the left yellow box and the terminal state is the right yellow box. The robot can perform four *actions* at each state, i.e., moves toward north (up), south (down), east (right), and west (left) directions. Notably, although the action can be taken, moves leading out of the maze are not permitted. The goal of the robot is to leave the maze or reach the terminal state in the least number of steps. For the nature of reinforcement learning problems, there is always a *reward* associated with each action. Given the goal of the robot is to reach the terminal state in the least number of steps, we assign a reward of -1

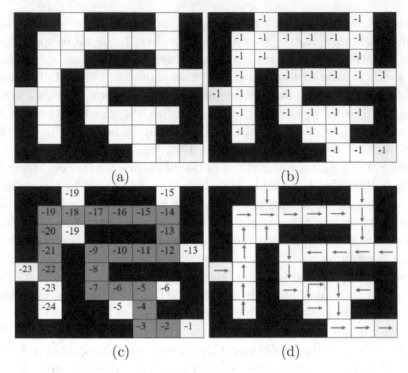

Figure 1.4: Solving a maze using reinforcement learning algorithm: (a) maze map: light gray boxes denote the initial and terminal states, and white boxes denote the maze; (b) reward assigned for each movement at each position; (c) the optimal value of each state, optimal path shown in dark gray; (d) the optimal move (arrow) at each position.

for every move it makes. The rationale behind the choice of negative reward value will become apparent as we walk through the explanation.

Under the above setup, the robot aims to find the optimal *policy* in order to achieve the maximum total or accumulated reward in the long run. We denote this accumulated reward of state s as $v(s)$, i.e., the total received rewards when the robot reaches the terminal state if starting from state s. The policy here refers to the strategy of action selection at each state. In other words, the robot wants to learn the best move for each of the boxes (or states) in the maze that will guide it toward the exit in the least number of steps. Given the state value $v(s)$ of neighboring states, the best action the robot should take is to move to the neighboring state with the highest value, implying that the robot will earn the largest total rewards in the long run. This strategy is widely known as "greedy policy." Next, we need to find the values of the neighboring states for each state such that the greedy policy may apply. Given the transition reward "-1," one can infer that the following relationship between the state (the robot staying at) and its neighboring states is true if using greedy policy,

$$v(s) = -1 + \max_a \sum_{s'} p(s_{t+1} = s' | s_t = s, a_t = a) v(s'), \qquad (1.1)$$

where $p(s_{k+1} = s' | s_t = s, a_t = a)$ represents the probability of visiting the neighboring state s' at time $t + 1$ when the robot stays at s and taking action a at time t. This equation is named the "Bellman optimality equation" which will be introduced in later chapters. Note that in our maze game, this state transition probability is always equal to one or zero for a given action. This implies that the summation over s' can be removed. Then Equation (1.1) is equivalent to the following:

$$v(s) = -1 + \max \Big\{ v(s' = \text{north box}), v(s' = \text{south box}),$$
$$v(s' = \text{east box}), v(s' = \text{west box}) \Big\}, \qquad (1.2)$$

where $v(s' = \text{north box})$ represents the state value of s', the north box to the state s. The key of reinforcement learning algorithms is to solve the above equations for all states. In this example, we have 31 states in total, meaning that we need to solve a system of 31 above equations. However, the max operator in (1.2) implies a nonlinear system, which is always nontrivial to solve analytically or even numerically. In fact, all reinforcement learning algorithms can be treated as algorithms to solve such a system of nonlinear equations. In this example, the solutions $v(s)$ are illustrated in Fig. 1.4(c). For instance, the above equation with the optimal solutions for the initial state using the greedy policy is verified as

$$-23 = -1 + p(s_{t+1} = \text{east box} | s_t = \text{initial state}, a_t = \text{move east}) * (-22),$$

in which the probability is equal to one. Overall, the optimal policy is shown in Fig. 1.4(d), at each position the robot makes a move toward the contiguous neighbor that has the highest state value among the four possible ones.

1.1.4 Applications of Reinforcement Learning

Reinforcement learning has paved the way to autonomy of a number of fields. Examples include industrial robot, autonomous car, share market trading, blackout protection in power sector, and of course gaming agents like *AlphaGo*. In what follows, we highlight a few use cases from the above sectors.

1. *Industrial robot*: In a manufacturing setting, robots are trained with reinforcement learning algorithms. For example, a sheet has to be cut following a curved line [102]. A robot is trained using Q-learning algorithm that can navigate along a curve to cut a metal sheet. Amazon has also started using industrial robots for inventory management.

2. *Autonomous car*: Self-driving car is much researched in the autonomous engineering community. The car can identify the lane lines, regulate its speed based on its surrounding vehicles, change lanes, and most importantly stop at the right signals. While autonomous cars exploit computer vision algorithms for identification and detection, reinforcement learning algorithms are used to regulate its telemetry and trajectory. For instance, the double deep-Q learning algorithm has been used in [205] to control a simulated car.

3. *Share market trading*: Financial giants like Goldman Sachs, JP Morgan Chase, and Morgan Stanley use deep reinforcement learning algorithms to regulate stock prices. A typical problem is when to sell stocks in the market so as to maximize stakeholder's profit. For this real-life challenge, reinforcement learning algorithms can calculate in real time the right price to bid with, and the optimal quantity of shares to present for sale in order to achieve near optimal profit for a given time horizon. For instance, a fusion of the popular Q learning algorithm and dynamic programming has been used in [117] to solve the above problem.

4. *Blackout protection in the power sector*: Blackout refers to a power outage when all generators in a connected grid shut down at the right time. It happens due to a chain of events when power demand peaks abruptly. For the generators to start and run in a power system, a spin-reserve is to be maintained. However, if a simultaneously large amount of power is drained out from different distribution centers around the country, sufficient spin-reserve cannot be maintained. As a consequence, generators shut down one by one and there is no power left in the grid. Such

a blackout is catastrophic because it results in power failure for essential needs such as cellular communication, internet connection, and heat or air conditioning. One such blackout happened in the northeastern region of the United States where 55 million people were affected. Nowadays, a reinforcement learning agent is delegated with the responsibility to monitor millions of distribution points to properly regulate power draining in order to prevent the blackout. A good survey is [49] that reviews recent research considerations in using reinforcement learning to solve electric power system decision and control problems.

5. *Games*: Google DeepMind created an intelligent computer that can beat a professional human player in the *Go* game in 2015. The computer is trained with a reinforcement learning algorithm such that after sufficient training, it can perform at a human level. The reinforcement learning era caught significant attention recently when it was able to beat a human in a game. In March 2016, it beat professional *Go* player Lee Sedol in a five-game match. The detailed methodology used in the intelligent computer *AlphaGo* is given in [150].

6. *Computer vision*: After the development and advancement of deep neural networks, given an image of a cow, car, or baby, the neural network can recognize the object correctly. However, the problem that is not yet adequately addressed is the real-time detection of the object. Take our previous shark sighting problem (Fig. 1.3) as an example, a deep reinforcement learning algorithm is shown to give a near-optimal bounding box deformation, e.g., shrinking, expanding, shifting right/left for each of the proposed regions so as to localize the object in the least number of steps [22].

7. *Natural language processing*: Natural language processing refers to understanding words from speech, parsing texts to produce a summary, or answering questions asked by a human. Nowadays, when we call the customer care center of any service, they allow us to say in a few words why we are calling them. Their automated system is capable of intelligently interacting with a human caller and serve his or her needs. Deep learning and reinforcement learning algorithms are widely used for this kind of speech-to-text conversation. A good survey is given in [204] that

covers the development of reinforcement learning systems trained with maximum likelihood word prediction from dialogue and non-repetitive summary production from texts.

1.2 HISTORY OF REINFORCEMENT LEARNING

The emergence of reinforcement learning dates back to 1850s when Alexander Bain addressed the phenomenon of learning by experiment. It can be also related to the use of the term *reinforcement* by psychologist Conway Morgan in 1894 to describe animal behavior. Later in 1957, Bellman introduced stochastic dynamic programming to find the optimal solution of *Markov decision processes* (MDPs). In the state of the art, deep learning algorithms are in place for solving complicated reinforcement learning problems. One perfect example is the development of deep-Q learning by Google DeepMind that defeated a professional human player in the *AlphaGo* game. The above journey is elaborated below.

1.2.1 Traditional Reinforcement Learning

As mentioned in earlier sections, reinforcement learning refers to learning from interaction and experience. In other words, the learning is through *trial-and-error*. Psychologist Edward Thorndike first formalized the theme of trial-and-error learning—actions that are followed by good or bad outcomes tend to be repeated or altered [50]. He termed this *law of effect* since it relates the tendency of reinforcing events with action selections. The *law of effect* involves trying alternatives and selecting among them by comparing their consequences. It also associates alternatives found by selection in particular situations. In other words, the *law of effect* is an amalgamation of search and memory, e.g., search in the form of trying out many actions and memory in the form of remembering what actions worked the best. A combination of search and memory poses an essential element to reinforcement learning. The two terms have been replaced by *exploration* and *exploitation* in modern reinforcement learning. In the early ages of reinforcement learning, several researchers explored trial-and-error learning as an engineering principle. One such work is the PhD dissertation of Minsky [107], where he discussed computational models of reinforcement learning and described his construction of an analog machine composed of components he called SNARCs (Stochastic Neural-Analog Reinforcement Calculators). Minsky in his paper in 1961 [106] discussed several issues relevant to reinforcement learning, such as how credit is distributed for success among the many decisions that may have been involved in producing it. On the other hand, Farley and Clark described another neural-network learning machine at the same time that learned through trial-and-error. In the 1960s, the term *reinforcement learning* was first used in the engineering literature [172].

In 1961, Donald Michie described [103] a trial-and-error based system for learning how to play tic-tac-toe called MENACE (Matchbox Educable Naughts and Crosses Engine). Years later, Donald Michie and Roger A. Chambers in [105] described another tic-tac-toe agent called GLEE (Game Learning Expectimaxing Engine) and a reinforcement learning controller called BOXES. They applied BOXES to the task of learning to balance a pole hinged to a movable cart. Michie and Chambers' version of pole-balancing is one of the best early examples of a reinforcement learning task under conditions of incomplete knowledge. It influenced much later work in reinforcement learning. Michie has consistently emphasized the role of trial and error and learning as essential aspects of artificial intelligence [104]. Reference [181] produced a reinforcement learning rule that could learn from success and failure signals instead of from supervised learning with training examples. This form of learning is called *learning with a critic* instead of *learning with a teacher*. The method was analyzed to learn playing blackjack.

Along another line, the reinforcement learning problem was mathematically formulated with notion of state, action, transition probability, reward and value functions formally introduced. Building upon the probabilistic formulation, the optimal action finding was aimed. The class of methods for the optimal control by solving probabilistic equation was termed as stochastic dynamic programming. Bellman first devised methods for solving stochastic dynamic programming equations in 1957 for both continuous and discrete state space. The latter version of the problem is known as *Markovian decision processes* (MDPs). Later, Ronald Howard proposed a policy iteration method for solving MDPs in 1960. The above mathematical formulation is the crux of modern reinforcement learning algorithms. However, the computational complexity of solving dynamic programming equation grows astronomically with increasing number of states. Yet, it is a widespread method of solving MDPs. Another disadvantage of dynamic programming is that it proceeds backward in time for the learning process making it difficult to realize how it learns in a process that proceeds forward in time. To alleviate that problem, Dimitri Bertsekas and John Tsitsiklis came up with neuro-dynamic programming amalgamating dynamic programming and neural networks in 1996. Their work paved the way to the understanding of a learning process that proceeds in the forward way. On the other hand, to tackle the curse of dimensionality as described in the above, people came up with approximate dynamic programming that significantly reduces the complexity. A set of intelligent approaches are discussed in Warren Powell's book *Approximate Dynamic Programming* (2007).

The other area of early reinforcement learning research is temporal-difference learning. These methods rely on the difference between temporal successive estimates of some values. Temporal differences can be viewed as an additional reinforcement agent that favorably shapes the actions of primary reinforcement agent. The earliest known work in the light of temporal difference learning is [185]. This work updates the value estimate for the current state node on the basis of one sample transition from it to the immediately following state, which will be discussed in detail in later chapters. This proposed method is termed as *tabular TD(0)* in Sutton and Barto's book (2012) for an adaptive controller intended to solve MDPs. In addition, Sutton and Barto did some impactful work on temporal difference learning. Sutton [157] established a link between temporal difference learning and animal learning, emphasizing learning rules driven by changes in temporally successive predictions. He and Barto embellished these ideas and developed a psychological model for classical conditioning based on temporal-difference learning [158, 14]. In their book, they developed a method for using temporal-difference learning in trial-and-error learning, known as the *actor-critic* architecture, and applied this method to Michie and Chambers's pole-balancing problem described earlier. Sutton studied this method in his PhD. dissertation (1984). This method was also extended in backpropagation neural networks in Anderson's (1986) PhD. dissertation. As a final refinement, the temporal-difference method was combined with optimal control in solving MDPs which is known as Chris Watkins's Q-learning (1989). The introductory chapter of their book is a good read regarding the development of the temporal difference learning method and their contribution to it.

1.2.2 Deep Reinforcement Learning

As will be discussed in later chapters, the traditional reinforcement learning approaches always suffer from the curse of dimensionality. Consequently, they are inherently limited to fairly low-dimensional problems. Rising in recent years, however, deep reinforcement learning algorithms allow solving complex problems with high-dimensionality. As the word *deep* suggests, there are multiple layers in the end-to-end training process. Deep reinforcement learning can be viewed as a combination of deep neural network and reinforcement learning. That is, use deep learning algorithms within reinforcement learning via function approximation and representation learning properties of deep neural networks. For example, we want to design a robot that will drive away the birds from a corn field and run away to warn human workers in that facility. On the input side, video is fed into a learning algorithm in the robot. The video containing high-dimensional pixels in each frame first goes through several layers of manipulation in a neural network, extracting the low-dimensional key features of video frames. Based on that, the robot applies reinforcement learning to decide whether to engage the object or run away from it. As it is shown, this kind of end-to-end learning involving high dimensional data poses astronomical computation complexity, which can be dealt with using deep learning. A nice survey on deep reinforcement learning [6] covers a variety of deep reinforcement learning algorithms including the deep Q-network, trust region policy optimization, and asynchronous advantage actor-critic.

Recently, deep reinforcement learning has already been proved by a wide range of applications. Considering the potential impact of deep reinforcement learning algorithms, tech giants like IBM Watson and Google have established their own specialized research centers and conducted extensive research. For example, *feature engineering* is an important step in the process of predictive modeling. It involves the transformation of given feature space for reducing the modeling error for a given target. Given the unavailability of a well-defined basis for performing effective feature engineering, an automated feature engineering framework is proposed in [70] that uses Q learning with function approximation to find the appropriate feature. On the other hand, the IBM Watson machine is gaining momentum in natural language processing, text parsing, and medical record retrieval-based disease diagnosis. One of its many applications is open domain *question answering* (QA). In this problem, given a passage or set of passages, the machine should be able to answer questions that are answered in one or many of the passages.

Google DeepMind is a leading artificial intelligence research center based in London, UK. It has been prolific over the past decade in producing work that made a positive impact on many problems. One such work is about making an automated Go game player that defeated a professional human player [150]. The Go game is deemed as one of the most challenging board games for artificial intelligence due to its enormous search space, difficulty in evaluating board positions, and predicting the right moves among many possibilities. Their designed Go game player achieved a 99.8% winning rate against other Go programs, and defeated the human European Go champion by 5 games to 0. This is the first time that a computer program has defeated a human professional player in the full-sized game of Go. Another such work is the development of the deep Q-network [109] that was tested on the challenging domain of classic Atari 2600 games. The agent, receiving only the pixels and the game score as inputs from Atari game, was able to surpass the performance of all previous algorithms and achieve a level comparable to that of a professional human games tester across a set of 49 games. This work bridged the gap between high-dimensional sensory inputs and actions. Very recently, Google DeepMind leveraged the computational functions of grid cells, thought to provide a multi-scale periodic representation used for path integration/navigation, to develop a deep RL agent with mammal-like navigational abilities [13]. This astonishing achievement strongly supports neuro-scientific theories that see grid cells as critical for vector-based navigation.

To conclude, despite the successful stories of deep reinforcement learning, many problems remain open before we can apply this technique to a wide range of real-world problems. Nowadays, in the machine learning community many research topics in this field are actively under investigation and the overall technique is evolving day by day.

1.3 SIMULATION TOOLKITS FOR REINFORCEMENT LEARNING

As discussed above, reinforcement learning is essentially a computational approach in which an agent interacts with an environment by taking actions to maximize its accumulated rewards. Therefore, to evaluate a reinforcement learning algorithm in simulations, one has to create an environment and the agent-environment interface. If the environment is complicated, this job could be very non-trivial and time

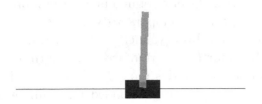

Figure 1.5: Snapshot of an OpenAI Gym environment: CartPole.

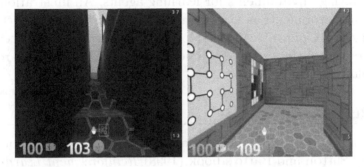

Figure 1.6: Snapshot of DeepMind Lab environments: Stairway (left) and Nav Maze (right).

costly. As motivated by this fact, several reinforcement learning toolkits have been developed as a collection of environments designed for testing, developing and comparing reinforcement learning algorithms. Among these toolkits, the most well known is the open-source OpenAI Gym which supports training agents in everything from walking to playing the "pong" game. For example, as shown in Fig. 1.5 , CartPole is one of the simplest environments in OpenAI Gym. As introduced in Gym, "a pole is attached by an un-actuated joint to a cart, the system is controlled by applying a force of +1 or −1 to the cart. The pendulum starts upright, and the goal is to prevent it from falling over. A reward of +1 is provided for every time step that the pole remains upright. The episode ends when the pole is more than 15 degrees from vertical, or the cart moves more than 2.4 units from the center." The agent-environment interface on the environment state observations and action inputs are also provided in Gym. Therefore, developers only need to focus on their core business—implementing the proposed algorithms, without concerns with the environments. Furthermore, we remark that OpenAI Gym supports developers to write agents using an existing numerical computation library, such as TensorFlow or Theano. Other toolkits or testbeds for (deep) reinforcement learning with more complicated environments includes OpenAI Universe and DeepMind Lab. OpenAI Universe is a platform intended for training an agent across the world's supply of games, websites and other applications. It enables us to train a single agent on any task a human can complete with a computer by looking at screen pixels and operating a virtual keyboard and mouse. DeepMind Lab provides a set of 3D navigation and puzzle-solving environments for learning agents. An illustration of the sampled environments is shown in Fig. 1.6. Furthermore, DeepMind and Blizzard Open StarCraft II provide a very challenging environment of the real-time strategy game StarCraft II to accelerate research on reinforcement learning.

1.4 REMARKS

Regarding the review of the development of traditional reinforcement learning, Sutton and Barto's book (1998) *Reinforcement Learning: An Introduction* is a good read. The review of the development of traditional reinforcement learning in this book, is inspired by their book. Additionally, the reader can take a look at the book by Bertsekas and Tsitsiklis (1996) for more examples and methodologies pertinent to reinforcement learning problems. Bellman's book on dynamic programming (1957a) and Markov decision processes (1957b) also covers a breadth of solutions methods for reinforcement learning problems. Regarding deep reinforcement learning, there is not a comprehensive textbook or reference book out there as this theory keeps evolving very fast in recent years. But readers can easily find valuable papers in the literature which introduce the up-to-date results in the field. Also, if interested in the implementation of basic deep reinforcement learning algorithms (e.g., using Python), readers can find several instruction books available online, such as *Deep Reinforcement Learning Hands-On* by Maxim Lapan (2018).

CHAPTER 2

Overview of Cyber-Physical Systems and Cybersecurity

CONTENTS

Cyber-Physical Systems (CPSs) are a kind of control system composed of networks of embedded sensors and actuators. CPSs are often compared to the Internet of Things (IoT). Their principal difference lies in that CPSs focus more on physical systems, thus containing more physical elements than IoTs. Examples of CPSs are smart grids, robots, and self-driving vehicles. CPSs have recently attracted wide attention from researchers, with their theories and applications being repeatedly challenged. This chapter is intended to provide a high-level description of CPS so as to help readers better understand this emerging and promising multi-disciplinary concept. First, we introduce the concept and present a big picture of CPSs, followed by several examples of identified research areas, including resource allocation, transmission and management, energy control, and model-based software design. We then briefly discuss the cybersecurity issues of CPSs.

2.1 INTRODUCTION

Traditional control systems are mostly implemented with embedded systems. Parameters of the system are detected by sensors and sent to embedded signal processors. The processor performs routine computations on sensor data, and emits commands to the actuators. The complexity of the system depends on its embedded processor, which is often severely restricted by its limited battery and computation speed. Cyber-Physical Systems (CPSs) alleviate this problem, by replacing the embedded system with a network. In CPSs, sensor data are sent wirelessly to a computer system, possibly a cloud system. By leveraging the computing power of full-weight computers, more powerful manipulations can be performed on sensor data in real time, thus control systems can become more intelligent.

More precisely, CPSs are control systems which interface the physical system to software, by providing abstractions and models of the system, as well as techniques for designing and analyzing physical systems. In general, a CPS consists of two main functional components: (1) the advanced connectivity which ensures real-time data acquisition from the physical world and information feedback from cyberspace, a.k.a. the physical process; and (2) intelligent data management, analytics and computational capability that constructs cyberspace, a.k.a. the cyber-system [82]. Fig. 2.1 is a diagrammatic layout for typical CPSs, where the shaded area on the left and the shaded area on the right represent the cyber-system and the physical process, respectively.

The advantages of CPSs, of course, does not come without challenges. For example, there is an unavoidable time delay in sending data to and from the computer system. It is said that "controlling large, physically distributed plants is hard enough using analog methods, but it's even harder using digital systems" [186]. To cope with these challenges, in 2006, the National Science Foundation (NSF) awarded a huge amount of funds to promote progress in such techniques. Since then,

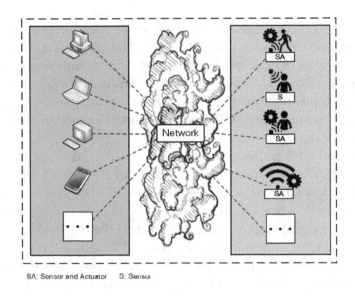

SA: Sensor and Actuator   S: Sensor

Figure 2.1: A diagrammatic layout for CPSs.

a large number of universities and companies have been participating in this project. A more detailed discussion on the history of CPS can be found in [81]. As a consequence, nowadays one may claim that the field of CPS is no longer in its infant stage. However, many challenging problems, such as cyberattack detection/prediction or security maintenance, remain open.

CPSs are closely related to the Internet of Things (IoT). The two concepts are similar in many aspects, but CPSs contain more physical and computing elements. It represents a wide variety of networked information technology (IT) systems accessed from and connected to the physical world. To be more specific, CPSs monitor, coordinate, control, and integrate, by one or more computation and communication cores, the operations of a physical and engineered system [132]. On the other hand, CPSs could be viewed as the brains of machines or systems. That is, CPSs enable devices to report or even rule themselves. This makes creating artificial intelligence robots or even silicon-based organisms possible. Furthermore, CPSs are changing the way we interact with the physical world around us. Application of CPSs might be or even has already been the IT revolution of our time. Plenty of areas are evolving to deploy CPSs in order to achieve better effectiveness. These areas include innovative medical devices and systems, assisted living, traffic control and safety, advanced automotive systems, process control, energy conservation, environmental control, avionics, and instrumentation. CPSs have also been applied to critical infrastructure control such as electric power, water resources, and communications systems, distributed robotics such as telepresence and telemedicine, defense systems, manufacturing, and smart structures. In light of these developments, nowadays CPSs and the maintenance of their security are of great significance.

A typical CPS architecture, known as 5C, is given in [82]. As shown in Fig. 2.2, The 5C architecture consists of 5 levels of functions: the connection level, conversion level, cyber level, cognition level, and configuration level. The connection level consists of sensors gathering data about the physical system, which are sent to the conversion level to extract meaningful information from them. The cyber level collects and synthesizes the extracted information from all machines in the system, to gain additional insight into the overall status of the system. The cognition level presents the system status as info-graphics to the users and assists them in making decisions over the system, or it may draw decisions on its own to achieve self-regulation. These decisions are executed by the configuration level.

From this design one can see that 1) computers play a significant role in regulating CPSs, as opposed to traditional models where humans are dominant controllers; and 2) CPSs are networked and accessible. These two properties of the CPS might be the advantages of the new IT era, but they can also be flaws and make a CPS vulnerable to cyber attacks [25]. In the rest of this chapter we will discuss the frontiers of various aspects of CPS research, but special emphasis will be placed on its cybersecurity issues.

2.2 EXAMPLES OF CYBER-PHYSICAL SYSTEMS RESEARCH

Since early 2007, considerable effort has been devoted to the understanding of CPS concepts, the development of CPS technologies and the real-world applications of CPSs. In this section, we list a few CPS research topics and review some relevant results in the literature, along the line of which more advanced technologies can be developed in the near future.

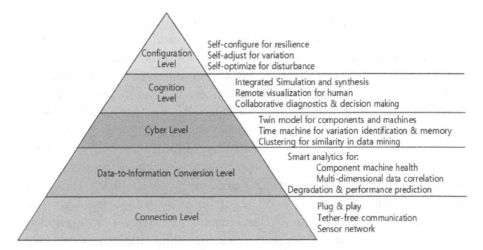

Figure 2.2: 5C architecture for implementation of CPSs [82].

2.2.1 Resource Allocation

Resource allocation refers to distributing the resources owned by the system, such as storage space, computational power, and network bandwidth, to the various devices in the network. Since resources are not unlimited, as one fundamental element in a CPS, the resource allocation algorithm has to consider multiple constraints, including cost, energy efficiency, and resource availability. Attempting to achieve optimization in all these aspects often leads to NP-hard combinatorial problems, which can only be solved with heuristic algorithms. In what follows, we introduce some typical examples of CPS resource allocation.

One example can be found in [189]. In this paper, the authors proposed an online algorithm, based on *Lyapunov optimization theory*, to approximate the optimal solution of reserved bandwidth allocation in cloud-integrated cyber-physical systems (CCPS). Under this modified CPS model, multiple CPS services may communicate with each other through a central cloud platform. However, the total bandwidth that these services may utilize is limited, forcing one to carefully arrange each service's bandwidth usage. In this work, the authors modeled the bandwidth allocation as a queue servicing problem. Roughly speaking, at each time slot, each CPS service requests the bandwidth it currently needs, which the allocator may or may not satisfy. If not satisfied, the unfulfilled part is added to the queue for the service, and will roll over to the next time slot. When designing the allocator, the authors considered the *stability* and the *cost*, and optimized the objective function (a linear combination of *stability* and *cost*) using heuristic algorithms.

Another example of resource allocation for industrial cyber-physical IoT systems based on 5G technologies is presented in [87]. A framework that multiple sensors and actuators establish communication links with a central controller in full-duplex mode with low bandwidth requirement is considered. In [87], the authors segregated the non-convex optimization problem with the objective to maximize the sum energy efficiency of the system into two sub-problems: power allocation and channel allocation. Various techniques are employed to tackle these subproblems, including *Dinkelbach*'s algorithm, the *Hungarian* algorithm, and game-theoretic methods. Dinkelbach's algorithm is a method for solving convex fractional programming [37]. The Hungarian algorithm is a polynomial algorithm for solving the linear assignment problem [72].

Moreover, a framework for the optimal defense resource allocation is proposed in [110] to minimize the unsupplied demand of CPS under uncertain cyber-attacks. Given that attacks over CPSs are mostly unpredictable and uncertain, which mathematically makes the optimization of defense resource allocation a nonlinear and nonconvex problem, the authors applied *Particle Swarm Optimization* (PSO) theory to tackle this problem, in which each resource allocation scheme is considered a "particle" in PSO. We refer the interested readers to [110] for details.

Finally, an interesting heuristic algorithm, called *Maximum Predicted Error First* (MPEF), is presented in [170]. The problem at stake here is to allocate wireless resources (bandwidth and time) for a control system network, a fundamental part of CPS. MPFE is a variation of an older heuristic algorithm, named *Maximum Error First* (MEF), introduced by Walsh and Ye [171]. Both techniques stem from the observation that data packets in control system networks usually contain less information than those in data networks. Hence, larger transmission errors may be tolerated, and we may trade transmission accuracy for performance [171]. As Walsh and Ye put it, "sending fewer packets, perhaps sending more important packets at the expense of others, has far more potential." MPFE works by giving packets which, if blocked from transmission, would cause a larger error in system status estimation, higher priority for allocation. In this way it minimizes the expected network-induced error of the network to achieve better control effects.

Generally speaking, there exists no unified framework to rank the various heuristic methods in the literature. However, one can often compare these algorithms on the following dimensions:

- *Information Demand*: Some heuristic algorithms require continuous input about the current status of the system. Such algorithms are called *online*, or *dynamic*, since they can adapt themselves to the changing system environment. However, it also means that they require more energy to run, thus being unsuitable for lightweight systems. In this regard, almost all algorithms introduced above are online, with the exception of the MPEF algorithm. Here the authors assumed that channel quality is fixed for given sensor and frequency, and does not vary with time. With this assumption, which is held for low-mobility applications [170], it becomes possible to run the scheduler offline.

- *Efficiency and Accuracy*: Some works, such as [189] and [87], calculate optimal solutions under certain assumptions. Such algorithms usually have polynomial time complexity. However, their accuracy, the gap between their output and the actual optimal solution, depends upon the strength of the assumption. Other heuristic algorithms, such as that in [110], calculate the global optimal solution. These algorithms are usually iterative, meaning they have to run a number of times before the solution converges. In such cases, one has to consider the speed of convergence. In [149], the authors discussed methods for conducting experiments to compare heuristic algorithms for specific problems, which can be easily adapted to CPS-related problems.

2.2.2 Data Transmission and Management

All CPSs contain many sensor devices. This leaves us with a big problem of managing all the data generated by them. More specifically, in order to avoid traffic jams in the system, we need to investigate the transmission and the management of data in CPSs.

Along this line, in [28] the authors presented a novel architecture for reducing the data transmission for a large-scale sensor-enabled CPS. Following this architecture, one can not only reduce the amount of information sent back from sensors but ensure that the backends get what they need. Also, Hao Wang *et al.* in [176] proposed a dynamic gateway bandwidth allocation strategy, in order to improve the communication efficiency between devices with different kinds of wireless technologies in CPSs. In [42], the authors combined retransmissions with real-time scheduling analysis to handle retransmission attempts of erroneous data without damaging the guaranteed delay bounds of other packets in CPSs.

2.2.3 Energy Control

Energy efficiency is a common topic for all network systems. Since lower energy consumption may lead to a lower efficiency of the whole system, there is always a trade-off in energy optimization problems. Especially for large-scale CPSs, the optimal solution between energy cost and efficiency often cannot be found in polynomial time, meaning that we need to solve most of those problems by using heuristic algorithms.

In paper [201], an improved *Krill Herd* (KH) algorithm [47, 92] was presented to solve the energy optimization problem in CPS. The KH Algorithm is similar to the Particle Swarm Optimization (PSO) method, in that both algorithms employ a large number of "particles." In addition to considering the minimal power consumption in the design phase, the effective management of power consumption during operation of the system is also a key to reducing the overall energy budget. Therefore, another paper targeted at improving the energy consumption of CPS using multiple operating modes is presented in [71]. Their target CPS architecture consists of a set of sensor and actuator modules, a communication network, and a computation and control unit. The components in the system have multiple operating modes such as active mode, idle mode, and some low-power operating modes. In their theory, if a component has not been used for a certain time period, the component is placed into lower operating modes gradually. Once a sensor detects an activity, all the components go into an active operating mode and the system responds to the environmental change.

2.2.4 Model-Based Software Design

There is no doubt that CPSs contain a variety of applications that need to communicate with each other, humans and the physical world all the time, meaning that a CPS requires a hardware-platform big enough to accommodate and manage those applications.

At present, the main model-based software design methods include Model-Driven Development (MDD) (e.g., UML), Model-Integrated

Computing (MIC), Domain-Specific Modeling (DSM), etc. Fig. 2.3 shows an abstraction in the design flow for DSM.

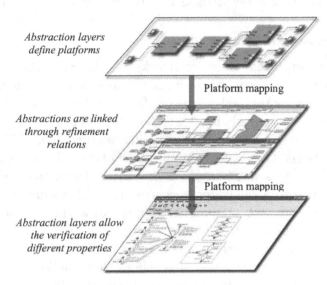

Abstraction layers define platforms

Platform mapping

Abstractions are linked through refinement relations

Platform mapping

Abstraction layers allow the verification of different properties

Figure 2.3: Abstractions in the design flow for DSM [161].

In [100], the authors presented a novel CPS hardware-software platform, which uses a parallel programming model. Its performance can be scaled conveniently by adding multiple boards (multiple boards can run in parallel). This platform also supports a task-based programming model based on OmpSs and leverages a high-speed, inexpensive communication interface. In addition, this board provides programmable logic, such as FPGA, to accelerate portions of an application. In addition, a model-based approach to generate configurable software architectures named Cloud-based Cyber-Physical Systems (CCPS) is elaborated in [33]. In this paper, improvements in the processing time for a CPS platform are shown and the solution to energy optimization is provided as well. In addition, this paper also presented an optimal cost-effective solution for the designed platform, a result that made this work a benchmark in the domain of model-based CPS software design during the last few years.

2.3 CYBERSECURITY THREATS

Cyber-systems do not have ethics like human beings: given a formally specified problem, they will automatically pump out an answer at lightning speed. This fact enables people to take advantage of CPSs in both good ways and bad ways. In this section, we formally introduce the well-known types of cyber attacks and the objectives of cybersecurity.

2.3.1 Adversaries in Cybersecurity

There are numerous examples of attacks over CPSs in the real world, some of which can cause severe damage to the aimed physical processes. One famous instance is the hacking of Maroochy Shire Council's sewage control system in Queensland, Australia [153]. The perpetrator used a laptop computer and a radio transmitter to gain control of 150 sewage pumping stations. Over a three-month period, he released one million liters of untreated sewage into a stormwater drain, from which the sewage flowed into local waterways. Awfully, this example is merely an epitome of the adversary model of the real-world CPSs attackers. A CPS can also be attacked or threatened by normal cybercriminals, disgruntled employees, terrorists, criminal groups or even spies from other nations [24]. For instance, some claim that the Soviet Union was the victim of an attack during the cold war (in 1982) when a logic bomb caused a gas pipeline explosion in Siberia [135]. More types of attacks on CPSs can be found in [175]. Hence, it is no surprise that most military organizations have been looking into advanced attack technologies, including cyber-attacks against the physical infrastructure of other nations.

The security issues of CPSs is only a part of a much larger trend of growing security concerns over computer systems in general. It has been reported in [46] that, on average, a computer network intrusion occurs every 20 seconds in the world, incurring billions of dollars of economic loss each year. Nowadays, floppy disk, CD, DVD, and USB are likely to carry malicious code; E-mail, Internet browsing, software downloading, and instant messaging are likely to be hijacked by hackers. A new computer, once it connects to the Internet, will be scanned by a hacker in less than 15 minutes. Our network environment is simply no longer trustworthy. In the specific context of wireless networks, deemed as the fundamental infrastructure of CPSs, the common adversaries are as follows:

Spoofing: A spoofing attack is a situation in which one person or program successfully makes itself up as another by doctoring data, thereby gaining an illegitimate advantage. This attack is made possible by the fact that many of the protocols in the TCP/IP suite do not provide mechanisms for authenticating the source or destination of a message. There are various types of spoofing attacks in cyber world. The most common one is IP spoofing. In IP spoofing, the attacker forges its own IP address and sends malicious requests to the target system. As the target is unable to verify the source of the request, it may easily trust the attacker, and leak confidential information.

Sybil: The basis of a sybil attack is that in a peer-to-peer network, a single node can have multiple identities. If one has control over a majority of identities on the network, the role of redundant backup is weakened. A Sybil attack is the use of a few nodes in the social network to control multiple false identities, and use these identities to control or influence a large number of normal nodes.

DoS and DDoS: Denial of Service (DoS) is a type of network attack that is often used to paralyze a server or network. Distributed Denial of Service (DDoS) is a common way to launch DoS attacks. To perform a DDoS, a hacker first gains control over a large number of computers. This can be done with the help of a Trojan virus or malware. Then the hacker commands all these computers to send a particular request to the network under attack. By exhausting the bandwidth or the computing capacity of the network, these requests effectively paralyze the attacked service, and block other users from accessing it.

The defense against these increasingly diversified adversaries must necessarily require a systematic investigation of cybersecurity. Cybersecurity is a socio-technical system which addresses problems related to technology infrastructure, applications, data, and human interactions. In designing network systems, in general one has two approaches to improve cybersecurity: *threat management* is an approach in which particular kinds of adversary models are identified and then special solutions are built to deal with them; *infrastructure management*, however, intends to improve the robustness of the system infrastructure, such as using cryptography to eliminate any possibility of privacy leak.

2.3.2   Objectives of Cybersecurity

Overall, there are four common security goals in CPSs: confidentiality, integrity, availability, and authenticity.

- *Confidentiality:* Confidentiality refers to the capability to prevent the disclosure of information to unauthorized individuals or systems [52].

- *Integrity:* Integrity means that data or resources cannot be modified without authorization [175].

- *Availability:* CPSs with good availability can provide services reliably by preventing computing, controlling, and communication interruptions from hardware failures, system upgrades, power outages or denial-of-service attacks [188].

- *Authenticity:* Last but not least, authenticity requires CPSs to enforce authentication in all end-to-end processes, including sensing, communications and actuations [156]. Authenticity also includes *controllability* and *auditability*. Controllability means that the owner of the system has the ultimate authority to control the network system. Auditability means that the basis and means of investigation can be provided when cybersecurity problems arise.

One should be clear that the above four objectives are not isolated but indeed closely interconnected. For example, the definitions of confidentiality and integrity explicitly depend upon authenticity. Availability is tied to the stability of data within the system, which in turn requires integrity. In the rest of this section we summarize some works on these four aspects of security so as to help readers ramp up on cybersecurity problems and the approaches to resolve such problems. The following content is much more like a brief literature review. Therefore, we strongly suggest the interested readers study the cited papers for details.

2.3.2.1 Confidentiality

One way to enforce confidentiality is to use formal models to check the flow of confidential information. Akella *et al.* [3] presented a semantic model for information flow analysis in a CPS. An interesting point, uniquely pertaining to CPSs, is made in this paper. That is, in traditional computing, a confidentiality breach is usually a leak of digital data from the servers. However, since CPSs can control physical systems, information can also be leaked through the behaviors of the systems they control. For example, if one observes that the throughput of a gas pipeline suddenly increases, then it must be the case that someone in the downstream of the pipeline has increased his or her demand. As the authors summarized, "an observation about commodity flow could permit an observer to infer possibly sensitive cyber actions."

Starting from this premise, the authors proposed a formal language to describe the correlation between cyber and physical processes in a CPS. This description may be analyzed with formal verification methods to ensure confidentiality of the whole system.

On the other hand, researchers have been trying to create new types of CPS architecture to simplify the maintenance of confidentiality in them. Reference [162] is a comprehensive survey of security-aware architectures for smart grids, but the techniques are easily adapted to other CPSs. Zhu *et al.* [208] proposed to adopt a hierarchical viewpoint of these security issues, addressing security concerns at each level of this viewpoint and emphasizing a holistic cross-layer philosophy for developing security solutions. A particular embodiment of this hierarchical security idea is presented in [173]. In this paper, the authors designed a Vehicular Cyber-Physical Systems and Mobile Cloud Computing Integration Architecture (VCMIA), which provides secure mobile services for potential users such as drivers and passengers to access a mobile traffic cloud. The network in this system is divided into three layers: the macro, meso, and micro layers (Fig. 2.4). The micro layer consists of the vehicle itself. The meso layer is a vehicular ad hoc network formed from spatially adjacent vehicles. The macro layer connects the vehicles to the central cloud server, which ultimately controls the system. Different security approaches may be applied to each level. For example, on the macro level, the authors proposed to adopt a hybrid cloud architecture to protect user privacy. Sensitive data could be stored on a private cloud, while other computations can be done on a public cloud.

In [197], the authors explored application of homomorphic encryption in CPSs. Homomorphic encryption is an emerging cryptographic technique which allows computation on encrypted data without decrypting it. In this way, even an attacker who has full access to the computation unit cannot extract confidential information from it (Fig. 2.5). But homomorphic encryption is still in its nascent stage, with only limited types of operations supported.

2.3.2.2 Integrity

Malicious data or behavior detection is one vital approach to handle the integrity issue. One example is presented in [164], which investigated the deception attacks on power grids. A deception attack is a special type of spoofing. In a deception attack, the attacker pretends to be a sensor in the system, and reports false data to the computing

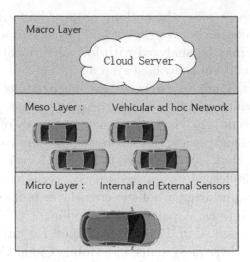

Figure 2.4: The three-level structure of the VCMIA architecture.

Table 2.1: Summary of Approaches to Confidentiality in CPSs

References	Highlight
[3]	Proposes a semantic model for information flow analysis in CPSs
[162]	A comprehensive survey of security-aware architectures
[208]	Proposes to adopt a hierarchical viewpoint to CPS security issues
[173]	Proposes a hierarchical architecture for mobile cloud services
[197]	Explores application of homomorphic encryption in CPSs

units, resulting in a breach of integrity. A CPS may combat this type of attack with a malicious data detector, which removes spurious data from the sensors. However, Teixeira and others showed that the more accurate the model the attacker has access to, the more devastating the deception attack he or she can perform undetected. More specifically, they quantified the trade-off between the model accuracy and the possible attack impact for different malicious data detection schemes.

Furthermore, [76] presented an analytical approach for evaluating the methods for CPSs to detect stealthy deception attacks, considering that these attacks become more and more erratic. Within this frame-

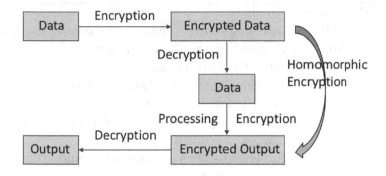

Figure 2.5: Operating principle of homomorphic encryption.

work one can derive the conditions under which a particular attack will succeed, and a particular malicious data detector will fail.

Techniques from machine learning are often employed to detect cyber attacks in sensor data. This whole subject is the focus of Chapter 7 in this book. Therefore, we only briefly survey this topic as follows. To relax the requirement about cyber state dynamics, a game theoretical actor-critic neural network structure was developed in [43] to efficiently learn the optimal cyber defense strategy online. Moreover, in this paper, to further improve the practicality of the proposed scheme, a novel deep reinforcement learning algorithm has been designed and implemented into actor-critic neural network structure. In paper [148], the authors proposed an intelligent sensor attack detection and identification method based on Deep Neural Network (DNN) techniques, which made it possible to identify deceptions as cyber attacks when multiple and heterogeneous sensors are attacked. The proposed strategy in [180, 96, 7] implemented the deep learning technique to analyze real-time measurement data from the geographically distributed Phasor Measurement Units (PMUs) and leveraged the physical coherence in the power systems to probe and detect the data corruption. These instances of implementing ML in CPSs' defensive strategy show that ML is a promising approach to improve the security maintenance of CPSs.

Table 2.2: Summary of Approaches to Integrity in CPSs

References	Highlight
[164]	Investigates deception attacks on power grids
[76]	Proposes an analytical framework for evaluating CPS attack detection
[43]	Develops a neural network structure to learn cyber defense strategy
[148]	Proposes an intelligent sensor attack detector using a deep neural network
[180, 96, 7]	Implements deep learning technique to detect data corruption

2.3.2.3 Availability

In contrast to the above techniques which are focused on detecting cyber attacks or compromised data, works on availability are concerned with minimizing performance lost under stress of cyber attacks or other adversary environments.

A novel attack compensator framework which can stabilize the CPS with a nearly desired system performance is presented in [61]. This specific technique can automatically fortify the CPS under a condition that an attack may occur without triggering an alarm.

In the scenario of networks of large data centers carried out as service function chaining by linking ordered lists of functions, selecting a service function path along which the service functions are executed, is challenging and necessary to improve the CFS availability. Islam *et al.* [64] proposed a strategy to select the link which has the minimum end-to-end delay.

The implementing of machine learning in the management of CPSs is also a hot research topic in recent years. With the help of this intelligent self-learning technique, a CPS can manage its defects autonomously and effectively [67]. An example of implementing ML in a water treatment system is presented in [63]. Fig. 2.6 presents the exact testbed used in this article, based on which two anomaly detection methods using DNN and SVM are presented and compared.

2.3.2.4 Authenticity

In the discussion of integrity we considered defensive approaches based on *data*. Specifically, we intercept attacks by identifying spurious and

Figure 2.6: The Secure Water Treatment (SWaT) testbed [63]

Table 2.3: Summary of Approaches to Availability in CPSs

References	Highlight
[61]	Stabilizes CPS with desirable system performance under cyber attack
[64]	Automatically selects transmission route that has least delay
[63]	Detects anomaly in water treatment systems

deviated data. In what follows, we review some defensive approaches based on the *identity* of corrupted devices.

In [207], Zhang *et al.* proposed a CPS health monitor system. The idea is to introduce a number of new sensors into the system, which monitor observable parameters of the system. When spurious data are detected, the monitor system utilizes input from these additional sensors to pinpoint the device that is not working properly. Since the new sensors require additional energy, however, the authors introduced a scheduler for these diagnostic sensors. By activating them on need, the health monitor is able to detect deception attacks without impacting the system performance much.

Reference [142] also introduced a technique for identifying compromised sensors. The basic idea is to introduce a random component into the decision by the controller. If the sensor is reliable, then its reported data would reflect the added random component. But if the correlation could not be detected, then it is highly probable that the sensor has been compromised.

Table 2.4: Summary of Approaches to Authenticity in CPSs

References	Highlight
[207]	Proposes a CPS health monitor system
[142]	Introduces a technique for identifying compromised components

2.4 REMARKS

In this chapter, we have introduced the concept of cyber physical systems and cybersecurity. To provide entry-level knowledge of the development and research on CPS and cybersecurity, we have concisely reviewed some state-of-the-art work related to this domain. Based on the individual's background and interest, readers are encouraged to follow the works cited throughout this chapter for details. As discussed in this context, machine learning has been seen as a powerful tool to handle many challenging issues in CPSs, and has taken up a bulk of public attention over the past few years. In the next part of this book, we will see how reinforcement learning plays a vital role in CPS design and implementation.

Overall, the deeper one explores the world of CPS, the more intriguing ideas about this area one will obtain. This emerging and promising domain has attracted significant interest in the last decade and surely will continue for the years to come.

2.5 EXERCISES

2.1. Explain the following terms:
   a) Cyber-physical System
   b) Homomorphic Encryption
   c) Sybil Attack
   d) 5C Architecture
   e) Authenticity of CPSs

2.2. What are some current examples of CPS?

2.3. What makes CPSs different from Internet of Things?

2.4. Compared with traditional control systems, what are the unique features of CPSs?

2.5. What are the common challenges faced in implementing CPSs?

2.6. What kinds of current technology can be used to implement the 5C architecture of CPSs?

2.7. Given the common types of cyberattacks on computer networks, consider how each type may affect a CPS.

2.8. What are some common cybersecurity approaches in CPSs? Classify these approaches into threat management and infrastructure management.

2.9. What are the relationships between the four cybersecurity objectives: confidentiality, integrity, availability, and authenticity?

The following exercises require you to explore beyond the textbook and synthesize knowledge from related fields.

2.10. Since CPSs rely on wireless sensor networks, they are subject to wireless data interception and modification. Review current network cryptography technologies, and decide whether they can meet the real-time requirements of CPSs.

2.11. Machine learning has been increasingly applied in cybersecurity. One way machine learning can recognize attacks is by recognizing malicious activities. This has been implemented in servers and personal computers in the form of host-based intrusion prevention. Review research on this topic, and consider whether it can be applied to CPSs.

2.12. The authenticity requirement mandates that the identity of each sensor be verified before it can upload data to the server. This prevents hijacked sensors from uploading forged data. Suppose that each sensor can check the integrity of any other sensors. Of course, only verdicts from sensors not controlled by hackers are reliable. Suppose further that more than half of the sensors are reliable. Propose an algorithm to reliably tell reliable and unreliable sensors apart. Hint: first find an algorithm that can always find a reliable sensor.

2.13. Model-based design is a fundamental tool in CPS development. Unified modeling language (UML) diagrams are a powerful tool to represent models of CPS components. In this exercise, suppose that a factory produces bottles at a fixed rate. A sensor checks the quality of each bottle, and emits 0 for each defective bottle, 1 otherwise. If three consecutive defective bottles are found, the system should alert the managers. Design a finite-state machine model for the CPS system, and represent it with an UML diagram.

2.14. In this exercise we consider the confidentiality requirement of the system. We follow the discrete synchronous model in Exercise 2.13. Furthermore, suppose that the internal state of a component is a finite state machine, and that you know its state diagram. In a realistic scenario, you cannot observe the input data of the system. However, you can observe its output, which are actions executed by actuators. Propose an algorithm to determine the most likely input data. This is an example of a side-channel attack.

II

Reinforcement Learning for Cyber-Physical Systems

II

Reinforcement Learning Problems

CONTENTS

In this chapter we formally introduce the reinforcement learning (RL) problem and its framework. We begin with two important simplified versions of the RL problem: Bandits and Contextual Bandits. The transition from Bandits to Contextual Bandits and then Contextual Bandits to Reinforcement Learning should seem natural and straightforward.

3.1   MULTI-ARMED BANDIT PROBLEM

The multi-armed bandit (MAB) problem, also referred to as the k-armed bandit problem, is one where the bandit has to pick among a discrete set of actions to maximize the expected return. The problem takes its name from a toy example where an agent has entered a casino and seeks to maximize earnings at a row of slot machines. However, upon entering the casino, the agent does not know which of the machines has the highest expected payout. The agent must therefore devise a strategy to both simultaneously learn the payout distribution for each slot machine and exploit his existing knowledge as to which machine is most lucrative. For now, we assume the payout distribution is stationary, that is, the payout distribution does not change over time. Despite its name, the MAB is constrained to play according to the following repetitive process: choose a slot machine to play, pull the selected machine's lever, and observe the machine's payout. As we build up to the full reinforcement learning problem, we want to point out some common elements and themes that emerge from the MAB problem that will also be common and critical to the RL problem.

First, we identify two entities in the problem: the agent and the row of slot machines. Our goal is to develop strategies to maximize the agent's return. Also, the slot machines and their true payout distributions are referred to as the *environment*, which is unknown to the agent.

Next, we introduce the concepts of *reward* and *return*. In the MAB problem, the *reward* is the money earned or lost after each arm pull. Whereas, the *return* is our cumulative profit or loss across all arm pulls since the agent entered the casino. The agent seeks to develop an algorithm that uses the history of the arm choices and the associated *rewards* to maximize the *return*. Formally, the return G is just the sum of the rewards r_t across time,

$$G = \sum_{t=1}^{T} r_t. \tag{3.1}$$

Upon entering the casino, the agent knows nothing about his environment (the payout distribution of each machine). To maximize the return, the agent must somehow reliably identify the machine with the highest expected reward and then play that machine repeatedly. With no prior machine knowledge, the agent must first *explore* his environment in order to learn how to most effectively *exploit* it. Since slot machine rewards are assumed to be stochastic or non-deterministic, the agent must play each machine multiple times to learn its reward distribution. As these distributions become more robust with sufficient arm pulls allocated to each machine, the agent should transition from exploration (learning the distribution) to exploitation (picking the machine

Figure 3.1: MAB problem structure: the arrow from action a to reward r represents the dependence of r on a.

with the highest expected output). This transition is widely known as the trade-off between exploration and exploitation, and the transition strategy directly determines the agent's performance. As we introduce algorithms to solve this MAB problem, one will see that they all incorporate mechanisms to balance *exploration* and *exploitation*.

The MAB problem has many algorithmic solutions. Often the appropriateness of a solution is dictated by the underlying assumption about the reward distributions. For example, a slot machine that can output any amount of money may be modeled with a Gaussian distribution. Whereas a machine that outputs \$0 or \$1 might be modeled as a Bernoulli distribution. However, the three algorithms we present for the MAB problem will be agnostic to the distribution family.

Let's first review the problem setup as shown graphically in Fig. 3.1. This figure shows the relationships in the MAB problem. The stochastic reward r from the selected machine by taking action "a" is a random variable with an unobserved probability distribution. Recall that our agent must simultaneously balance exploration (learning the distribution for each machine) and exploitation (playing the machine with the highest estimated payout). Before we dive into algorithms that do so, let's first introduce some mathematical concepts related to estimating the reward distribution for each machine. These concepts will be relevant to each MAB algorithm.

Recall that the expectation of a random variable is the weighted average over all values the random variable could assume. Here, the weights for a given value are simply the probability of the random variable assuming that value. Formally, this relationship is captured in equations (3.2) and (3.3) for continuous and discrete random variables, respectively.

$$\mathbb{E}[x] = \int_x p(x) \cdot x \ dx, \tag{3.2}$$

$$E[x] = \sum_x p(x) \cdot x. \tag{3.3}$$

In the MAB problem, we do not know the true reward distributions for each machine denoted as $p(r|a = j)$: this conditional probability means the probability of receiving reward r given that the agent's action a was to play the jth machine. If the agent knew these distributions for every slot machine, then it could use them to compute the expected reward for each machine using either Equation (3.2) or (3.3), respectively, according to whether the rewards were continuously or discretely distributed. As such, our bandit must either approximate the expected reward for each machine, $E[r|a]$, or learn the distribution $p(r|a)$. We will focus on the former. Assuming each realization of a random variable is independent and identically distributed (i.i.d.), the *law of large numbers* states that the empirically estimated expectation approaches the true expectation as the number of samples goes to infinity. That is,

$$E[x] = \lim_{N \to \infty} \frac{1}{N} \sum_{i=1}^{N} x_i. \tag{3.4}$$

Thus for large N, one can reasonably approximate the expectation according to Equation (3.5).

$$E[x] \approx \frac{1}{N} \sum_{i=1}^{N} x_i. \tag{3.5}$$

Applying this result to the MAB problem, we can estimate the expected reward for each machine by simply keeping an average of all rewards collected from each machine since the bandit started playing. In particular, we define the estimated expected payout of the jth machine as μ_j,

$$\mu_j = \frac{1}{N_j} \sum_{i=1}^{N_j} r_{i,j}. \tag{3.6}$$

Here, N_j is the number of times we played the jth machine, and $r_{i,j}$ is the reward from the ith time we played the jth machine. Note that this quantity can be computed in an iterative manner, an approach in which the agent does not need to record all historical rewards. Mathematically,

$$
\begin{aligned}
\mu_j(n) &= \frac{1}{n} \sum_{i=1}^{n} r_{i,j} \\
&= \frac{1}{n} \left(\sum_{i=1}^{n-1} r_{i,j} + r_{n,j} \right) \\
&= \frac{1}{n} \sum_{i=1}^{n-1} r_{i,j} + \frac{1}{n} r_{n,j} \\
&= \frac{n-1}{n} \cdot \frac{1}{n-1} \sum_{i=1}^{n-1} r_{i,j} + \frac{1}{n} r_{n,j} \\
&= \frac{n-1}{n} \mu_j(n-1) + \frac{1}{n} r_{n,j}.
\end{aligned}
\tag{3.7}
$$

Now we revisit the important theme of *exploration* and *exploitation* in light of this mathematical tool. According to the *law of large numbers*, our estimated expected reward μ_j for the jth machine approaches the true expected reward as N_j tends toward infinity. However, when N_j is small, our estimates can be very wrong. Imagine a simple example with two machines. The first machine pays out $1, 35% of the time and $0 the rest of the time. The second machine pays out $1, 55% of the time and $0 the rest of the time. Obviously, the agent is best off playing the second machine. However, let's say the agent is greedy and chooses to explore each machine once before deciding which machine to play repeatedly. One possible outcome is that the agent plays the first machine and wins $1 and plays the second machine and wins $0. This greedy and naive agent then concludes that the expected payout for the first machine is $1 and for the second machine is $0 according to Equation (3.6). Our greedy agent then sub-optimally exploits the casino!

Alternatively, we consider a very conservative agent that never trusts his estimated payouts μ_j. This agent enters the casino and endlessly explores the machines but never begins to exploit them according to the gained knowledge. If that agent explores by randomly selecting between the same two machines as the greedy agent, then he only chooses the optimal machine 50% of the time.

It should be clear now that a good algorithm for the MAB problem must balance *exploration* (learning reliable μ_j) and *exploitation* (picking the machine with the largest μ_j). This balance can be accomplished in many ways. The manner in which this balance is struck distinguishes various MAB algorithms presented later.

3.1.1 ϵ-Greedy

We now introduce our first algorithm for the MAB problem: ϵ-greedy. The ϵ-greedy algorithm is a straightforward algorithm that nicely illustrates the concept of balancing *exploration* and *exploitation*. According to ϵ-greedy, the agent chooses to explore (pick an arm uniformly art random) with probability ϵ and to exploit (pick the arm with the highest μ_j) with probability $(1-\epsilon)$. In an environment with k action choices, the probability for picking the jth arm, $Pr(A_t = j)$, is distributed with probabilities according to Equation (3.8).

$$
\begin{aligned}
Pr(A_t = j) &= \begin{cases} 1 - \epsilon + \frac{\epsilon}{k} & \text{if } j = \underset{j=1,\dots,k}{\arg\max}\ \mu_j, \\ \frac{\epsilon}{k} & \text{otherwise.} \end{cases} \\
&= \begin{cases} 1 - \frac{(k-1)\epsilon}{k} & \text{if } j = \underset{j=1,\dots,k}{\arg\max}\ \mu_j, \\ \frac{\epsilon}{k} & \text{otherwise.} \end{cases}
\end{aligned}
\tag{3.8}
$$

For those readers unfamiliar with the *argmax* operator, it simply returns the argument that maximizes the following term. In Equation (3.8), it returns the index of the largest μ_j. Note that there could be a tie for maximum value across all μ_j. In this scenario, one can take the first index or randomly break any ties. Also observe in Equation (3.8) that the probability of exploration, ϵ, is evenly divided and allotted to the k arms including the greedy arm (that with the highest estimated expected payout). As such, all arms other than the maximum are selected with probability $\frac{\epsilon}{k}$. The greedy arm is then selected with remainder of the probability, $1 - \frac{(k-1)\epsilon}{k}$.

We present the full ϵ-greedy algorithm in Algorithm 1. It initializes the expected payout and observation counters for all k arms to zero at the beginning. Thereafter, it loops over T trials (slot machine plays). In each play, the algorithm assigns categorical probabilities for each arm and then samples and performs an action from this distribution. This action induces a reward sampled from the environment's unknown true distribution (the chosen slot machine's true reward distribution). After observing the reward, the algorithm updates its expected reward for the recently played arm. Note that we use the iterative update for the expected reward estimate from Equation (3.7) in Algorithm 1.

Algorithm 1 ϵ-greedy Algorithm for MAB

Initialize estimates: $\mu_j := 0$ for $j = 1, \ldots, k$
Initialize play counters: $N_j := 0$ for $j = 1, \ldots, k$
for $t = 1$ **to** T **do**
   maxSelected = **false**
   for $j = 1$ **to** k **do**
      if $\mu_j = \max(\mu_1, \ldots, \mu_k)$ **and** maxSelected = **false then**
         $\theta_j := 1 - \frac{(k-1)\epsilon}{k}$
         maxSelected := **true**
      else
         $\theta_j := \frac{\epsilon}{k}$
      end if
   end for
   Sample and perform action: $a \sim \text{Categorical}(\theta_1, \ldots, \theta_k)$
   Observe reward: r
   Increase the number of observations for the played arm: $N_a := N_a + 1$
   Update expected payout for the played arm: $\mu_a := \frac{N_a - 1}{N_a}\mu_a + \frac{1}{N_a}r$
end for

Let's highlight a few takeaways from the ϵ-greedy algorithm.

1. It employs a small probability, $\epsilon \in (0, 1)$, such that exploration never stops.

2. It is agnostic to each arm's reward distribution family. In fact, each arm could have a different distribution family (Gaussian, Bernoulli, etc...) and ϵ-greedy would still work.

3. It is the engineer's responsibility to choose an appropriate ϵ to balance exploration or exploitation. As such, one can start with a large ϵ and reduce it over time. Setting ϵ to 1 would amount to uniform exploration with zero exploitation. Decaying ϵ to zero would transition the algorithm to become completely exploitative (greedy).

It is noteworthy that, if the payout distribution is nonstationary, that is, that the payout distribution changes over time, exploration is always needed to make sure that the best machine always has a chance to be chosen. By doing so, we can simply use a fixed $\epsilon > 0$. In fact, as we will see in the next few chapters, most reinforcement learning problems encounter nonstationarity.

3.1.2 Softmax Algorithm

The softmax algorithm follows a similar structure as the ϵ-greedy algorithm. In fact, the only difference is the construction of the categorical action generating distribution. Instead of Equation (3.8) we replace it with the softmax distribution as

$$Pr(A_t = j) = \frac{e^{\mu_j/\tau}}{\sum_{i=1}^{k} e^{\mu_i/\tau}}, \tag{3.9}$$

where τ is a positive parameter called the temperature. The softmax distribution draws its name from the fact that it approximately gives a probability of 1 to the largest element. The exponential function e^x is a monotonically increasing function that makes large numbers larger. The temperature, τ, is analogous to ϵ from before: a hyper-parameter that the engineer must set to balance exploration and exploitation. The denominator is simply a normalizing constant that ensures the probability distribution sums to 1. From an implementation perspective, it is best to compute the numerator for each j and then divide each numerator by their sum as opposed to directly implementing Equation (3.9) j times. With this slight change, we now present the algorithm in Algorithm 2.

Algorithm 2 Softmax Algorithm for MAB

Initialize estimates: $\mu_j := 0$ for $j = 1, \ldots, k$
Initialize play counters: $N_j := 0$ for $j = 1, \ldots, k$
for $t = 1$ **to** T **do**
　$Z := 0$
　for $j = 1$ **to** k **do**
　　$\phi_j := \exp(\mu_j/\tau)$
　　$Z := \phi_j + Z$
　end for
　for $j = 1$ **to** k **do**
　　$\theta_j := \phi_j/Z$
　end for
　Sample and perform action: $a \sim \text{Categorical}(\theta_1, \ldots, \theta_k)$
　Observe reward: r
　Increase the number of observations for the played arm: $N_a := N_a + 1$
　Update expected payout for the played arm: $\mu_a := \frac{N_a-1}{N_a}\mu_a + \frac{1}{N_a}r$
end for

Let's examine some properties of the softmax algorithm.

1. Ignoring τ for the moment, i.e., pretending $\tau = 1$, one can see that our softmax probabilities θ_j will always be positive for finite μ_j. This result comes from the fact that we take the exponential: $\exp(\mu_j)$. Ignoring τ, we see that this algorithm will never truly stop exploring since the probability of selecting an arm is always non-zero.

2. Like ϵ-greedy, the softmax algorithm is agnostic to each arm's reward distribution family.

3. Once again though, we must choose the hyper-parameter, τ, to balance exploration and exploitation. Again, one can start with a large τ. Setting τ to infinity would amount to uniform exploration with zero exploitation. Decaying τ to zero would transition the algorithm to be completely exploitative (greedy).

3.1.3 UCB Algorithm

So far, the algorithms we presented for the MAB problem balance exploration and exploitation, but the degree to which they do so is controlled by a hyper-parameter and its decay. Recall that our impetus to explore stems from the fact that we need a reasonable number of samples to robustly estimate the expected payouts. Even after we have robust approximations, there always (for a finite number of samples) exists a small probability that our estimated expectations are incorrect. If our expected payouts are incorrect, then we may be playing a suboptimal arm. Thus it seems we should slowly transition from uniform exploration to near greedy exploitation as our estimates become more robust. In the ϵ-greedy and softmax algorithms, we would have to pick initial ϵ and τ and decay them over time with some user-defined decay function and hope that the decay was in accordance with our estimated reliability. Would it not be great to develop an algorithm that controls the "decay" according to our estimation uncertainty? Deriving an upper confidence bound (hence the name UCB) for our μ_j in the MAB problem is outside the scope of this book, but it stems from Hoeffding's bound, which at a high-level bounds the probability of our estimation error as a function of the number of samples collected. More discussions on UCB can be found in [77, 2, 9]. Applying this result to the

MAB problem results in the UCB algorithm where we select actions according to Equation (3.10):

$$A_t = \arg\max_a \left[\mu_t(a) + c\sqrt{\frac{\ln t}{N_t(a)}} \right], \qquad (3.10)$$

where $\in$ is the natural logarithm, $N_t(a)$ is the number of times that action a has been selected prior to time t, and $c > 0$ is the parameter that controls the exploration.

In the ϵ-greedy and softmax algorithms, we sampled actions stochastically according to a constructed probability distribution to enforce exploration. Here, we act greedily but we add an uncertainty term to our estimate. This uncertainty term, $c\sqrt{\frac{\ln t}{N_t(a)}}$, inflates the estimated payout according to our uncertainty. Actions with uncertain estimated payouts will have their estimates heavily inflated, whereas actions with very certain estimates will receive little to no inflation. How does this work? Remember the number of times that we tried an action is $N_t(a)$ and the current time step is t. It should be clear that as we increase $N_t(a)$ by trying action a, our estimate becomes more confident and this term shrinks. Also because $\ln t$ has a sub-linear growth rate, we can perform action a fewer times than t and still have high confidence. The square root further shrinks this inflation. The constant c is still a hyper-parameter we must set to control the effect of the confidence bound. We integrate this action selection into a MAB algorithm below.

Algorithm 3 UCB Algorithm for MAB

Initialize estimates: $\mu_j := 0$ for $j = 1, \ldots, k$
Initialize play counters: $N_j := 0$ for $j = 1, \ldots, k$
for $t = 1$ **to** T **do**

Perform action: $A_t = \arg\max_a \left[\mu_t(a) + c\sqrt{\frac{\ln t}{N_t(a)}} \right]$

Observe reward: r
Increase the number of observations for the played arm: $N_t(a) := N_t(a) + 1$
Update expected payout for the played arm: $\mu_t(a) := \frac{N_t(a)-1}{N_t(a)}\mu_t(a) + \frac{1}{N_t(a)}r$
end for

A few highlights of the UCB algorithm:

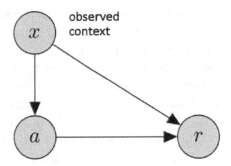

Figure 3.2: Contextual Bandit Problem Structure.

1. Compared to ϵ-greedy and softmax, UCB does not explore by sampling but rather inflates the estimated expected payout according to its uncertainty. UCB then takes the maximum of these inflated terms such that exploration still occurs despite the deterministic action selection.

2. While we still must set the hyper-parameter, c, we no longer need to consider decaying it over time as the confidence bound naturally shrinks the more we try an action.

3. The UCB algorithm is also agnostic to each arm's reward distribution family.

3.2 CONTEXTUAL BANDIT PROBLEM

We now expand the MAB problem by introducing context. Context is nothing more than an observation made by the agent before choosing an action. Let's leave the casino example and consider a real-world application of contextual bandits: online advertising. In this scenario, an ad-serving algorithm might observe a user's cookies, web browsing data, etc. Using this information (context), the algorithm then selects an advertisement (action) catered to this user's interests. If the user clicks the ad, then the algorithm is rewarded. Otherwise the algorithm receives no reward. Unlike our toy casino example for the MAB problem, this real-world contextual bandit has the potential to make a company a lot of money! The contextual bandit problem structure appears in Fig. 3.2.

The main differences between the MAB and contextual bandit

problem is that the observed context, x, influences the reward (denoted by a directed edge). For example, a user with an interest in outdoor equipment may not respond to ads for video games. As such, the agent should select an action, a, according to the observed context, x, indicated by an arrow between them. This notion of selecting an action according to an observation is a theme common to reinforcement learning problems. We call the mapping from observation (context) to action a *policy*. As before, our goal is to maximize the return, the sum (or weighted sum) of rewards over time. Thus, the primary goal of the contextual bandit is to learn a *policy* that selects the action with the largest expected payout according to the observed context. From a probability perspective, we now seek to estimate the expected reward coming from the distribution: $p(r|a, x)$—read as "the probability of receiving reward r for taking action a after observing context x." The conditioning on the context captures its effect on the reward's distribution.

Unfortunately, it is outside the scope of this book to cover contextual bandit algorithms in detail. We introduce them because they are a convenient building block to the full reinforcement learning problem as they introduce the notion of selecting an action according to an observation. Part of the difficulty with presenting turn-key algorithms for contextual bandits is that any algorithm must make some sort of assumption about the underlying environment. For example, an algorithm must assume some type of mapping from context to reward (i.e., linear or non-linear). Alternatively, an algorithm must select how to model the reward and context distributions (i.e., Gaussian, Bernoulli, etc...). These choices heavily influence algorithm selection and derivation. As such we will only present one algorithm that follows directly from the UCB algorithm for MAB.

3.2.1 LinUCB Algorithm

In this algorithm, we assume that the agent gets to make an observation prior to selecting an action. Further, we assume that this observation is a d-dimensional vector $\mathbb{R}^d$. This algorithm includes two parts as its name suggests. First, it seeks to construct a linear mapping from context to estimated reward for all k possible actions. Second, it applies an upper confidence bound to this estimated reward just like we did in UCB for MAB. This algorithm's derivation is outside the scope of this book and can be found in [84]. However, we hope its presentation

(Algorithm 4) seems structurally similar to that of UCB algorithm for MAB (Algorithm 3).

Algorithm 4 LinUCB Algorithm

Initialize model: $H_a := I_{d \times d}$ and $b_a := 0_{d \times 1}$ for $a = 1, \ldots, k$, and hyper-parameter $\alpha > 0$.

for $t = 1, \ldots, T$ **do**

    Observe context: x

    for $a = 1, \ldots, k$ **do**

        Construct context-to-reward map: $\theta_t(a) := H_a^{-1} b_a$

        Estimate reward with uncertainty inflation: $\mu_t(a) := \theta_t(a)^T x + \alpha \cdot \left(x^T H_a^{-1} x \right)^{1/2}$

    end for

    Perform action: $A_t := \arg\max_a \mu_t(a)$ (with ties broken arbitrarily)

    Observe reward: r

    Update model: $H_a := H_a + x x^T$

    Update model: $b_a := b_a + r x$

end for

In this algorithm, x is a vector in $\mathbb{R}^d$ and x^T represents its transpose. $I_{d \times d}$ represents an $d-by-d$ identity matrix. H^{-1} represents the inverse of matrix H. One should note the striking similarity of $\theta_t(a)^T x + \alpha \cdot \left(x^T H_a^{-1} x \right)^{1/2}$ to the UCB for MAB problems (Equation (3.10)). The first term is our estimated reward for taking action j given the observed context x. The second term is our UCB on this estimate. The only structural difference between LinUCB and UCB is that we are now creating a context-to-estimated-reward model instead of an empirical reward estimate. This change captures our assumption that context influences the reward.

3.3 REINFORCEMENT LEARNING PROBLEM

We are now ready to introduce the full reinforcement learning problem. In contextual bandit problems, the agent is allowed to make an observation before choosing an action. In the reinforcement learning problem, we replace the observable context variable with an environmental state variable. In RL problems, the agent will observe (at least in part) the environment's state before choosing an action. The major departure

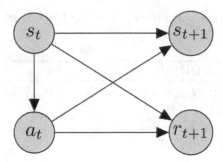

Figure 3.3: Reinforcement learning problem structure: the arrows from element A to element B represent the dependence of B on A.

from contextual bandit problems, is that the agent's action at time t affects the state it will observe at $t + 1$. In this manner, RL problems can be thought of as contextual bandit problems with feedback. This relationship is captured in Fig. 3.3.

3.3.1 Elements of RL

In RL problems, we consider two entities: the agent and the environment. The agent needs to be trained to accomplish some task within its operating environment. RL provides a very intuitive framework to algorithmically train an agent. In the RL framework, an agent must choose and perform an action at each time step. This action will then alter the environment in some way. For instance, consider the maze example in Section 1.1.3. At each time step, the agent notes its current position on the grid and must select a direction to move. If the agent chooses a direction that is not blocked by the boundary, then this action will result in the agent staying at a new position—an environmental change particular to this example. This turn-based process is repeated until the agent finds the exit. In Section 1.1.1, we briefly introduced the main elements of the reinforcement learning framework. In what follows, we reiterate these main elements with emphasis on four of them: *reward signal*, *policy*, *value function*, and optional *environmental model*.

First of all, like most traditional machine learning and optimization problems, RL must introduce an objective value: a scalar value that we seek to minimize or maximize. In the RL framework, the environment is responsible for issuing the agent a reward after each of its performed actions. This reward is what we formally call the *reward signal*. An environment's *reward signal* is always a function of two inputs: the state of the environment and the agent's action. We will consider many RL algorithms, but in general the mapping of state and action may be either deterministic or stochastic. We can now define our maximization objective. We want our agent to maximize some variant of long-term return or equivalently a weighted sum across time of all the received rewards. The good (and bad) news is that we as engineers must define the *reward signal* according to the application and problem we are considering. Remember we are *not* maximizing the reward at each time step. Rather we seek to maximize the long-term return, i.e., the sum of all rewards across time or an episode. Again consider the maze example in Figure 1.4 in Chapter 1. How can we define the *reward signal* as a function of action and state such that the sum of rewards for finding the exit quickly is large and the sum of rewards for meandering aimlessly is small? We posit that a *reward signal* that rewards -1 for every action taken that does not move the agent to the exit will work. In this example, the agent accumulates negative rewards until it finds the exit. Thus, the return (sum of rewards) will be very low for aimless wandering. The agent can maximize this value by finding the exit as quickly as possible. It may seem too simple to work at this point, but that is the beauty of reinforcement learning!

Next, we consider the *policy*. In essence, this is the agent's strategy (i.e., taking an action in a given state) to maximize the return with the real-time environment states as inputs. As before, the agent must balance exploration and exploitation when developing its policy to ensure that it does not get stuck on a sub-optimal policy. Thus the policy can be either deterministic or stochastic at a given time.

Next and perhaps the most critical to the algorithmic framework is the *value function*. In reinforcement learning, there are actually two flavors of *value functions*. The first is called the state-value function. The second is called the state-action-value function (often abbreviated to action-value function). As their names imply, the former is a function of just state while the latter is a function of state and action. Generally speaking, these functions assign a value to either a current state (state-value function) or current state and potential actions (state-action value function). The numerical value seeks to capture the agent's potential to maximize return given its current situation. These functions must be learned by the agent through experience. Again in the maze example, Figure 1.4 (c) in Chapter 1 shows the optimal state-value function.

Finally, we have the *environmental model*. Reinforcement learning algorithms fall into multiple categories, one of which is model-based vs. model-free algorithms. As such, this element is optional to some algorithms. The *environmental model* seeks to model the influence an agent's action has on the environment. In particular, given a current state and potential action, can we predict the resulting next state and its *reward signal*? Imagine if we introduce random patches of impassable terrain to our grid world such that the agent does not know the terrain is impassible. Thus if the agent chooses to move into the impassable terrain it simply remains in its current position. Taking a probabilistic approach, the probability of an action of moving in impassable terrain is zero (i.e., the agent can never move into this terrain). Conversely, actions toward passable terrain result in the agent moving in that direction with probability one (i.e., the agent has complete control of its position in passable terrain).

3.3.2 Introduction of Markov Decision Process

Now we introduce the reinforcement learning problem in its mathematical form. Most reinforcement learning tasks satisfy the probabilistic model of the Markov Decision Process (MDP). Recall that a (first-order) Markov process means that the next time-step only depends on the previous time step. In general, probabilities fall into two categories: discrete and continuous. MDPs that consider discrete states and actions are called finite MDPs. This book will mostly focus on finite MDPs given their prevalence, simplicity, and well-established theory. MDPs that treat either state or action as continuous are called continuous MDPs and remain an active area of research. Let's examine the stationary Markovian relationship as follows:

$$p(s', r|s, a) = \Pr[S_{t+1} = s', R_{t+1} = r|S_t = s, A_t = a]. \qquad (3.11)$$

Equation (3.11) captures the probability of entering the next state, $s' \in \mathcal{S}^+$ ($\mathcal{S}^+$ is $\mathcal{S}$ plus a terminal state if the MDP is episodic), and receiving the reward, $r \in \mathcal{R}$, given the current state, $s \in \mathcal{S}$, and the proposed action, $a \in \mathcal{A}$. As one can readily tell, the future $t+1$ only depends on the present t. This is a formal first-order Markov relationship. Note that a first-order Markov descriptor is often abbreviated as just Markov. Given this MDP, one can compute the expected rewards for state-action pairs as

$$r(s,a) = \mathbb{E}[R_{t+1}|S_t = s, A_t = a]$$
$$= \sum_r r \sum_{s'} p(s', r|s, a). \quad (3.12)$$

Here, we marginalize out the next state variable, s', and take the expectation of r. Similarly, we can marginalize out the reward, r, in Equation (3.11) to produce the state-transition probabilities in (3.13).

$$p(s'|s,a) = \Pr[S_{t+1} = s'|S_t = s, A_t = a]$$
$$= \sum_r p(s', r|s, a). \quad (3.13)$$

3.3.3   Value Functions

In this section we formalize both the state value and action value functions for a finite MDP. However, first we introduce the notion of a probabilistic policy, π, in Equation (3.14).

$$\pi_t(a|s) = p(a|s)$$
$$= \Pr[A_t = a|S_t = s]. \quad (3.14)$$

This policy $\pi_t(a|s)$ captures the agent's preference for taking an action $A_t = a$ given its state $S_t = s$ at time t. Like the contextual bandit problem, the agent observes the state and then samples an available action according to the current policy. Note that a policy can be deterministic simply by making all action probabilities zero except for the one deterministic action. As with contextual bandits, reinforcement learning algorithms generally will begin with a stochastic (random exploration) policy and eventually converge to a deterministic (exploitative) policy. We emphasize that the goal of all reinforcement learning problems is to learn an optimal (or near-optimal) policy for the agent.

Recall that our notion of a good policy seeks to maximize the sum of rewards across an episode. To generalize the sum rewards over an entire episode to the sum of rewards available beyond a certain time-step within an episode, we introduce the discounted return (sum of future rewards) in Equation (3.15).

$$G_t = \sum_{k=0}^{\infty} \gamma^k \cdot R_{t+k+1}$$
$$= R_{t+1} + \gamma \cdot G_{t+1}. \quad (3.15)$$

Here, G_t is the sum of potential future (i.e., those beyond time t) rewards R_k. The $\gamma \in [0, 1]$ term is a discount factor that diminishes the value of rewards further in the future. Setting this value close to 1 inspires the agent to truly consider the long term. Conversely, lowering the value makes the agent more myopic in that it values near-term rewards more and more. If the sum is taken over a finite number of terms, i.e., an episode, $\gamma = 1$ can be used because the sum remains finite. Note the recursive relationship between the first and second line: the return at time t can be expressed as the reward and the discounted return at time $t + 1$. With this formalization of discounted return of future rewards, for a given state, the state-value function following a policy π is defined as

$$v_\pi(s) = \mathbb{E}_\pi[G_t | S_t = s],$$

where the expectation $\mathbb{E}_\pi$ is taken over random values given the agent follows policy π. In fact, the value $v_\pi(s)$ can be obtained recursively from its successor state value functions. That is, for all $s \in \mathcal{S}$,

$$
\begin{aligned}
v_\pi(s) &= \mathbb{E}_\pi[G_t | S_t = s] \\
&= \mathbb{E}_\pi[R_{t+1} + \gamma \cdot G_{t+1} | S_t = s] \\
&= \sum_a \pi(a|s) \sum_{s'} \sum_r p(s', r|s, a) \left(r + \gamma \cdot \mathbb{E}_\pi[G_{t+1} | S_{t+1} = s'] \right) \\
&= \sum_a \pi(a|s) \sum_{s'} \sum_r p(s', r|s, a) \left(r + \gamma \cdot v_\pi(s') \right).
\end{aligned}
$$

$$(3.16)$$

This recursive equation is also known as the *Bellman Expectation Equation* for the state-value function. Let us parse this equation and its importance. The first line simply says our current state's value is the expected return for all future states visited when following our policy— after all the policy is a distribution such that we can take an expectation with respect to it. The second line introduces the recursive relationship of returns as presented in Equation (3.15). The third line expands out the expectation with respect to policy π, takes an expectation of the next reward, and represents the next time step's return as an expectation also with respect to π. The last line simply identifies the remaining expectation as the value function of the next state. Here one clearly see the recursion between the value function of the current state and the value function of the next state. While it seems trivial or unimpressive now, this relationship empowers many of the finite MDP algorithms.

Next we consider a similar treatment of the action value function in Equation (3.17), known as the *Bellman Expectation Equation* for the state-action value function or action value function. First of all, the action value $q_\pi(s, a)$ following policy π is defined as

$$q_\pi(s, a) = \mathbb{E}_\pi[G_t | S_t = s, A_t = a].$$

Then, the action value $q_\pi(s, a)$ can be represented in terms of the action values, $q(s', a')$, of possible successors to the state-action pair (s, a).

$$
\begin{aligned}
&q_\pi(s, a) \\
&= \mathbb{E}_\pi[G_t | S_t = s, A_t = a] \\
&= \mathbb{E}_\pi[R_{t+1} + \gamma \cdot G_{t+1} | S_t = s, A_t = a] \\
&= \sum_r r \cdot p(r|s, a) + \gamma \cdot \sum_{s'} \sum_{a'} p(s', a'|s, a) q(s', a') \\
&= r(s, a) + \gamma \cdot \sum_{s'} \sum_{a'} p(a'|s', s, a) p(s'|s, a) q(s', a') \\
&= r(s, a) + \gamma \cdot \sum_{s'} \sum_{a'} \pi(a'|s') p(s'|s, a) q(s', a')
\end{aligned}
\tag{3.17}
$$

Similar to the state value derivation, we demonstrate the recursive relationship in the action value function. However, we note that the next action a' will be defined by the policy π. This recursive property is not to be overlooked as it also empowers many of the finite MDP algorithms. Additionally, the recursive relationship of the state value and action value functions empowers much of the theory. In fact, we use this relationship to define whether a policy is the optimal policy! What does it mean to be optimal? It means that no other policy exists that will produce a better expected return. In other words, a policy is better than all other policies, $\pi^* \geq \pi$, if and only if $v_{\pi^*}(s) \geq v_\pi(s)$ for all state $s \in \mathcal{S}$. Note that the optimal policy is not necessarily unique. Let's formally define the optimal state-value and action-value functions below,

$$v_{\pi^*}(s) = \max_\pi v_\pi(s), \tag{3.18}$$

for all $s \in \mathcal{S}$, and

$$q_{\pi^*}(s, a) = \max_\pi q_\pi(s, a), \tag{3.19}$$

for all $s \in \mathcal{S}$ and $a \in \mathcal{A}(s)$. Rather simply, the optimal policy, π^*, is the policy that maximizes the respective value functions. Following the definitions of state value function $v_\pi(s)$ and action value function $q_\pi(s, a)$, we can write the optimal action-value function for taking action, a, and following the optimal policy as follows.

$$q_{\pi*}(s,a) = \mathbb{E}_\pi[R_{t+1} + \gamma \cdot v_{\pi*}(s')|S_t = s, A_t = a]. \tag{3.20}$$

From here, we can derive the important *Bellman Optimality Equation* for the state-value function in Equation (3.21) by recognizing that the optimal policy implies taking the action that maximizes the action-value function.

$$
\begin{aligned}
v_{\pi*}(s) &= \max_a q_{\pi*}(s,a) \\
&= \max_a \mathbb{E}_{\pi*}[R_{t+1} + \gamma \cdot v_{\pi*}(s')|S_t = s, A_t = a] \\
&= \max_a \sum_{s'}\sum_r p(s',r|s,a)\left(r + \gamma \cdot v_{\pi*}(s')\right) \\
&= \max_a r(s,a) + \gamma \cdot \sum_{s'} p(s'|s,a)v_{\pi*}(s').
\end{aligned} \tag{3.21}
$$

A similar derivation can be used to show the Bellman optimality equation for the action-value function as follows.

$$
\begin{aligned}
q_{\pi*}(s,a) &= \mathbb{E}_\pi[R_{t+1} + \gamma \cdot v_{\pi*}(s')|S_t = s, A_t = a] \\
&= \sum_{s'}\sum_r p(s',r|s,a)\left(r + \gamma \cdot v_{\pi*}(s')\right) \\
&= \sum_{s'}\sum_r p(s',r|s,a)\left(r + \gamma \cdot \max_{a'} q_{\pi*}(s',a')\right) \\
&= r(s,a) + \gamma \cdot \sum_{s'} p(s'|s,a) \cdot \max_{a'} q_{\pi*}(s',a').
\end{aligned} \tag{3.22}
$$

Typically, for finite MDPs with N states, the Bellman optimality equation (3.21) has a unique solution independent of the policy. If the model $p(s',r|s,a)$ is known, (3.21) implies a system of N equations with N unknown variables. Therefore, if N is small, one can always solve the Bellman optimality equation by simply solving the corresponding system of nonlinear equations. Once $v_{\pi*}(s)$ is obtained for all states, the optimal policy is easy to determine by one-step searching the action that leads to the best $v_{\pi*}(s')$. Similarly, if $q_{\pi*}(s,a)$ is known for all state-action pairs (s,a), the optimal policy at state s is simply choosing the action that achieves $q_{\pi*}(s,a)$.

3.4 REMARKS

In this chapter, we have first introduced the multi-armed bandit problem, which can be viewed as a simplified RL problem and has been studied since the 1930s [165, 137, 17]. From the bandit problems, one can see how RL works in practice and get insight on the fundamental tradeoff of RL—*exploration* and *exploitation*. Next, we have presented the framework of RL problems and MDP. The resulting Bellman expectation equations (3.16) and (3.17) and the Bellman optimality equations (3.21) and (3.22) are the foundation for all RL algorithms in this book. In other words, all RL algorithms/solutions are essentially designed to solve these Bellman equations. If the transition $p(s', r|s, a)$ in the equations is completely and accurately known, the collection of RL algorithms to compute the solutions of the Bellman equations is the so-called model-based solutions, such as dynamic programming. Otherwise, if the transition is unknown, the collection of RL algorithms is the so-called model-free solutions, such as the Monte Carlo methods and temporal-difference learning. We will present all these methods in the rest of this book.

3.5 EXERCISES

3.1. For the softmax action selection, show the following,

a). In the limit as $\tau \to 0$ (*temperature*), softmax action selection becomes the same as greedy action selection.

b). In the case of two actions, the softmax operation using the Gibbs distribution becomes the logistic, or sigmoid, function commonly used in artificial neural networks.

3.2. In the n-armed bandit problem, if using the sample-average technique to estimate the action-value, why could the greedy method perform significantly worse than the ϵ-greedy method in the long run?

3.3. As shown in the k-arm UCB algorithm with update

$$a = \arg \max_j \left[\mu_j + c\sqrt{\frac{\ln t}{N_j}} \right],$$

for $j = 1, 2, \cdots, k$, the term $\sqrt{\frac{\ln t}{N_j}}$ helps us avoid always playing the same arm without checking out other arms. Consider the 2-arm example with $c = 1$: the first arm has a fixed reward 0.25 and the second arm has a $0-1$ reward following a Bernoulli distribution with probability 0.75. If using a greedy strategy, with probability 0.25, arm 2 yields reward 0, upon which we will always select arm 1 and never revisit arm 2. If using UCB in this situation, we do not have this problem. Denote t as the time step and assume arm 1 is played for $t = 1$ and arm 2 is played for $t = 2$ with reward 0 (with the probability 0.25 that this occurs), then which arm will be played for $t = 3$ and $t = 4$?

3.4. In a simple MDP as shown in Fig. 3.4, there are two actions—up or down—starting from the initial state S_0. All rewards R are deterministic. Assume that the terminal state T has 0 value, find the optimal policy with respect to $\gamma = 0, 0.5$ and 1.

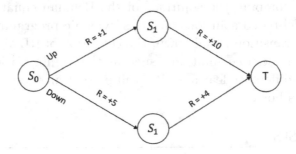

Figure 3.4: A simple MDP.

3.5. Compute the state value for S_t in all the MDPs in Fig. 3.5—3.7. The decimal number above lines refers to the probability of choosing the corresponding action. The value r refers to reward, which can be deterministic or stochastic. Assume $\gamma = 1$ for all questions and all terminal states (i.e., no successors in the graph) always have zero values.

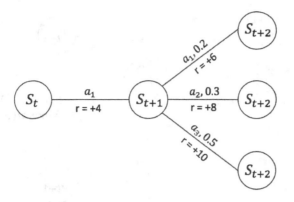

Figure 3.5: MDP with deterministic transitions.

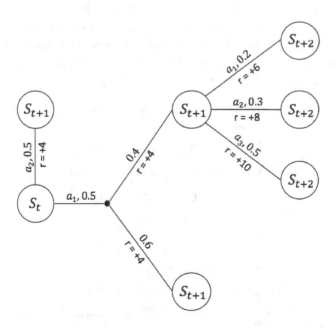

Figure 3.6: MDP with stochastic transitions.

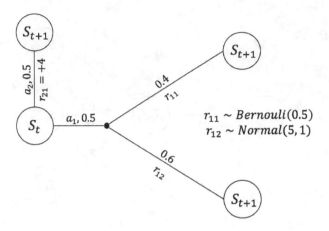

Figure 3.7: MDP with stochastic rewards.

3.6. Consider the 4×4 grid world in Fig. 3.8, in which T represents the terminal state. The number in the grids corresponds to the value of that state (i.e., position). Terminal state always has 0 value. There are four actions (up, down, left, right) possible in each state. Any actions leading out of the grid leave the state unchanged.

	1	2	3	4
1	0	0.7	0.6	0.9
2	0.6	0.8	0.7	0.6
3	0.8	1.2	1	0.7
4	0.9	1.4	T	0.5

Figure 3.8: Grid world.

a). Suppose that one robot starts from the position $(1,1)$, based on the grid values what is the optimal path if the robot follows the greedy method?

b). Suppose that the reward for each action is in the sequence of $-1, -2, \ldots, -n$ for the path you choose in question (a). Given $\gamma = 0.5$, compute the return $G_1, G_2, \ldots, G_N$, where N is the total number of actions in the chosen path.

c). Suppose that the reward is 0 for all actions and the robot follows equiprobable policy (i.e., take actions with equal probability), prove the value in $(2, 2)$ position using Bellman expectation equation (with $\gamma = 1$).

3.7. Given an arbitrary MDP with reward function $R(s)$ and a given constant $\beta > 0$, consider a modified MDP where everything remains the same, except it has a new reward function $R'(s) = \beta R(s)$. Prove that the modified MDP has the same optimal policy as the original MDP.

3.8. Given an MDP model, express the Bellman expectation Equation (3.16) and provide the solution to $v(s)$ for all s in matrix form. One will see that directly solving the matrix-based equation has computational complexity in the order of n^3 where n is the number of states. Therefore, such direct solution is only possible for small models. For large models, iterative methods introduced in later chapters have to be employed.

3.9. Derive the Bellman optimality equation for the state value functions when the transitions are deterministic.

3.10. (Expected Regret Bounds) Assume a reinforcement learning algorithm A for discounted infinite-horizon MDPs has expected regret

$$\mathbb{E}_* \left[\sum_{t=1}^{T} r_t \right] - \mathbb{E}_A \left[\sum_{t=1}^{T} r_t \right] = f(T)$$

for all $T > 0$, where $\mathbb{E}_*$ is over the probability distribution with respect to the optimal policy π_* and $\mathbb{E}_A$ is the expectation with respect to the algorithm's behavior. We assume that $\gamma \in [0, 1)$ is the discount factor and that rewards are normalized, i.e., $r_t \in [0, 1]$.

a). Let π be an arbitrary policy or algorithm. Show that for any $\epsilon' > 0$

and $T' \geq \log_{\frac{1}{\gamma}} \frac{H}{\epsilon'}$ where $H = \frac{1}{(1-\gamma)}$, we have

$$\left| v_\pi(s) - \sum_{t=1}^{T'} \gamma^{t-1} \mathbb{E}_\pi[r_t | s_1 = s] \right| \leq \epsilon',$$

for all state s. Note that v_π is the value function associated with π and $\mathbb{E}_\pi$ is the expectation with respect to the randomization of π.

b). From the regret guarantee of algorithm A and Part a), show that for any $\epsilon' > 0$ and $T' \geq \log_{\frac{1}{\gamma}} \frac{H}{\epsilon'}$, we have

$$\mathbb{E}_*\big[v_*(s_{T+1})\big] - \mathbb{E}_A\big[v_A(s_{T+1})\big] \leq f(T' + T) - f(T) + 2\epsilon',$$

for $T > 0$, where v_A is the value function of the (possibly non-stationary) policy that algorithm A follows.

c). Assume $f(T) = \sqrt{T}$, and show that for any $\epsilon > 0$ and $t \geq 1 + \frac{1}{\epsilon^2}(\log_{\frac{1}{\gamma}} \frac{4H}{\epsilon})^2$, we have

$$\mathbb{E}_*\big[v_*(s_t)\big] - \mathbb{E}_A\big[v_A(s_t)\big] \leq \epsilon.$$

Hint: set ϵ' to be some function of ϵ.

CHAPTER 4

Model-Based Reinforcement Learning

CONTENTS

4.1   INTRODUCTION

Starting from this chapter, we will systematically introduce algorithms for reinforcement learning. This chapter is intended to present model-based solutions. Recall that the goal of reinforcement learning is to let the agent learn how to make sequential decisions based on a series of input/observations from the environment, e.g., the states of the environment, such that the total reward is maximized or the task is accomplished. To do so, model-based reinforcement learning methods always assume a perfect mathematical model on the environment's dynamics, upon which an optimal action can be derived for each state. In contrast to the model-free methods, which will be introduced in the next chapter, the advantage of model-based methods is that it can use fewer samples to complete training. However, model-based methods could highly rely on their model hypothesis. For some problems, if the model of the environment dynamics cannot be known accurately in advance, it is inappropriate to apply model-based reinforcement learning.

As introduced in the previous chapter, MDP can be considered a classic and common model for reinforcement learning problems. MDP breaks a sequential decision-making problem into a sequence of single-step decision-making problems, which can be effectively solved by *dynamic programming*. In this chapter, we first assume the environment is a finite MDP, i.e., finite state, action sets, and thus a finite set of transition probabilities $p(s', r|s, a)$, and present the algorithms to solve the Bellman expectation equations and the Bellman optimality equations. Then, we briefly discuss the partially observable MDP and the continuous MDP.

Let us first provide one CPS example of a smart grid that can be modeled as a continuous MDP. This example is intended to help readers get a sense of how to model a real-world problem as an MDP. Readers without background on control and estimation theory may skip this example. Without this example, readers will not be affected in their understanding of the rest of the content in this chapter.

4.1.1 Example

Example (*Optimal Attack to CPS* [78])

With the advent of modern *information and communication technologies* (ICTs), much critical infrastructure, such as power grids or transportation systems, are undergoing a transformation into remote-controllable and autonomous systems. However, when ICT increases the operational efficiency, it also makes the system vulnerable to cyber attacks. One typical class of attacks is *false data injection* (FDI), i.e., to inject false sensor data and/or control commands into the industrial control systems in order to cause the system to deviate from its normal state. Take power grids as an example. If the attacker injects a sequence of small-magnitude false sensor data, it will mislead the control algorithm into sending out a wrong command to adjust the bus voltage in a wrong direction and eventually cause catastrophic safety incidents. However, as the deviation becomes larger, the attacker needs to send out larger-magnitude false signals as compensation such that the combined data still looks reasonable and the detector would not

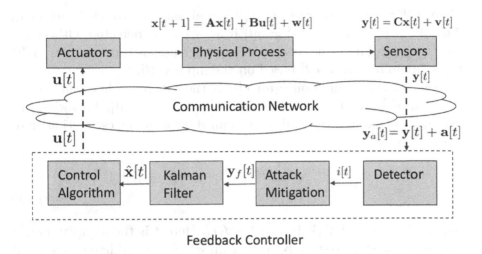

$$x[t + 1] = \mathbf{A}x[t] + \mathbf{B}u[t] + \mathbf{w}[t] \qquad y[t] = \mathbf{C}x[t] + \mathbf{v}[t]$$

Figure 4.1: Discrete-time linear time-invariant (LTI) system model.

raise the alarm. Definitely, this will increase the attacker's power cost. An optimal attack refers to a sequence of false data injections, which maximize the estimation error of the system with a limited power cost to the attacker. Therefore, to evaluate the safety of a control system, it is always necessary to investigate the possibility and the cost of generating such an effective sequence of attack signals. We next show how this problem can be mathematically represented as an MDP.

Consider a discrete-time power grid, as shown in Fig. 4.1, comprising a physical power grid, a communication network and a discrete-time linear time-invariant (LTI) feedback controller. In this model, $x[t]$ represents the state of the power grid at time instant t, $y[t]$ represents the sensor measurement and $u[t]$ represents the control signal to adjust $x[t]$. The dynamics of the power grid is modeled as a linear process parameterized by matrices A and B. Assume that the (A, B) pair is controllable. Besides, $w[t]$ is the random noise of the physical process of power grid, following the normal distribution $\mathcal{N}(0, Q)$. The observation process of the sensor is model as $y[t] = Cx[t] + v[t]$, in which matrix C is the measurement matrix and $v[t]$ is the measurement noise following the normal distribution $\mathcal{N}(0, R)$. Assume that the (A, C) pair is detectable. The attacker is assumed to add an interrupting signal $a[t]$ to $y[t]$ through the communication network, leading to a corrupted measurement signal $y_a[t]$. Next, the system is assumed to have a chi-squared (χ^2) attack detector and a perfect attack mitigation mechanism $\delta[t] = a[t]$ to recover the $y[t]$ signal once an attack is detected. That is, $y_f[t] = y_a[t] - \delta[t] = y[t]$ if an attack is detected. Otherwise, $y_f[t] = y_a[t]$. Then, the feedback controller uses a Kalman filter (KF) to estimate the state $\hat{x}[t]$ based on the input $y_f[t]$.

In KF, the estimation error $e[t]$ is the difference between the estimated $\hat{x}[t]$ and the real $x[t]$, i.e., $e[t] = \hat{x}[t] - x[t]$. Following the evolution of the KF dynamics, one can show that the estimation error is evolving as

$$e[t+1] = A_K e[t] + W_K w[t] - K(a[t+1] - i[t+1]\delta[t+1]) - Kv[t+1], t \geq 0, \tag{4.1}$$

where $A_K = A - KCA$, $W_K = I - KC$. Here I is the identity matrix and K is the steady-state Kalman gain which is considered a constant matrix. Moreover, $i[t]$ in (4.1) denotes a χ^2 detector defined in (4.2). In (4.2), $g = r[t]^T P_r r[t]$ (g is a scalar) where P_r is a pre-assigned constant matrix and $r[t]$ is a residual signal defined in (4.3). It should be noted that $g \sim \chi^2(k)$ (non-central chi-distribution) where k denotes the dimension of measurement $y[t]$. Besides, η is a pre-set threshold.

$$i[t] = \begin{cases} 0, & \text{if } 0 \leq g \leq \eta \\ 1, & \text{otherwise.} \end{cases} \tag{4.2}$$

$$r[t] = y[t] + a[t] - C(A\hat{x}[t-1] + Bu[t-1]) = CAe[t-1] + a[t] + Cw[t-1] + v[t]. \tag{4.3}$$

The goal of an optimal attack is to maximize the KF controller's cumulative expected estimation error. Mathematically, over a horizon of T steps, the optimal attack sequence is given by solving (4.4),

$$\max_{a[1],...,a[T]} \sum_{t=1}^{T} \mathbb{E}[||e[t]||^2] \tag{4.4}$$

$$s.t. \ \ KF \ error \ dynamics \ (4.1),$$
$$||a[t]|| \leq a_{max}, t \geq 0,$$

where $||\cdot||$ denotes the 2-norm and a_{max} reflects the maximal attacking capability of the attacker. In the literature, this is realized as an optimal control problem, or essentially an MDP problem. The MDP state is the error $e[\cdot]$ in (4.1), which depends only on the previous one-step error and the additive noises. The sequence of MDP actions are the attacker sequential injections $a[1], ..., a[T]$ depending on the states of the systems. Then, the transition probability is given by

$$p(e[t+1]|e[t], a[t]),$$

which is determined by (4.1). By expanding the objective function, one can find that the immediate expected reward used in this MDP at time step t is given by

$$\int_{e'} p(e'|e[t], a[t]) \cdot ||e'||^2 de'.$$

4.2 DYNAMIC PROGRAMMING

Overall, there are three basic methods for solving MDP problems: linear programming, heuristic search and dynamic programming. Linear programming obtains the optimal state value via solving a minimization problem with respect to the value of different states based on the Bellman equations. Heuristic search models MDP by a graph in which the node is the state and the arc between nodes represents the transition under a specific action, so MDP can be solved using many effective graph-based searching methods [53]. In this chapter, however, we focus on dynamic programming due to its superior scalability and converging speed.

In computer science or mathematics, *dynamic programming* (DP) can be perceived as a type of method that finds out the solution of a complicated problem by breaking it into multiple small sub-problems with similar structures. As the sub-problem is always tractable and its solutions are coupled with other sub-problems, the solution of the whole problem can be achieved by storing solutions of small sub-problems and then combining the solutions based on their interconnections. In the context of MDP, the task of making a sequence of decisions that maximizes the expected cumulative reward can be simplified as finding the optimal policy for each state. Therefore, the long-term decision problem can be divided into short-term decision problems for each state. The connection among the sub-problems is established by the Bellman equations.

To solve RL problems, one approach is to find the optimal state or action value functions, from which the optimal action can be directly obtained via the greedy strategy. Recall that the optimal value functions, i.e., value functions following the optimal policy π^*, are characterized by the Bellman optimality equations:

$$v_{\pi*}(s) = \max_a \sum_{s'} \sum_r p(s',r|s,a)\Big(r + \gamma \cdot v_{\pi*}(s')\Big), \qquad (4.5)$$

and

$$q_{\pi*}(s,a) = \sum_{s'} \sum_r p(s',r|s,a)\Big(r + \gamma \cdot \max_{a'} q_{\pi*}(s',a')\Big). \qquad (4.6)$$

Then, the key idea of DP is to obtain π^* by solving $v_{\pi*}(s)$ or $q_{\pi*}(s,a)$ in a recursive manner. In the following sections, we will introduce the DP methods of *policy iteration* and *value iteration* to solve the above Bellman optimality equations.

4.2.1 Policy Iteration

To recursively find the optimal policy, we need to first address a one-step problem, i.e., how to find a better policy than the current one. Toward this end, it is essential to evaluate the current policy quantitatively. One measurement for evaluating the current policy is the value function $v(s)$, which represents the long-term expected reward starting from s and following the current policy.

Policy evaluation: Given the transition matrix (MDP model) $p(s',r|s,a)$ for all $s \in \mathcal{S}$, $a \in \mathcal{A}$, $r \in \mathcal{R}$ and $s' \in \mathcal{S}^+$ ($\mathcal{S}^+$ is $\mathcal{S}$ plus a terminal state if the MDP is episodic), and policy π, the state value function $v_\pi(s)$ for each state can be obtained by solving the Bellman expectation equation in (3.16), i.e.,

$$v_\pi(s) = \sum_a \pi(a|s) \sum_{s'} \sum_r p(s',r|s,a)\Big(r + \gamma \cdot v_\pi(s')\Big). \qquad (4.7)$$

This implies that for N-state MDP we need to solve a system of N Bellman equations. However, when the state space is large, solving a large number of simultaneous linear equations could be computationally tedious. Alternatively, we herein use DP to iteratively approximate the value functions, where in a sequence of approximate value functions, each successive approximate value is obtained by using the Bellman equation. Note that in (4.7) the update of $v_\pi(s)$ for $\forall s \in \mathcal{S}$ at time instant $k+1$ is determined from the Bellman expectation equation using values $v_\pi(s')$ at time instant k. Under the same conditions that guarantee the existence of the fixed point/solutions to the Bellman equations, the convergence of such a sequence to the fixed point is guaranteed. Concretely, this iterative algorithm is given in Algorithm 5.

Algorithm 5 Policy Evaluation

1: **Input**: MDP model and policy π
2: **Output**: value array $v_\pi(s)$ for each state
3: Initialize a random value array, $v(s), \forall s \in \mathcal{S}$
4: **repeat**
5:     $\Delta \leftarrow 0$
6:     **for** $s \in \mathcal{S}$ **do**
7:         $v \leftarrow v_\pi(s)$
8:         Update $v_\pi(s)$ based on (4.7)
9:         $\Delta \leftarrow \max(|v - v_\pi(s)|, \Delta)$
10:    **end for**
11: **until** $\Delta < \theta$ (a pre-assigned small positive number)

Policy Improvement: Given the value functions for a given policy, it is straightforward to improve the policy following a greedy strategy. The priority of actions in one state can be decided by $q_\pi(s, a)$. It is true that

$$q_\pi(s, a) = \mathbb{E}_\pi[R_{t+1} + \gamma v_\pi(S_{t+1})|S_t = s, A_t = a] \tag{4.8}$$

$$= \sum_{s'} \sum_{r} p(s', r|s, a)[r + \gamma v_\pi(s')]. \tag{4.9}$$

Therefore, the action with the maximal Q-value can be selected as

$$\pi^*(s) = \text{argmax}_a q_\pi(s, a)$$

$$= \text{argmax}_a \sum_{s'} \sum_{r} p(s', r|s, a)[r + \gamma v_\pi(s')], \tag{4.10}$$

where argmax_a denotes the value of a that maximizes the expression (with ties broken arbitrarily).

Following the *policy improvement theorem* [159], it is known that such a greedy selection of actions is always better (or at least cannot be worse) than the current policy. Based on this fact, one can see that if iterating the *policy evaluation* and *policy improvement*, as illustrated in Fig. 4.2, the algorithm can converge to a policy and a stable value function. This is referred to as *policy iteration*. The pseudocode is given in Algorithm 6.

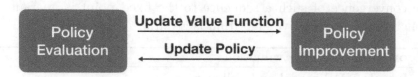

Figure 4.2: Policy iteration: The interaction between value function and policy function continues until convergence to the optimum.

Algorithm 6 Policy Iteration

1: **Input**: MDP model and an arbitrary policy π
2: **Output**: policy $\pi \approx \pi^*$
3: Initialize a random value array $v_\pi(s), \forall s \in \mathcal{S}$
4: **repeat**
5:     $\hat{v}(s) \leftarrow v_\pi, \forall s \in \mathcal{S}$
6:     Update v_π by policy evaluation in Algorithm 5
7:     Update π based on policy improvement (4.10)
8:     $\Delta \leftarrow \max\{|v_\pi - \hat{v}(s)|, \forall s \in \mathcal{S}\}$
9: **until** $\Delta < \theta$ (a pre-assigned small positive number)

It is straightforward to prove that policy iteration always converges to an optimal policy. The convergence is guaranteed when the terminal states exist or discounting factor $\gamma < 1$. Actually, these two conditions are mathematically similar. As long as the length n of decision making increases, $\gamma^n \to 0$. Once $\gamma^n \to 0$, the follow-up states will exert no impact on the current state and the sequence can be perceived as "terminated." Either condition assures that the decision-making process will end within finite steps.

4.2.1.1 Example

Example: *Grid world*

Grid world is a classic and widely used example for RL algorithm testing. The goal of the grid world problem is to navigate a robot to bypass obstacles and reach its home. Fig. 4.3 displays a grid map. It is assumed that the robot knows the map information in advance. The MDP model is given below.

State ($\mathcal{S}$): Each grid is represented by (row index, column index)

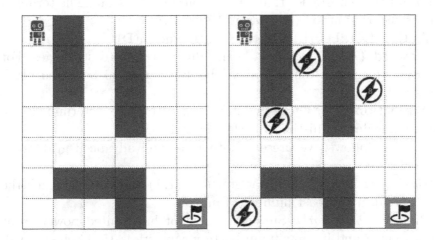

Figure 4.3: Grid world maps. The left map is the basic grid world and the right map is the advanced grid world, where the "lightning" icon indicates a power station and the number inside shows the corresponding power storage.

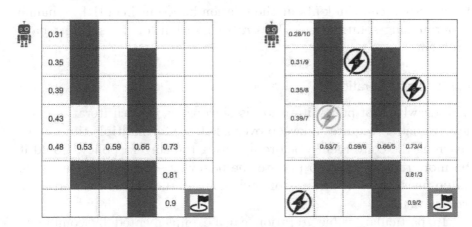

Figure 4.4: Solutions to the two grid world problems. Suppose $\gamma = 0.9$. The track of numbers on the map shows the optimal trajectory with each value representing the state value. The value (A/B) on the right map refers to the state value A as well as the remaining power B of the robot in that box and the half-transparent charger means that this charger has been used.

except for those obstacles that can be considered a state. The terminal state is the destination (the flag in Fig. 4.3).

Action ($\mathcal{A}$): Left(L), right(R), up(U), down(D).

Reward ($\mathcal{R}$): There exist many different reward strategies. For instance, we can set the arrival at the destination to be 1 and other states to be 0.

Transition ($\mathcal{T}$): Once the state and action are determined, the transition is deterministic, e.g., $p((1,1)|(2,1), U) = 1$.

In what follows, we present both basic and advanced grid world problems.

Basic grid world: The robot starts at $(1,1)$ and aims to reach the end at $(7,6)$ in the least number of moves.

Advanced grid world: Suppose the robot has limited power 10 at the beginning and its maximum battery capacity is 15. Each step will consume 1 unit of power. At each step, the robot can only choose to walk or charge. Meanwhile, there are some power supply stations with different power storage shown as numbers in the map. Each power supply station can only be used once.

The model-based solutions to the above two RL problems are given in Fig. 4.4. Readers can write the program to check these solutions, and if interested, can think about the relation between this MDP dynamic programming solution and *Dijkstra*'s algorithm for the shortest path problem.

4.2.2 Value Iteration

The drawback of policy iteration is obvious: as in each iteration, policy evaluation requires a sweep over all states for multiple times until reaching the convergence before updating the current policy. Could it be more time-efficient to update the policy as soon as it updates the value function? The answer, of course, is yes and this is referred to as *value iteration*.

In particular, value iteration can be implemented by combining (4.7) and (4.10), i.e., rather than updating value functions with the expectation value, it uses the maximum value among all actions, i.e.,

$$v(s) = \max_{a \in \mathcal{A}} \sum_{s'} \sum_{r} p(s', r|s, a) \Big(r + \gamma \cdot v_\pi(s') \Big)$$

$$= \max_{a \in \mathcal{A}} \Big(r(s, a) + \gamma \sum_{s'} p(s'|s, a) v(s') \Big). \tag{4.11}$$

Note that in (4.11) the update of $v(s)$ for $\forall s \in \mathcal{S}$ at time instant $k+1$ is determined from the Bellman optimality equation using values $v(s')$ at time instant k. The complete algorithm is shown in Algorithm 7. Even though value iteration changes the update order in comparison with policy iteration, it is proved that both algorithms yield the same optimal policy.

Algorithm 7 Value Iteration

1: **Input**: MDP model and an arbitrary policy π
2: **Output**: policy $\pi \approx \pi^*$
3: Initialize a random value array $v_\pi(s), \forall s \in \mathcal{S}$
4: **repeat**
5:     $\Delta \leftarrow 0$
6:     **for** $s \in \mathcal{S}$ **do**
7:       $v' \leftarrow v(s)$
8:       Update $v(s)$ based on (4.11)
9:       $\Delta \leftarrow \max(\Delta, |v(s) - v'|)$
10:    **end for**
11: **until** $\Delta \leq \theta$ (a pre-assigned small positive number)
12: $\pi \leftarrow \mathrm{argmax}_a r(s, a) + \gamma \sum_{s'} p(s'|s, a)v(s'), \forall s \in \mathcal{S}$
13: **return** π.

Readers are encouraged to rewrite the grid world program using value iteration, and compare this algorithm with policy iteration, e.g., discussing the convergence speed and convergence values.

4.2.3 Asynchronous Dynamic Programming

So far, we have discussed the synchronous DP methods. However, one can notice some major drawbacks of such methods. On the one hand, they require a sweep over the entire state space at each iteration. This sweep could be prohibitively costly if the state space is very large. On the other hand, since the update on the state value is synchronous, the agent needs to store two copies of value functions in each sweep over the states, e.g., all new values obtained from (4.11) and all old values used for the update in (4.11). For a very large state space, the storage memory could be an issue. Thus motivated, asynchronous DP can be viewed as an approach to speed up the iteration by updating the state values in some order using whatever values are available. However, due to this asynchronous nature, some states might be updated multiple times before a certain state is updated for its first time. In addition, asynchronous DP does not assure that it will converge faster than the synchronous DP, e.g., policy iteration or value iteration. But it can always help get rid of a long sweep of a large state space.

Typically, there are two types of asynchronous strategies: real-time update and prioritized sweeping. For real-time updates, at each time step the agent selects a particular state s_t to update the state value $v(s_t)$ following the Bellman equation (4.11). The state selection at each time step is based on agent's experience and thus the selection rule can be appropriately designed. Prioritized sweeping, however, ranks the states based on their Bellman error

$$\left| r(s,a) + \gamma \sum_{s' \in \mathcal{S}} p(s'|s,a)v(s') - v(s) \right|,$$

and always first updates the state with the maximum Bellman error. In summary, the pseudocode for both asynchronous DP algorithms are given in Algorithm 8 and Algorithm 9, respectively.

Algorithm 8 Asynchronous DP - Real-Time Update

1: **Input**: MDP model and an arbitrary policy π
2: **Output**: policy $\pi \approx \pi^*$
3: Initialize a random value array $v_\pi(s), \forall s \in \mathcal{S}$
4: $\Delta \leftarrow 0$
5: **repeat**
6:    select state s_t using agent's experience
7:    $v' \leftarrow v(s_t)$
8:    Update $v(s_t)$ by (4.11)
9:    $\Delta \leftarrow \max(\Delta, |v(s_t) - v'|)$
10: **until** $\Delta \leq \theta$
11: $\pi(s) \leftarrow \operatorname{argmax}_a r(s,a) + \gamma \sum_{s' \in \mathcal{S}} p(s'|s,a)v(s'), \forall s \in \mathcal{S}$
12: **return** π.

4.3 PARTIALLY OBSERVABLE MARKOV DECISION PROCESS

In MDP, it is assumed that the agent has full knowledge about the environment. However, in reality, *partially observable MDP* (POMDP) is more common. In POMDP, the agent has no direct information about the current state. It can only make an indirect observation of the underlying state and make an estimation on the true state based on the observation history.

Algorithm 9 Asynchronous DP - Prioritized Sweeping

1: **Input:** MDP model and an arbitrary policy π
2: **Output:** policy $\pi \approx \pi^*$
3: Initialize a random value array $v_\pi(s), \forall s \in \mathcal{S}$
4: $\Delta \leftarrow 0$
5: **repeat**
6:     **if** not exist a priority queue **then**
7:         Initialize a new priority queue with $v(s)$ as its elements
8:     **end if**
9:     Select the state s with the maximum Bellman error from the priority queue
10:     $v' \leftarrow v(s)$
11:     Update $v(s)$ by (4.11).
12:     Calculate Bellman error $e \leftarrow |v(s) - v'|$.
13:     $\Delta \leftarrow \max(\Delta, e)$
14:     Update the priority queue with e.
15: **until** $\Delta \leq \theta$
16: $\pi(s) \leftarrow \text{argmax}_a r(s,a) + \gamma \sum_{s' \in \mathcal{S}} p(s'|s,a)v(s'), \forall s \in \mathcal{S}$
17: **return** π.

Figure 4.5: Partially observable grid world. Given the light gray and dark gray squares as the only observable neighboring grids, the robot doesn't know on which grid on the map it is standing.

Take the grid world as an example. If a robot only has knowledge about its neighboring grids as shown in Fig. 4.5, then the problem of navigating the robot to home can be better modeled by POMDP, rather than MDP. If we still apply the classic MDP here and use the neighboring grids information to define the state, then the agent will take the same action when its surroundings are similar. Apparently, by doing so, it is very likely that the agent will fall into some dead loop. In practice, POMDP has a broad range of applications in many fields, such as robotics, finance, and medical applications, in which the information received by the agent is always incomplete or noisy. For instance, when doctors are making a therapy plan, they may not have full and perfect information about the patient's body. All they can do is to rely on different bio-markers as well as their past experience to make a decision.

Different from MDP, POMDP introduces a new observation variant Ω and the corresponding observation function $\mathcal{O}$ into the original MDP. Thereby, POMDP can be represented as a tuple of $(\mathcal{S}, \mathcal{A}, \mathcal{R}, \mathcal{T}, \Omega, \mathcal{O})$:

1. $\mathcal{S}, \mathcal{A}, \mathcal{R}, \mathcal{T}$: As described in MDP, $\mathcal{S}$ and $\mathcal{A}$ respectively represent the state and action space. $\mathcal{R}(s, a)$ is the reward function with respect to the state s and action a. $\mathcal{T}(s, a, s')$ represents the transition probability $p(s'|s, a)$;

2. Ω: Observation space;

3. $\mathcal{O}$: The observation function. For an action a and the resulting state s', it gives a probability distribution over the possible observations as $Pr(O_{t+1} = o|A_t = a, S_{t+1} = s') \in \mathcal{O}$.

4.3.1 Belief MDP

As the agent cannot identify its current state, the best choice is to maintain a probability distribution over the states and then updates this probability distribution based on its real-time observations. Following this idea, we can convert POMDP to MDP, or "belief MDP." Specifically, the belief MDP consists of a state estimator and a policy/controller, as shown in Fig. 4.6. The state estimator updates an internal belief state b which summarizes the past experience, while the controlling part (policy π) generates the optimal action based on the belief state b rather than the real state of the world.

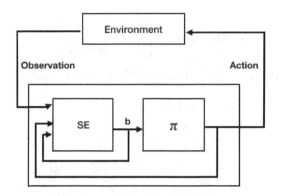

Figure 4.6: POMDP decomposition. SE represents a state estimator and π is a control policy.

In particular, the belief state $b_t(s)$ is defined as the probability of staying at state s at time t given the past experience,

$$b_t(s) = Pr(S_t = s | b_0, a_0, o_1, ..., b_{t-1}, a_{t-1}, o_t)$$
$$= Pr(S_t = s | b_{t-1}, a_{t-1}, o_t).$$

The second equality is true because $b_t \in \mathcal{B}$, defined in the first equality, is a *sufficient statistic*, implying that no other statistic calculated from the same history can provide more information [182]. Additionally, we have $\sum_{s \in \mathcal{S}} b_t(s) = 1$. According to the definition of b_t, the corresponding transition function in terms of the belief state b is given by

$$
\begin{aligned}
p(b'|b,a) &= \sum_{o \in \Omega} p(o, b'|a, b) \\
&= \sum_{o \in \Omega} p(b'|a, b, o) p(o|a, b) \\
&= \sum_{o \in \Omega} p(b'|a, b, o) \sum_{s' \in \mathcal{S}} p(o, s'|a, b) \\
&= \sum_{o \in \Omega} p(b'|a, b, o) \sum_{s' \in \mathcal{S}} p(o|a, s', b) p(s'|a, b) \\
&= \sum_{o \in \Omega} p(b'|a, b, o) \sum_{s' \in \mathcal{S}} p(o|a, s') p(s'|a, b) \\
&= \sum_{o \in \Omega} p(b'|a, b, o) \sum_{s' \in \mathcal{S}} p(o|a, s') \sum_{s \in \mathcal{S}} p(s'|a, s) b(s),
\end{aligned}
\tag{4.12}
$$

where

$$p(b'|a, b, o) = \begin{cases} 1, & b_o^a = b' \\ 0, & \text{otherwise,} \end{cases}$$

and given a and o the belief state $b_o^a(s')$ can be updated as

$$\begin{aligned} b_o^a(s') &= p(s'|b, a, o) \\ &= \frac{p(s', o|b, a)}{p(o|b, a)} \\ &= \frac{p(o|s', b, a) \sum_{s \in S} p(s'|s, a)b(s)}{\sum_{s' \in S} p(o|s', b, a)p(s'|b, a)} \\ &= \frac{p(o|s', b, a) \sum_{s \in S} p(s'|s, a)b(s)}{\sum_{s' \in S} p(o|s', a)p(s'|b, a)} \\ &= \frac{p(o|s', a) \sum_{s \in S} p(s'|s, a)b(s)}{\sum_{s' \in S} p(o|s', a) \sum_{s \in S} p(s'|s, a)b(s)}. \end{aligned}$$

Here we use the fact that $p(o|s', b, a) = p(o|s', a)$, which is known as part of the model. For the belief state transition, the agent simply executes the action following the policy and then updates the belief state according to the above equation. Given the belief state, the goal becomes maximizing the expected sum of the discounted belief reward

$$r(b, a) = \sum_{s \in S} r(s, a)b(s).$$

Overall, any POMDP can be equivalently transformed into the above continuous belief MDP. As a result, the algorithms for finding the optimal policy to MDP, e.g., value iteration and policy iteration, can also be used here to search for the optimal policy to POMDP. For instance, to perform value iteration, the Bellman optimality equation for the belief MDP can be characterized in (4.13):

$$v(b) = \max_{a \in \mathcal{A}} \left[r(b, a) + \gamma \sum_{b' \in B} p(b'|a, b)v(b') \right], \qquad (4.13)$$

where $p(b'|a, b)$ is obtained by (4.12).

Note, however, that b is a continuous variable, which means the value function $v(b)$ has infinite space. Therefore, it is essential to find out the underlying pattern and make a good approximation about the value function in order to reduce the searching space. It has been proved by Sondki [154] that the value function with respect to the belief state is a *piece-wise linear convex* (PWLC) function. To understand the reason why (4.13) is a PWLC function, new concepts, the *policy tree* and *alpha vector*, should be introduced. We refer interested readers to the literature on this topic for details.

4.4 CONTINUOUS MARKOV DECISION PROCESS

Continuous MDP consists of continuous state MDP and continuous-time MDP. Continuous state MDP is a collection of MDPs in which $\mathcal{S}$ or $\mathcal{A}$ is a continuous space rather than a finite set. Hence, the transition function $p(s'|a, s)$ becomes a continuous function with respect to (s, a, s'). In contrast, in continuous-time MDP, the agent is moving along a continuous time horizon instead of step by step, meaning that the interval between decisions is not constant but a controlled variable. In what follows, we discuss continuous state MDP and we refer interested readers to [51, 19] for more detailed tutorials on both types of continuous MDP.

In the real world, continuous state MDP is omnipresent. For example, in Example 4.1.1, the state is the continuous estimation error and the attack signal (action) is also a continuous variable. If we still want to use the methods for the discrete MDP on the continuous state MDP, the discretization method (DM) is most straightforward. The idea is to discretize the continuous space into a finite set and then apply either policy iteration or value iteration to find the optimal policy. To discretize the space, one could adopt the evenly split strategy like grid world or use advanced clustering methods to split the space like continuous U-Tree [168]. However, DM suffers from the *curse of dimensionality*. Suppose a continuous space $\mathcal{S}$ in $\mathbb{R}^n$. Then if we divide each dimension into k equal intervals, the size of the discrete state space will be k^n, which grows exponentially with respect to the dimension n. Therefore, DM cannot provide a feasible solution to many real complex applications. Next, we briefly introduce alternative techniques to deal with the continuous state MDP.

4.4.1 Lazy Approximation

So far, the optimal value function is always represented by a lookup table where each state is associated with a unique value. However, as the state becomes a continuous variable, the lookup table does not scale well in this situation and thus it is essential to adopt a function

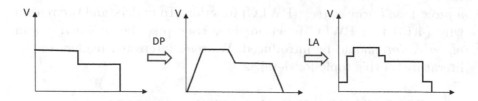

Figure 4.7: Value function update in lazy approximation.

approximation instead of a lookup table. As mentioned in the previous section about POMDP, the value function with respect to the belief state can be generalized to be a piecewise linear convex function represented by a set of linear vectors. Lazy approximation (LA) [85] takes advantage of similar ideas and provides a more effective solution than DM.

First, LA approximates the continuous transition function $p(s'|a, s)$ as a piecewise linear (PWL) function. Then the Bellman optimality equation of the continuous state MDP is given by

$$v_{t+1}(s) = \max_{a \in \mathcal{A}} \left[r(s, a) + \int_{\mathcal{S}} p(s'|a, s)v_t(s)ds \right], \quad (4.14)$$

where the integral is in fact a convolution of the transition function and the value function.

As $p(s'|a, s)$ is a PWL function, then suppose the initial value function v_0 is a piecewise constant (PWC) function. After the one-step Bellman update in (4.14), the value function will evolve into a PWL function. However, if we take one more update, PWL will turn into a piecewise quadratic function. To reserve the PWL nature of the value function, the LA algorithm re-approximates the PWL function into a PWC function. This process is illustrated in Fig. 4.7.

As the value function remains PWC periodically, some neighboring states share the same state value. This is, to some extent, similar to DM. However, DM would evenly discretize the space while LA's PWC approximation is based on the previous PWL function, where the intervals will not be identical. Moreover, LA uses a continuous transition function to execute the Bellman update while DM discretizes the continuous transition function by introducing additional error. Therefore, generally speaking, LA outperforms DM in applications.

4.4.2   Function Approximation

Now let us discuss more on *function approximation* (FA). One can see that lazy approximation is a special case of FA where it approximates the continuous value function as a piecewise constant function. In general, many other function approximation methods have been investigated in the literature in the past decades, including the basic linear approximation or deep neural networks. Concretely, suppose an FA is represented by $v(s) = f(s; w)$ where w refers to the parameters of FA, then the optimal value function (or parameter w) can be achieved by minimizing the Bellman residual value L, i.e., the error between the current state value and the estimate from its successors, i.e., $r + \gamma v(s')$, based on the Bellman equation,

$$L = \frac{1}{N} \sum_{i=1}^{N} \sum_{s} [r_i + \gamma v_i(s') - v_i(s)]^2, \qquad (4.15)$$

where n denotes the N samples from the agent's training experience. A gradient-based method, or backpropagation if using neural network [140], can be adopted to update w iteratively until the optimal w is achieved. We will discuss FA in detail in the chapter on deep reinforcement learning. Related topics such as the optimality and time-efficiency of different FAs can be found in [184, 12].

4.5   REMARKS

Model-based reinforcement learning is very useful in the applications where the underlying dynamics of the environment can be perfectly concluded. As the model of the dynamics is known, much less training samples are needed compared with the model-free methods (to be discussed in the next chapter). In addition, for some particular applications where training samples are sparse, model-based methods could be more useful than model-free methods. For instance, in the clinician-in-loop decision support, the agent is requested to learn from the patient's electronic health record (EHR) and alert the caregivers when the patient is ready for medical treatment such as ventilation. In such medical applications, the data is sparse and irregular. Therefore, it is necessary to set up a *good* model for more efficient learning.

In this chapter, we have introduced two dynamic programming-based solutions to MDP: policy iteration and value iteration. Policy iteration is a two-stage method, including first evaluating the value function and then updating the current policy by the greedy strategy. Value iteration integrates these two steps and updates the policy immediately when the value function has been updated. Next, motivated by the case that the state space could be very large, we have introduced the asynchronous value iteration to save memory and speed up updates. However, fundamentally all dynamic programming-based methods are subject to the curse of dimensionality, implying that this type of method would be intractable or substantially time-consuming when the state space is super large or continuous. Function approximation is a widely used technique to handle this issue, which will be discussed in later chapters. Furthermore, since in real-world applications the agent may not directly access the states, we have introduced the *partially observable MDP* (POMDP) and shown that all POMDP can be converted into an MDP called the belief MDP.

To end this chapter, we remark that all MDPs that we have discussed so far are centralized problems. That is, there is only one agent in the environment. However, many real cyber physical systems are actually characterized as multi-agent systems. For instance, in a sensor network, tens of distributed sensors need to coordinate with each other to perform a large-scale sensing task. Many of these problems can be modeled as the so-called *decentralized MDP* (Dec-MDP). One major difference between the centralized and the decentralized MDP is that in Dec-MDP there exists latency among agents. One agent could not know the current states or actions of other agents in a timely manner. Hence, the methods for addressing the centralized MDPs cannot be directly applied to Dec-MDP. Much research has been conducted in this area [16, 35].

4.6 EXERCISES

4.1. In which cases would you prefer to use dynamic programming? Approximate dynamic programming?

4.2. Explain what the purpose of the discount factor in infinite horizon problems is. What effect does a small discount factor have? What about a large one?

4.3. Consider the model-based MDP problem as shown in Fig. 4.8. The number above the line refers to the probability of taking that action and r is the reward for the corresponding action.

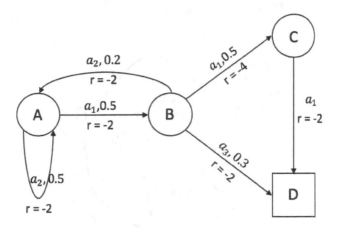

Figure 4.8: Model-based MDP.

a). Use matrix-form Bellman equation to find the value of states $(\gamma = 0.5)$.

b). Suppose that the initial values of all states are 0. The agent follows the policy given in the graph and assumes the discount factor $\gamma = 1$. Find the values of all states in the first two steps $k = 1$ and $k = 2$ in the algorithm of iterative policy evaluation.

c). Following the results of question (b), update the values of all states for $k = 3$ using the value iteration method.

d). Summarize the difference between value iteration and policy iteration.

4.4. [129] Consider the following MDP in Fig. 4.9 with discount factor $\gamma = 0.5$. Uppercase letters A, B, C represent states; arcs represent state transitions; lowercase letters ab, ba, bc, ca, cb represent actions; signed integer fractions represent transition probabilities.

a). Consider the uniform random policy $\pi(s, a)$ that takes all actions from state s with equal probability. Starting with an initial value function of $V_1(A) = V_1(B) = V_1(C) = 2$, apply one synchronous iteration of iterative policy evaluation (i.e., one backup for each state) to compute a new value function $V_2(s)$;

b). Apply one iteration of a greedy policy improvement to compute a new, deterministic policy $\pi(s)$.

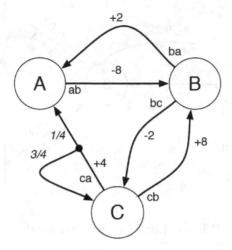

Figure 4.9: ABC MDP model [129].

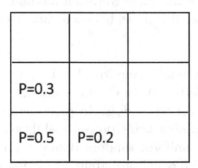

Figure 4.10: Grid world with partial state observation: the number in the box represents the probability that the agent stays in that box.

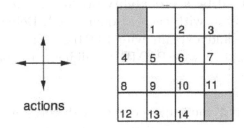

Figure 4.11: Small grid world [159].

4.5. At each iteration of value iteration algorithm, the current best policy can be extracted as a result of the "max" operation. Provide an example that the best policy at step k is the same as the best policy at step $k + 1$. In such a case, can the policy ever change again with further iterations of the value function?

4.6. Given a model of the reward and transition functions, derive the update equation in a value iteration using the Q-values instead of the state values.

4.7. Explain the difference between the asynchronous value iteration and the standard value iteration, and the importance of the state ordering in the asynchronous value iteration.

4.8. (Small Grid World, Example 4.1 in [159]) Consider the 4×4 grid-world shown in Fig. 4.11. The nonterminal states are $1, 2, 3 \cdots 14$. There are four actions (up, down, left, right) possible in each state. The reward is -1 on all transitions until the terminal state is reached. Any actions leading out of the grid leave the state unchanged. The terminal state (two places) is shaded in the figure. Suppose the agent follows the equiprobable random policy (all actions equally likely) and the discount factor $\gamma = 1$. If we run an iterative policy evaluation (synchronous update) based on the Bellman expectation equation and initialize all state values $V(i) = 0$ for $i = 1, 2, \cdots 14$ at step $k = 0$ (terminal states have zero values for all steps). What is the state value of $V(1)$ and $V(2)$ at $k = 1$ and $k = 2$?

4.9. Consider the grid world in Fig. 4.10, in which the position of the agent is represented by a probability distribution over possible states (i.e., 9 states in total with each a square box). Define the belief-state for this example and explain why POMDPs are called "belief-state MDPs." Also, explain why POMDP is difficult to solve, for example, using value iteration.

4.10. Consider that you are concerned with collision avoidance of two vehicles in close proximity and the agent in one vehicle wants to find a policy to avoid collision. Do we need to model this as a POMDP or MDP? Why?

CHAPTER 5

Model-Free Reinforcement Learning

CONTENTS

5.1 INTRODUCTION TO MODEL-FREE RL

In the previous chapter we introduced model-based reinforcement learning, in which the agent knows the reward function and the transition function of the environment. In other words, the agent knows all elements of an MDP and is able to compute the solution before executing an action in the real environment. In the literature, this is typically called *planning*. All algorithms in the previous chapter, e.g., value iteration, policy iteration, etc., are referred to as classic planning algorithms.

However, in most cases, it is hard for the agent to know the environment before interacting with it. Specifically, the agent has no clue how the environment will response to its action and what immediate reward it will receive for doing so. For example, a navigating robot explores an unknown underground caves; an autonomous driving vehicle is designed to avoid all kinds of unpredictable collisions on the roads. This challenging fact leads to the most merit of reinforcement learning, model-free reinforcement learning, which is completely apart from a planning problem. The basic idea of model-free reinforcement learning is that the agent tries to take some actions based on its historical experience, observe how the environment responses, and then find an optimal policy in the long run.

In this chapter, we first introduce the model-free methods for policy evaluation, a.k.a. *RL prediction*, in which the value function $v_\pi(s)$ is estimated for a fixed arbitrary policy π. Next, we discuss the model-free methods for the optimal policy search, a.k.a. *RL control*, in which a policy is found in an iterative manner to maximize the value functions.

5.2 RL PREDICTION

There are several approaches to evaluate a given policy by estimating the value function $v_\pi(s)$. In this section, two typical approaches, *Monte Carlo* and *Temporal Difference*, are introduced, upon which more sophisticated approaches can be studied.

5.2.1 Monte Carlo Learning

Different from dynamic programming, the Monte Carlo method does not require the agent to explicitly know the model, instead, the Monte Carlo method learns directly from sampled experience. In most cases, the Monte Carlo method is applied to episodic tasks, in which the agent always has a start state, a terminal state and rewards in a finite time period no matter what actions are taken in each step of the episode.

In order to evaluate the state value, in dynamic programming we use the Bellman expectation equation to obtain the value $v_\pi(s)$ by leveraging the known MDP model. In the Monte Carlo approach, however, the agent averages the return values from a set of episodes to estimate the actual expectation. Specifically, to evaluate the current policy, the agent runs multiple episodes following the current policy. One complete episode is defined as an experience, which consists of a randomly selected start state and a terminal state with a return value. To evaluate the state value, we compute the mean of the return value for such a state based on multiple episode experiences. Basically there are two widely used Monte Carlo methods: first-visit Monte Carlo and every-visit Monte Carlo.

First-visit Monte Carlo: For each episode, an agent may visit a particular state multiple times before reaching the terminal state. However, to calculate the value of one state, i.e., the mean of the total return from that state, only the return from the first time the agent visits this state will be counted for the total return. We use $G_{ij}(s)$ to represent the return of the state s in the *i-th* episode when visiting the state s for the *j-th* time. Then for the first-visit Monte Carlo, the value of state s is calculated as

$$v_{t+1}(s) = \frac{G_{11}(s) + G_{21}(s) + G_{31}(s) + \cdots G_{t1}(s)}{N_t(s)},$$

where $N_t(s)$ is the total number of the *first visits* to state s in t episodes. One can see that each return $G_{ij}(s)$ in the above formula is an independent, identically distributed (i.i.d.) estimate of $v_\pi(s)$. Therefore, according to the *law of large numbers*, as $N_t(s) \to \infty$ we have $v(s) \to v_\pi(s)$. This first-visit MC method is summarized in Algorithm 10.

Algorithm 10 First-Visit Monte-Carlo Prediction

1: **Input:** Policy π to be evaluated, an arbitrary state-value function $v(s)$, an empty list of total return $\hat{G}(s)$ for all $s \in \mathcal{S}$
2: **Output:** State value function $v(s)$
3: **Repeat forever:** Use current policy π to generate an episode i
   In the episode, for each state s:
   1. Record the return $G_{i1}(s)$ following the first occurrence of s
   2. Append return to the total return $\hat{G}(s)$
   3. Assign the average return $\frac{\hat{G}(s)}{N(s)}$ to the corresponding state value function $v(s)$

Every-visit Monte Carlo: In each episode, the return for every time the agent visits that state is added to the total return. Then for every-visit Monte Carlo, the value of state s is calculated as

$$v_{t+1}(s) = \frac{G_{11}(s) + G_{12}(s) + \cdots + G_{21}(s) + G_{22}(s) \cdots + G_{t1}(s) + G_{t2}(s) + \cdots}{N_t(s)},$$

where $N_t(s)$ is the total number of *visits* to state s in such a set of episodes and t is the total number of episodes. Different from the first-visit Monte Carlo formula, the return $G_{ij}(s)$ is no longer i.i.d. since the returns from visiting a state multiple times in one episode are somewhat correlated. However, it is shown in [152] that $v(s)$ also converges to $v_\pi(s)$.

Notice that one major downside for the above averaging algorithms is that the agent needs to memorize all returns $G_{ij}(s)$ before estimating the state value $v_\pi(s)$. One way to handle this issue is to implement the above algorithms in an iterative manner, i.e., episode by episode. For instance, the first-visit Monte Carlo method can be implemented as follows. When completing the $(t+1)$-th episode where $G_{t+1}(s)$ denotes the return from the $(t+1)$-th episode, the state value can be updated below:

$$
\begin{aligned}
v_{t+1}(s) &= \frac{G_{11}(s) + G_{21}(s) + \cdots + G_{t1}(s)}{N_t(s)} \\
&= \frac{v_t(s)N_{t-1}(s) + G_{t1}(s)}{N_t(s)} \\
&= \frac{v_t(s)(N_t(s) - 1) + G_{t1}(s)}{N_t(s)} \\
&= v_t(s) + \frac{1}{N_t(s)}\Big(G_{t1}(s) - v_t(s)\Big).
\end{aligned}
\tag{5.1}
$$

By doing so, the agent only needs to store the value $v_t(s)$ and $N_t(s)$ in each iteration. To search for an optimal policy, knowing state values alone is not sufficient. Starting in a state, the best policy is to take the action that leads to the largest return, i.e., the sum of the reward (of taking such an action) and the next state value. In other words, the state-action value $q_\pi(s, a)$, the expected return when starting in state s and taking action a, needs to be estimated. Similarly, the Monte Carlo method can be used for estimating $q_\pi(s, a)$ in the same way as that used for estimating $v_\pi(s)$. However, one should notice that some state-action pairs may be never visited for the training episodes. Specifically, consider a deterministic policy π, one can only estimate one action value starting in one state s. In other words, all other action values starting in such a state will be always zero. This fact will cause trouble if the agent wants to improve the policy, which requires to compare all possible action values starting in a state. One approach to deal with such a problem, named *exploring starts*, is to have each episode start from any state-action pair with non-zero probability. As the number of episodes increases to infinity, all state-action pair will be visited an infinite number of times.

Thus far it is assumed that the environment or process is stationary. However, most of the real-world episodes are non-stationary. Therefore, one should assign more weight on the recent returns than the past ones. In particular, the Monte Carol method for a non-stationary process can be implemented in an iterative manner as follows,

$$v_{t+1}(s) = v_t(s) + \alpha(G_t - v_t(s)), \tag{5.2}$$

where $\alpha \in (0, 1]$ refers to the fixed step size. By expanding the above iteration, it yields,

$$v_{t+1}(s) = (1 - \alpha)^t v_1(s) + \sum_{i=1}^{t} \alpha(1 - \alpha)^{t-i} G_i,$$

from which we see that the weight decays exponentially on the past returns.

5.2.2 Temporal-Difference (TD) Learning

Recall that for dynamic programming the agent requires the knowledge of the environment model, e.g., reward and state transition matrix, and the update of the current state value depends on the value of other states, a.k.a. *bootstrapping*. The Monte Carlo method, however, conducts learning based on the episodic experience and does not bootstrap. In other words, the Monte Carlo method must keep collecting the rewards, for example, until the end of the episode for the first-visit MC and then updates the value $v(s)$ in (5.2). This fact results in a significant delay of learning when an episode is long. Essentially, this is one of the major disadvantages of non-bootstrapping RL methods. In this section, we introduce a new method called Temporal-Difference (TD) learning, which combines the advantages of the DP and MC methods, namely, the bootstrapping of DP and the model-free sampling of MC. In the following discussion, we assume RL in a non-stationary environment, which is likely to be the most application scenarios.

5.2.2.1 TD(0)

We start with the recursive Monte Carlo method in (5.2). Specifically, the update of the estimate V of v_π depends on the current estimated state value $V(S_t)$ and the latest actual return G_t of the episode task:

$$V(S_t) \leftarrow V(S_t) + \alpha(G_t - V(S_t)).$$

Then the basic idea of TD(0) is to use the estimated return $R_{t+1} + \gamma V(S_{t+1})$ to replace the actual episodic return G_t. It yields,

$$V(S_t) \leftarrow V(S_t) + \alpha(R_{t+1} + \gamma V(S_{t+1}) - V(S_t)), \tag{5.3}$$

where $R_{t+1} + \gamma V(S_{t+1})$ is called the TD-target and $\sigma_t = R_{t+1} + \gamma V(S_{t+1}) - V(S_t)$ is called TD-error. This formula indicates that the state value $V(S_t)$ is updated based on the observed instantaneous reward R_{t+1} and the current estimate $V(S_{t+1})$ when moving to the next state S_{t+1} at time step $t + 1$. That is, the bootstrapping (i.e., learn a guess from a guess) is employed to resolve the latency issue in MC. This method is referred to as TD(0) in the literature. The reason why we can use $R_{t+1} + \gamma V(S_{t+1})$ in TD(0) to replace G_t can be found in the way we calculate the state value. That is,

$$
\begin{aligned}
v_\pi(s) &= \mathbb{E}_\pi[G_t | S_t = s] \\
&= \mathbb{E}_\pi[\sum_{k=0}^{\infty} \gamma^k R_{t+k+1} | S_t = s] \\
&= \mathbb{E}_\pi[R_{t+1} + \sum_{k=1}^{\infty} \gamma^k R_{t+k+1} | S_t = s] \\
&= \mathbb{E}_\pi[R_{t+1} + \gamma \sum_{k=1}^{\infty} \gamma^{k-1} R_{t+k+1} | S_t = s] \\
&= \mathbb{E}_\pi[R_{t+1} + \gamma \sum_{k=0}^{\infty} \gamma^k R_{t+k+2} | S_t = s] \\
&= \mathbb{E}_\pi[R_{t+1} + \gamma v_\pi(S_{t+1}) | S_t = s].
\end{aligned}
\tag{5.4}
$$

5.2.2.2 TD(λ)

Recall that in the MC method, the update of the estimated state value is given by

$$V(S_{t+1}) = V(S_t) + \alpha(G_{t+1} - V(S_t))$$
$$= V(S_t) + \alpha(R_{t+1} + \gamma R_{t+2} + \cdots + \gamma^{T-t-1} R_T - V(S_t)),$$
$$(5.5)$$

where $G_{t+1} = R_{t+1} + \gamma R_{t+2} + \cdots + \gamma^{T-t-1} R_T$ is the return when the agent starts at time step t in state s and terminates at time step T of the episode. In TD(0), however, we estimate the return G_{t+1} by using $R_{t+1} + \gamma V(S_{t+1})$, where $V(S_{t+1})$ is the estimate of the expected return for the next state, i.e., the state that the agent visits at time step $t+1$. As previously discussed, MC uses the true return, e.g., collecting rewards until the end of the episode, as the target to update the state value. But this mechanism could lead to significant delay if the episode is long. In contrast, TD(0) only needs the instantaneous reward and the estimated state value in the next step to update the current state value. This means the update of TD(0) has minimal delay. However, the true next-step state value $V(S_{t+1})$ is not known and only the estimate can be used instead. Therefore, the accuracy of the update could be questionable. From these arguments, we see that MC and TD(0) can be viewed as extreme cases in the tradeoff of estimate delay and accuracy. Can we design a mechanism with performance in the middle?

Now, let us introduce another mechanism, named TD(λ), in which more than one-step estimated returns are considered and the weighted sum over the multiple estimated returns is used as the target to update $V(S_t)$. Mathematically, TD(λ) is defined as follows,

$$V(S_t) \leftarrow V(S_t) + \alpha(G_t^{\lambda} - V(S_t))$$

with

$$G_t^{\lambda} = (1 - \lambda) \sum_{n=1}^{\infty} \lambda^{n-1} G_t^n,$$

where $\lambda \in [0, 1]$ serves as the weight of each G_t^n and the sum of weights equal to one for $\lambda \in [0, 1)$. The final estimated return G_t^{λ} is the weighted sum of all the returns based on 1-step, 2-step, $\cdots$, n-step return values. Here the n-step return value is defined as

$$G_t^n = R_{t+1} + \gamma R_{t+2} + \cdots + \gamma^{n-1} R_{t+n} + \gamma^n V(S_{t+n}).$$

Assume a terminal state is reached at time step T where we use G_t to denote all subsequent n-step returns, then G_t^λ can be separated as

$$G_t^\lambda = (1 - \lambda) \sum_{n=1}^{T-t-1} \lambda^{n-1} G_t^n + \lambda^{T-t-1} G_t.$$

According to this equation, $G_t^\lambda = G_t$ when $\lambda = 1$. Thus, TD(λ) becomes the Monte Carlo algorithm in (5.2). In addition, $G_t^\lambda = G_t^1$ when $\lambda = 0$, implying that TD(λ) becomes TD(0) in (5.3). Therefore, TD(λ) can be viewed as the space of RL methods lying between Monte Carlo and TD(0).

From the definition of G_t^λ, one can notice that for $\lambda \in (0, 1]$ such a estimated return on the current step t depends on the complete episode in the future. In other words, the agent needs to wait until the end of the episode to obtain G_t^λ. This fact encounters the same downside as that in the Monte Carlo method. One breakthrough to handle this large delay issue is to implement TD(λ) via the mechanism of *eligibility trace*, which is comprehensively introduced in [159].

Finally, we remark that the method of estimating the state-action value $q_\pi(s, a)$ for the current policy π is the same as the methods of estimating $v_\pi(s)$ described above.

5.3 RL CONTROL

Knowing the method of estimating the value functions for a given policy, we are now ready to learn a (near-)optimal policy, a.k.a. RL control. In this section, we introduce several control algorithms that are widely used in real-world applications. Similar to the prediction algorithms, each control algorithm that stems from the corresponding prediction algorithm has its own *pros and cons*.

5.3.1 Monte Carlo Control

Overall, the Monte Carlo control updates the policy as the following process: it firstly evaluates the current policy (E) and obtains the resulting state-action pair value, then it improves the policy (I) and moves on to the next round for evaluation and improvement, i.e.,

$$\pi_0 \xrightarrow{E} q_{\pi_0} \xrightarrow{I} \pi_1 \xrightarrow{E} q_{\pi_1} \xrightarrow{I} \pi_2 \xrightarrow{E} ... \xrightarrow{I} \pi^* \xrightarrow{E} q_{\pi^*},$$

where π^* and q_{π^*} denote the optimal policy and the optimal state-action values, respectively. Note that in the step of evaluations, one can use the algorithm of Monte Carlo with *exploring starts* such that the state-action value function $Q(s, a)$ on all state-action pairs can be estimated over long run. In the step of policy improvement, greedy policy can be used in which the action starting in each state is determined as follows,

$$\pi(s) = argmax_a \ Q(s, a).$$

Based on the *policy improvement theorem*, as shown in Section 4.2 in book [159], such a greedy policy ensures that the policy is always improved until it is optimal.

Furthermore, the alternation between policy evaluation and policy improvement is not necessarily performed after all state-action values being updated. In other words, the alternation can be done on an episode-by-episode basis. Putting the above together, the Monte Carlo control algorithm is summarized in Algorithm 11.

Algorithm 11 Monte Carlo Control

1: **Input**: Arbitrary policy π_0; Arbitrary $Q(s, a)$ values for all states and actions.
2: **Output**: the optimal policy π^*
3: **Repeat forever**:
   1. Generate an episode with exploring starts by following the current policy π
   2. For each state-action pair (s, a) in an episode, update the $Q(s, a)$ based on the *first visit* or *every visit* Monte Carlo algorithm
   3. For each state s in the episode, update the policy as

   $$\pi(s) = argmax_a \ Q(s, a)$$

5.3.2 TD-Based Control

In the previous section, we have introduced TD prediction algorithms, e.g., TD(0) and TD(λ). Now we will form several new control algorithms based on TD prediction on the state-action pair. Before diving into the details of the TD-based control algorithms, we firstly introduce two concepts: on-policy learning and off-policy learning.

1. **On-policy learning** is a learning method in which the policy π is updated based on the experience following the current policy π.

2. **Off-policy learning** is a learning method in which the policy π is updated based on the experience following another policy μ.

We will discuss these two different learning methods in detail later.

5.3.2.1 Q-Learning

In TD(0) prediction, we update the state value at time step t based on the instantaneous reward and the estimated return on the next state, i.e.,

$$V(S_t) \leftarrow V(S_t) + \alpha(R_{t+1} + \gamma V(S_{t+1}) - V(S_t)).$$

Motivated by this state value update, the (one-step) TD control, a.k.a. *Q-learning* [179], is given below in which the state value is replaced with the state-action pair value.

$$Q(S_t, A_t) \leftarrow Q(S_t, A_t) + \alpha(R_{t+1} + \gamma \max_a Q(S_{t+1}, a) - Q(S_t, A_t))$$

Obviously Q-learning is an off-policy control method as it requires the agent to choose the maximum state-action value, no matter what the current policy is. The Q-learning algorithm is summarized in Algorithm 12.

Algorithm 12 Q-learning Algorithm

1: **Input:** Arbitrary $Q(S, A)$ and $Q(\text{terminal state}, \cdot) = 0$
2: **Output:** (near-) optimal policy π^*
3: **Repeat:** for each episode
4: Initialize S
5: **repeat**
6:     Choose action A from state S following the policy π derived by Q (e.g., ϵ-greedy policy)
7:     Take action A, obtain reward R and the next state S'
8:     Update Q values as

$$Q(S, A) \leftarrow Q(S, A) + \alpha(R + \gamma \max_a Q(S', a) - Q(S, A))$$

9:     $S \leftarrow S'$
10: **until** S is the terminal state

Under the conditions that all state-action pairs are consistently updated and the sequence of step-size satisfies the usual convergence condition, the Q-learning algorithm has been proved to converge to the optimal Q values.

5.3.2.2 Example

Example (*Adaptive embedded control of CPS* [21])

In a cyber-physical system, an *embedded control system* (ECS) is always needed to control a physical device. However, most of the current ECS has fixed system parameters, which are configured at design in advance. One approach to improve the efficiency of the ECS is to online adapt the ECS parameters, such as sampling rates and computation settings. Consider a cart-pole swing-up task as shown in Fig. 5.1. The processor/actuator, powered by a battery, generates force commands applied to the cart. The control task is to swing up the pole from fall position to upright position, and keep the pole upright as long as possible using the limited energy in the battery. The RL model for such a task is presented below:

States: The system state variables are

$$s = (x, \dot{x}, \theta, \dot{\theta}, e)^T,$$

where x is the cart position, θ is the pole angle and e is the current battery energy. $\dot{x}$ and $\dot{\theta}$ are the corresponding velocity/rate. $(\cdot)^T$ denotes the transpose of a vector.

Actions: the action vector consists of force command f and sampling time h,

$$a = (f, h)^T.$$

Both actions are continuous variables, but in this example they are considered as discrete quantities for simplicity, in which the sampling time can be chosen from some bounded number of available choices.

Policy: The policy π is defined as a mapping of the system states to the actions.

Reward: The reward is defined as the time period that the controller can keep the pole in the upright position. This means the agent should try to use longer sampling times to save processing power such that the pole can be balanced for a longer time.

For this case study, Q-learning was used for training this adaptive ECS. The resulting learning curve is presented in Fig. 5.2. Two sampling times $h_1 = 10 \, ms$ and $h_2 = 100 \, ms$ were used for the experiments. The adaptation refers to the switching between the two sampling times in real time. It is shown that the adaptive ECS identifies better settings after less than 10×10^6 learning steps and is able to balance the pole about $2s$ longer than the fast fixed sampling rate.

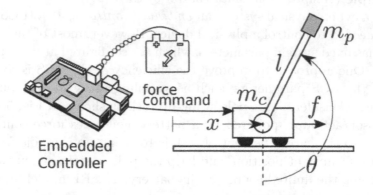

Figure 5.1: Cart-pole control: $m_c = 1kg$, $l = 20cm$, $m_p = 0.1kg$, $x \in [-6m, 6m]$, $f_{\max} = 200N$ and battery capacity $= 0.3J$ [21].

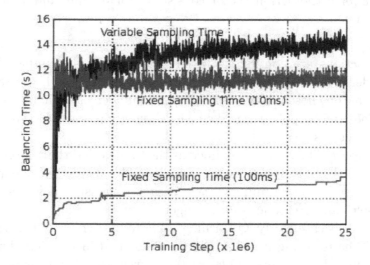

Figure 5.2: Maximum balancing time (return) achievable by the ECS in swing-up and balance task [21].

5.3.2.3 Sarsa

Now we introduce a TD-based on-policy control algorithm, named *Sarsa*. The update step of Sarsa is very similar to Q-learning except that the state-action pair is estimated using the current policy. Mathematically,

$$Q(S_t, A_t) \leftarrow Q(S_t, A_t) + \alpha(R_{t+1} + \gamma Q(S_{t+1}, A_{t+1}) - Q(S_t, A_t)).$$

The fact that each update is related to $S_t, A_t, R_{t+1}, S_{t+1}, A_{t+1}$ leads to the name *Sarsa*. For each non-terminal state, the agent uses the equation above to update the state-action value. If the next state is the terminal state, the agent will then put the action value function as $Q(S_{t+1}, A_{t+1}) = 0$.

The convergence of Sarsa to an optimal policy and the optimal state-action values is guaranteed if all state-action pairs are visited an infinite number of times and the sequence of step-size satisfies the usual convergence condition. In fact, the policy induced by Sarsa will always converge to the greedy policy. In practice, to achieve an infinite number of visits on each state-action pair, one can start with the ϵ-greedy policy or ϵ-soft policy and then have ϵ delaying to zero over the long run. We summarize the Sarsa algorithm in Algorithm 13.

If we apply the TD(λ) prediction method to state-action pairs rather than to states, then we can produce an on-policy TD control method—Sarsa(λ). The previous Sarsa can be viewed as *one-step* Sarsa, a special case of Sarsa(λ). Similar to the implementation of TD(λ), the implementation of Sarsa(λ) requires the use of eligibility trace. More details can be found in [159].

5.3.2.4 Example

Example (*Learning to Ride a Bicycle* [133])

In this example, Sarsa(λ) is used to teach a robot to ride a bicycle. The ultimate goal is to have the robot ride the bicycle to a target location. In what follows, an intermediate goal of balancing a bicycle is considered. In particular, at each time step, the robot acquires the information from the environment such as the angle of the handle bars and the velocity of the bicycle. Then the robot needs to choose actions to keep the balance of the bicycle. The number of seconds the robot can balance the bicycle is used to evaluate the trials. The task of trials is considered to complete once the number of seconds reaches 1000s. The RL model is described as follows.

Algorithm 13 Sarsa Algorithm

1: **Input:** Arbitrary $Q(S, A)$ and $Q(\text{terminal state}, \cdot) = 0$

2: **Output:** (near-) optimal policy π^*

3: **Repeat for each episode:**

Initialize: S

Choose A from S following the policy π derived by Q (e.g., ϵ-greedy)

Repeat: For each step of the episode:

1. Take action A, obtain reward R and the next state S'

2. Choose A' for state S' following the policy derived by Q (e.g., ϵ-greedy)

$$Q(S, A) \leftarrow Q(S, A) + \alpha(R + \gamma Q(S', A') - Q(S, A))$$
$$S \leftarrow S', A \leftarrow A'$$

3. Until S is the terminal state

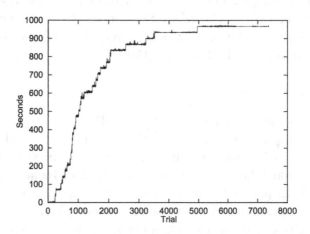

Figure 5.3: Number of seconds that the robot keeps balancing the bicycle *vs.* the number of trials [133].

Figure 5.4: Record of path of first 151 trials. The longest path is 7 meters [133].

States: The system state variables are

$$s = (\theta, \dot\theta, \omega, \dot\omega, \ddot\omega)^T,$$

where θ is the angle the handle bars are displaced from normal and $\dot\theta$ is the angular velocity of the angle. ω is the angle from vertical to bicycle, $\dot\omega$ is the angular velocity, and $\ddot\omega$ is the angular acceleration. Given the states are continuous variables, the states are discretized by non-overlapping intervals in the state-space. In particular,

1. the angle θ : $0, \pm 0.2, \pm 1, \pm\frac{\pi}{2}$ radians;

2. the angular velocity $\dot\theta$: $0, \pm 2, \pm\infty$ radians/second;

3. the angle ω : $0, \pm 0.06, \pm 0.15, \pm\frac{1}{15}\pi$ radians;

4. the angular velocity $\dot\omega$: $0, \pm 0.25, \pm 0.5, \pm\infty$ radians/second;

5. the angular acceleration $\ddot\omega$: $0, \pm 2, \pm\infty$ radians/second^2.

Actions: Overall, the agent has 6 possible actions including the selection of torque T being applied to the handle bars, and the center of mass d being displaced from the bicycle's plan,

$$T \in \{-2N, 0N, +2N\}$$

$$d \in \{-2cm, 0cm, +2cm\}.$$

Policy: The policy π is defined as a mapping of the system states to the actions.

Reward: The agent's reward corresponds to the number of seconds that the agent keeps balancing the bicycle.

As the result of the training, the number of seconds that the agent keeps balancing the bicycle as a function of the number of trials is presented in Fig. 5.3. The movement record of each trial during the early training process is visualized in Fig. 5.4, in which the bicycle is restarted at the starting point when it falls over. From both sets of results, one can see that the robot is learning over trials and performs better over time.

5.3.3 Policy Gradient

Till now, the approach we have learned to obtain the optimal policy is to learn the values of state-action pairs and then select actions based on these state-action pair values. Does this mean that if there is no estimate on the state-action pair values, no optimal policy can be found? In this section, we introduce a method, named *policy gradient*, in which a parameterized policy can be directly learned without resorting to a value function. Although the value function might be used to learn the policy parameter, it is not required to be used for action selection.

In general, a parameterized policy with parameter $w \in \mathbb{R}^n$ can be represented as follows,

$$\pi(a|s, w) = Pr(A_t = a|S_t = s, W_t = w).$$

One example can be the linear approximation of features $f(s, a) \in R^n$,

$$\pi(a|s, w) = w^T \cdot f(s, a) = w_1 f_1(s, a) + w_2 f_2(s, a) + \cdots + w_n f_n(s, a),$$

where $f_i(s, a)$ denotes the i-th feature at the state-action pair (s, a). To optimize the parameter w, an objective $J(w)$, a function of the policy parameter, needs to be well defined. Then, the iterative updates on the parameter w to maximize the performance $J(w)$ can be represented as

$$w_{t+1} = w_t + \alpha \nabla_{w_t} J(w_t),$$

where w_t is the estimate of parameter $w \in \mathbb{R}^n$ at time step t. $\nabla_{w_t} J(w_t)$ is the gradient of the performance measure with respect to its argument w_t. We call any method that follows this general scheme to find the optimal policy a *policy gradient method*.

In what follows, we consider the episodic case and thus define the performance measure as

$$J(w) = v_{\pi_w}(s_0) = E[R_1 + \gamma R_2 + \gamma^2 R_3 + ...|s_0, \pi(:, w)],$$

where $v_{\pi_w}(s_0)$ is the true value function on the starting state s_0 of every episode. Then the *gradient policy theorem* [160] provides that

$$\nabla_w J(w) = \sum_s p_\pi(s|w) \left[\sum_a Q^{\pi_w}(s,a) \nabla_w \pi(a|s,w) \right], \quad (5.6)$$

where $Q^{\pi_w}(s,a)$ is the state-action value of (s,a) under policy π_w, and $p_\pi(s|w) = \lim_{t\to\infty} Pr(S_t = s|s_0, w)$ is the stationary distribution of states under π, which we assume exists and is independent of s_0 for all policies. This yields

$$
\begin{aligned}
\nabla_w J(w) &= \sum_s p_\pi(s|w) \left[\sum_a Q^{\pi_w}(s,a) \pi(a|s,w) \nabla_w \log \pi(a|s,w) \right] \\
&= \sum_{s,a} Q^{\pi_w}(s,a) p_\pi(s|w) \pi(a|s,w) \nabla_w \log \pi(a|s,w) \\
&= \sum_{s,a} p_\pi(s,a|w) Q^{\pi_w}(s,a) \nabla_w \log \pi(a|s,w) \\
&= E_\pi \left[Q^{\pi_w}(s,a) \nabla_w \log \pi(a|s,w) \right],
\end{aligned}
\tag{5.7}
$$

where $\nabla_w \log \pi(a|s,w)$ is called a *score function*. Next, we present a concrete algorithm, named REINFORCE [183], which is recognized as the first policy-gradient algorithm in the literature. The basic idea of REINFORCE is to use sufficient samples to approximate the above expectation in $\nabla_w J(w)$. The samples are collected from episodes randomly generated as we did in Q-learning and Sarsa. Considering the reward discount factor γ in an episode, the policy gradient update can be approximated by

$$w_{t+1} = w_t + \alpha \gamma^t G_t \nabla_{w_t} \log \pi(a|s,w_t) = w_t + \alpha \gamma^t G_t \frac{\nabla_{w_t} \pi(a|s,w_t)}{\pi(a|s,w_t)},$$

where G_t, used to approximate $Q^{\pi_w}(s,a)$, is the return received starting from time step t at state-action pair (s,a) following the policy π_w. Notice that on the right-hand side, the second term is weighted by γ^t to preserve the expected value. The detailed derivation of this formula can be found in the original REINFORCE paper. Note that REINFORCE uses the return till the terminal state in each episode; it is essentially a Monte Carlo algorithm for the episodic cases. Thus, REINFORCE is

---

Algorithm 14 REINFORCE Algorithm

1: **Input:** A policy parameterization $\pi(a|s, w)$ which is differentiable.
2: **Output:** (near-) optimal policy π^*
3: **Initialize:** Initialize policy weights w
4: **Repeat forever:**
  Generate an episode $S_0, A_0, R_1, \cdots, S_{T-1}, A_{T-1}, R_T$, following the policy $\pi(\cdot|\cdot, w)$
  For each step of the episode $t = 0, 1, \cdots, T - 1$:
  1. Assign the return from step t to G
  2. Update parameter $w \leftarrow w + \alpha\gamma^t G\nabla_w \log \pi(A_t|S_t, w)$

---

also called Monte Carlo Policy Gradient. The REINFORCE algorithm is provided in Algorithm 14.

One drawback of REINFORCE is its high variance due to the Monte Carlo sampling. Specifically, in the above algorithm, updating the parameter w requires the discounted sum G of all sequential rewards in an episode, each of which is a random variable. This fact leads to the high variance. One approach to reduce such high variance is to subtract a baseline function $B(s)$ from the policy gradient (5.6), i.e.,

$$\nabla_w J(w) = \sum_s p_\pi(s|w)\left[\sum_a (Q^{\pi_w}(s, a) - B(s))\nabla_w \pi(a|s, w)\right]. \quad (5.8)$$

Note that introducing the baseline function will not change the expected value of the update. Mathematically, this is true because

$$\sum_a B(s)\nabla_w \pi(a|s, w) = B(s)\nabla_w \sum_a \pi(a|s, w) = B(s)\nabla_w 1 = 0.$$

Then the update of REINFORCE with the baseline function is given by,

$$w_{t+1} = w_t + \alpha\gamma^t \left(G_t - B(s_t)\right)\frac{\nabla_{w_t} \pi(a|s, w_t)}{\pi(a|s, w_t)}. \quad (5.9)$$

But how can we choose a baseline function $B(s)$? First of all, note that in REINFORCE the return G_t is an estimated value of the state-action pair $Q^{\pi_w}(s, a)$. Also, according to the Bellman optimality equation, it is known that

$$v^*(s) = \max_a q^*(s, a).$$

Since for any MDP there always exists a deterministic optimal policy, it is true that

$$Q^{\pi_w}(s, \pi_w(s)) - V^{\pi_w}(s) = 0$$

as the policy goes to the optimum. This observation motivates us to choose the state value $V^{\pi_w}(s)$ as the baseline function, i.e., $B(s) = V^{\pi_w}(s)$. For a large state space, we can alternatively use an estimate of the state value, $\hat{V}(s, \theta)$ with a weight vector $\theta \in R^m$, as the baseline function. Similarly, we can use a Monte Carlo method to learn the state value weights θ. The algorithm of using the baseline function in REINFORCE is given in Algorithm 15.

Algorithm 15 REINFORCE with Baseline Algorithm

1: **Input:** A differentiable policy parameterization $\pi(a|s, w)$ and a differentiable state-value parametcrization $\hat{V}(s, \theta)$ which is differentiable, step sizes α and β
2: **Output:** (near-) optimal policy π^*
3: **Initialize:** Initialize policy weights w and state-value weights θ
4: **Repeat forever:**
   Generate an episode following the policy $\pi(\cdot|\cdot, w)$ For each step of the episode $t = 0, \cdots, T - 1$:
   1. Compute the return G_t starting from step t
   2. Update $B(S_t) \leftarrow \hat{V}(S_t, \theta)$
   3. Update $\theta \leftarrow \theta + \beta(G_t - B(S_t))\nabla_\theta \hat{V}(S_t, \theta)$
   4. Update $w \leftarrow w + \alpha\gamma^t(G_t - B(S_t))\nabla_w \log \pi(A_t|S_t, w)$

5.3.3.1 Example

Example (*Multi-agent Autonomous Driving* [147])

It is envisioned that RL can be a highly useful tool for autonomous driving, an emerging technology that will be widely used in our daily life in the near future. Among all the tasks of autonomous driving, safety is highly prioritized, where the goal of the agent (autonomous car controller) is to keep the probability of an accident extremely low (i.e., 10^{-9}). In this example, a policy gradient-based RL solution, one of the first attempts along this line, is exploited to resolve the safety issue. The input to the agent is the information from the process of sensing, based on which the agent forms an environmental model consisting of the positions of the surroundings including vehicles, curbs, barriers and so forth. Then in RL the state space contains such an "environmental model" and other inputs including its own dynamics and the kinematics of moving objects from the previous frames (obtained from the embedded camera). Given the multi-variable continuous state space, the policy herein is parameterized and approximated by a deep layered network, e.g., recurrent neural networks (RNN). In this example, as shown in Fig. 5.5, the double merging maneuver is investigated, a problem which is notoriously difficult to resolve using conventional motion and path planning approaches. In the double merging problem, the agent should be able to choose to either continue on the current trajectory or merge to the other side in order to avoid accidents. The action space can be a set of discrete values capturing different levels of actions such as merge left, merge right, stay, accelerate, decelerate and so forth.

As usual, the policy π is defined as a mapping of the system states to the actions. Consider the reward function $R = -r(r > 0)$ for trajectories, which represents the event that the agent needs to avoid. For instance, if an accident occurs, the reward function $-r$ with large r value would provide a significantly high penalty to discourage this occurrence. In the test of this RL solution, the sensing information includes the static part of the environment represented as the geometry of lanes and the free space (all in ego-centric units), and the location, velocity, and heading of every other car within 100 meters away from it. One demo video showing the resulting performance of such an autonomous driving agent can be found in [141].

5.3.4 Actor-Critic

As discussed in the previous section, REINFORCE suffers from high variance due to the nature of Monte Carlo sampling. To deal with this issue, a baseline function $B(s)$ has been introduced to the state-action value function $Q^{\pi_w}(s, a)$. In this section, we present another approach to reduce the variance in which a *critic* is used to estimate the state value function $B(s) = V^{\pi_w}(s)$. That is, we use a parameterized state value function $\hat{V}(s, \theta)$ to approximate the true state value function $V^{\pi_w}(s)$ by *bootstrapping* for a given parameterized policy π_w. Here $\hat{V}(s, \theta)$ is parameterized by a vector θ in a way similar to the parameterization on π_w. Therefore, one can see that there are two coupled vectors of parameters to be optimized in this situation. We call this

Figure 5.5: The double merge scenario [147].

approach the *Actor-Critic (AC)* method, in which the following are defined:

1. Critic: update the state value function parameter θ to evaluate the current policy.

2. Actor: update the policy parameters w in the direction suggested by the critic to improve the policy.

Further equipped with the critic, the REINFORCE algorithm with baseline function (5.9) can be represented as follows,

$$
\begin{aligned}
w_{t+1} &= w_t + \alpha\gamma^t(G_t - \hat{V}(s_t, \theta))\frac{\nabla_{w_t}\pi(a|s, w_t)}{\pi(a|s, w_t)} \\
&= w_t + \alpha\gamma^t(R_{t+1} + \gamma\hat{V}(s_{t+1}, \theta) - \hat{V}(s_t, \theta))\frac{\nabla_{w_t}\pi(a|s, w_t)}{\pi(a|s, w_t)} \quad (5.10) \\
&= w_t + \alpha\gamma^t\delta\frac{\nabla_{w_t}\pi(a|s, w_t)}{\pi(a|s, w_t)},
\end{aligned}
$$

where $\delta = R_{t+1} + \gamma\hat{V}(s_{t+1}, \theta) - \hat{V}(s_t, \theta)$ refers to the TD error. To update the start value parameter θ, the critic can use semi-gradient TD(0) algorithm. Putting the above together, pseudocode for the complete AC algorithm is provided in Algorithm 16.

One may notice that, like the AC algorithm, the REINFORCE-with-baseline method also learns both the parameterized policy and

---

Algorithm 16 Actor-Critic Algorithm

1: **Input**: A differentiable policy parameterization $\pi(a|s,w)$ and a differentiable state-value parameterization $\hat{V}(s,\theta)$, step sizes α and β

2: **Output**: (near-) optimal policy $\pi^*(\cdot|\cdot,w)$

3: **Initialize**: Initialize policy weights θ and state-value weights w

4: **Repeat**:

   Initialize first state of episode S

   Assign initial value 1 to I

   While S is not terminal:

   1. $A \sim \pi(\cdot|S,\theta)$

   2. Take action A, observe S', R

   3. $\delta \leftarrow R + \gamma\hat{V}(S',\theta) - \hat{V}(S,\theta)$. ($\hat{V}(S',\theta) = 0$ if S' is terminal)

   4. $\theta \leftarrow \theta + \beta\delta\nabla_w\hat{V}(S,\theta)$

   5. $w \leftarrow w + \alpha I\delta\nabla_w log\pi(A|S,w)$

   6. $I \leftarrow \gamma I$

   7. $S \leftarrow S'$

---

state value. However, the REINFORCE-with-baseline method is not considered to be an AC algorithm. This is because it does not use bootstrapping (updating a state from the estimated values of subsequent states), a technique that would introduce bias in learning but reduce variance and accelerate learning. In particular, the AC method uses bootstrapping $\delta = R_{t+1} + \gamma\hat{V}(s_{t+1},\theta) - \hat{V}(s_t,\theta)$ (like TD(0)) in (5.10) while the REINFORCE-with-baseline method uses $(G_t - \hat{V}(s_t,\theta))$. That is, the parameterized state value $\hat{V}(s_t,\theta)$ in the REINFORCE-with-baseline method is only used as a baseline function, a fact that implies that REINFORCE with baseline is unbiased and will converge asymptotically to a (local) minimum. However, like all Monte Carlo methods (wait until the end of the episode to obtain return G_t) it tends to be slow to learn and thus inconvenient to implement online due to such delay in learning.

5.3.4.1 Example

Example (*Tracking Control in Robotics* [123])

Accurate reference tracking is of importance for most of robotic applications ranging from pick-and-place tasks to welding tasks. Since a manipulator arm itself is a complex system and also used in environ-

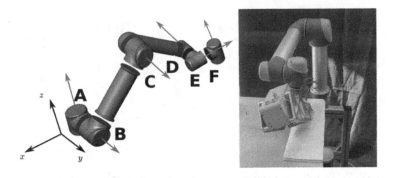

Figure 5.6: The tracking robot [123].

ments with uncertainties, it is always challenging to control the manipulator arm to complete a task with high accuracy. In this example, an AC-based RL algorithm is used to improve the tracking performance of a robotic manipulator. In general, there exists a feedback controller g provided by the manufacturer to help generate a control input to the arm such that the tracking error is minimized. That is, the control input u_t is determined by the tracking error e_t at time t, i.e., $u_t = g(e_t)$ with $g : R^n \rightarrow R^m$, $e_t \in R^n$ and $u_t \in R^m$. However, this manufacturer-provided feedback controller embedded in the device is not adaptive to the dynamic environment. As a result, the goal of RL-based compensator $h : R^n \rightarrow R^m$ is to further reduce the tracking error thanks to its online learning capabilities. That is,

$$u_t = g(e_t) + h(e_t).$$

One experimental evaluation of a robotic manipulator arm (Fig. 5.6) is done by comparing the AC-based compensator and a nominal controller. The states of the RL system include the velocity and position for each joint of the robotic arm, including base, shoulder, elbow, wrist 1, wrist 2 and wrist 3, denoted as A to F in the figure. The action space contains the values of the movement performed at each joint. The reward is measured by the position error in distance notation between the reference curve to the tracking curve. Two tasks of tracking square and circular references on a paper are tested in the experiment. The results of comparison with the nominal proportional-derivative (PD) controller on these two tasks are shown in Fig. 5.7, showing that the AC-based compensator can effectively reduce the tracking error.

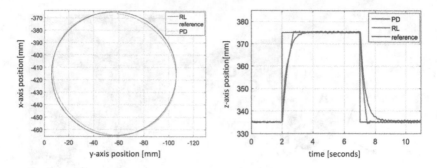

Figure 5.7: Tracking curve for circular task [left] and square task [right] [123].

5.4 ADVANCED ALGORITHMS

So far, we have introduced several classic model-free control algorithms including Monte Carlo control, Sarsa, Q-learning, policy gradient and actor-critic. Based on the classic algorithms, in this section we present some advanced model-free control algorithms, which can either further reduce the variance of value functions over the learning process (e.g., expected Sarsa) or can solve the over-estimate problem in Q-learning (e.g., double Q-learning).

5.4.1 Expected Sarsa

Recall that in Sarsa the Q function is updated as follows:

$$Q(S_t, A_t) \leftarrow Q(S_t, A_t) + \alpha(R_{t+1} + \gamma Q(S_{t+1}, A_{t+1}) - Q(S_t, A_t)).$$

As Sarsa is an on-policy algorithm, the stochastic nature of using $Q(S_{t+1}, A_{t+1})$ could introduce large variance into the update, leading to a slow convergence of the algorithm. Thus motivated, a variation on Sarsa, named *expected Sarsa*, is proposed in [145] to reduce the variance of learning. In particular, the expected Sarsa computes an expectation over all actions available in S_{t+1} instead of simply using the selected action. That is,

$$Q(S_t, A_t)$$
$$\leftarrow Q(S_t, A_t) + \alpha(R_{t+1} + \gamma \mathbb{E}[Q(S_{t+1}, A_{t+1})|S_{t+1}] - Q(S_t, A_t))$$
$$= Q(S_t, A_t) + \alpha(R_{t+1} + \gamma \sum_a \pi(a|S_{t+1})Q(S_{t+1}, a) - Q(S_t, A_t)).$$

$$(5.11)$$

It is proved in [145] that the expected Sarsa converges under the same conditions as Sarsa and has smaller variance. This lower variance could enable higher learning rates and thus faster learning in applications. In deterministic environments, the updates of expected Sarsa have zero variance, in which scenario a learning rate of 1 can be applied. The peusdocode of expected Sarsa is provided in Algorithm 17.

Algorithm 17 Expected Sarsa

1: **Initialize**: Initialize $Q(s, a)$ arbitrarily for all states and actions
2: **Repeat**:
   Initialize S
   For each step of the episode:
   1. Following the policy π derived from Q, at current state S, choose action A, observe S' and R
   2. Update $V(S') \leftarrow \sum_a \pi(a|S') \cdot Q(S', A)$
   3. Update $Q(S, A) \leftarrow Q(S, A) + \alpha[R + \gamma V(S') - Q(S, A)]$
   4. $S \leftarrow S'$
   Until S is terminal.

5.4.2 Double Q-Learning

Recall that in the stochastic MDPs for the Q-learning algorithm, the agent's estimate for the maximal action value for each action is based on a single sample, which may not be reused when the state is visited again. Since the sample distribution is unknown but depends on the whole experience of the agent, the samples of Q-learning could be biased, thus leading to an overestimate of the action values [55]. Hasselt in [54] proposed a new off-policy reinforcement learning algorithm, *Double Q-learning*, to mitigate this overestimation issue. The algorithm is summarized in Algorithm 18.

One can see that double Q-learning utilizes two Q functions Q^A and Q^B. At each step we update one value function, say Q^A, using the sum of the immediate reward R and the value of the next state. To determine the value of the next state, we first find the best action according to Q^A and then use the second value function Q^B to calculate this action value. Similarly, for updating the second Q function Q^B we use Q^B to determine the best action in the next state but then use Q^A to estimate the value of this action. By doing so, the selection of

---

Algorithm 18 Double Q-learning

1: **Initialize**: Initialize $Q^A(S, A)$ and $Q^B(S, A)$ arbitrarily and assume $Q^A(\text{terminal-state}, :) = 0$, $Q^B(\text{terminal-state}, :) = 0$

2: **Repeat**: For each episode:

Choose A from S following the policy derived from Q^A and Q^B, observe R and S'

Choose one of the following updates according to some randomness (e.g., each with 0.5 probability):

$$Q^A(S, A)$$
$$\leftarrow Q^A(S, A) + \alpha(R + \gamma Q^B(S', argmax_a Q^A(S', a)) - Q^A(S, A))$$

else:

$$Q^B(S, A)$$
$$\leftarrow Q^B(S, A) + \alpha(R + \gamma Q^A(S', argmax_a Q^B(S', a)) - Q^B(S, A))$$

$S \leftarrow S'$

Until S is terminal.

---

the best action and the evaluation of such a selection is decorrelated, a method that resolves the overestimate problem in Q-learning.

5.5 REMARKS

In this chapter, we have introduced several basic model-free RL algorithms. Each of them has its own *pros* and *cons*. We remark that one missing piece in this chapter is the *eligibility traces*, which is also one of the basic RL mechanisms. This mechanism is motivated by $TD(\lambda)$ algorithms. We know that in general $TD(\lambda)$ is a delayed learning process because the agent has to wait until the end of the episode to update the target value. However, a backward view of this algorithm, the nature of eligibility traces, provides a mechanism of updating the target in real time. In fact, almost any TD method, such as Q-learning or Sarsa, can be combined with eligibility traces to obtain a more general method that may learn more efficiently. A good tutorial on eligibility traces can be found in [159].

In this chapter, we have also introduced a new approach to find an optimal policy—policy gradient. This approach directly searches for the parameterized policy rather than first searching for the optimal action value function and then concluding the policy by greedy strategy. Furthermore, the AC algorithm with parameterization on both policy and value functions has been introduced to reduce learning variance, leading to fast convergence. We remark that the idea of parameterization is of importance to deal with large-scale and continuous real-world applications. The parameterization in a well-designed form can be very powerful and efficient when used to model complicated policy and value functions. One example is deep reinforcement learning in the next chapter, in which the parameterization is performed via deep neural network.

5.6 EXERCISES

5.1. Which of the following reinforcement learning algorithms estimate some quantity based on experience, from which we *cannot* approximately compute the *optimal policy*?
    a). Model-based Monte Carlo
    b). Model-free Monte Carlo
    c). SARSA
    d). Q-learning
    e). TD learning

5.2. Please indicate *True* or *False* for the following statements:
    a). Although both policy iteration and value iteration are widely used, it is not clear which, if either, is better in general.
    b). One drawback to policy iteration is that each of its iterations involves policy evaluation, which may itself be a protracted iterative computation requiring multiple sweeps through the state set.
    c). In the Monte Carlo estimation of action values, if a deterministic policy π is used, in most cases one agent (with the same starting state) could not learn the values of all actions.
    d). For a stationary problem, Sarsa converges with probability 1 to an optimal policy and action-value function as long as all state-action pairs are visited an infinite number of times and the policy converges in the limit to the greedy policy.
    e). In general, TD methods converge more quickly than Monte Carlo methods.

5.3. In real-world applications, we often encounter reinforcement learn-

Figure 5.8: Random Walk [159].

ing problems that are effectively non-stationary (e.g., the mean value of the random process is time-varying). In such cases, why do we usually use a constant step-size in the incremental update of a reinforcement learning algorithm, e.g., $Q_{k+1} = Q_k + \alpha[r_{k+1} - Q_k]$?

5.4. In reinforcement learning, what are the meanings of "on-policy" and "off-policy" methods?

5.5. Q-learning is on-policy or off-policy? why?

5.6. Why do we say the TD-method is a *bootstrapping* method?

5.7. Given an MDP task where you want to find the optimal policy. One question you are pondering is whether to compute and store v(s) or q(s, a). Name one argument in favor of v(s), and one different argument in favor of q(s,a).

5.8. Why is policy evaluation not directly applicable in some situations where TD-learning is able to compute the value function?

5.9. (Small Random Walk [159]) See Fig. 5.8. All episodes start in the center state, C, and proceed either left or right by one state on each step, with equal probability. Episodes terminate either on the extreme left or the extreme right. When an episode terminates on the right, a reward of +1 occurs; all other rewards are zero. For example, a typical walk might consist of the following state-and reward sequence: $C; 0; B; 0; C; 0; D; 0; E; 1$. Assume this task is undiscounted ($\gamma = 1$) and episodic, then the true value of each state is essentially the probability of terminating on the right if starting from that state.
a). What is the state value $V(C)$?
b). Then what are the state values $V(A), V(B), V(D), V(E)$?
c). Suppose we initialize state value $V(s) = 0.5$ for all state s. From

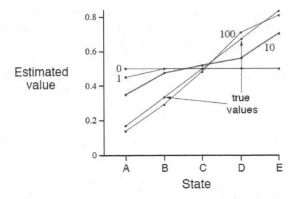

Figure 5.9: Values learned by TD(0) with a constant step-size $\alpha = 0.1$ after various numbers of episodes [159].

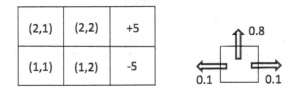

Figure 5.10: Grid world MDP and transition function.

Fig. 5.9 (the learning process), it appears that the first episode results in a change in only $V(A)$. What does this tell you about what happened on the first episode? Why was only the estimate for this one state changed? By exactly how much was it changed?

5.10. (Small Grid World) Consider the small grid world MDP as shown in Fig. 5.10. The states are grid squares, identified by their row and column number (row first). The agent always starts in state (1,1). There are two terminal goal states, (2,3) with reward +5 and (1,3) with reward -5. Rewards are 0 in non-terminal states. (The reward for a state is received as the agent moves into the state.) The underlying transition function is such that the intended agent movement (up, down, left, right) happens with probability 0.8. With probability 0.1 each, the agent ends up in one of the states perpendicular to the intended direction. For example, if the agent at (1,2) chooses to move up to (2,2), it can reach (2,2) only with probability 0.8. The agent may hit (1,1) or terminal state -5 with equal probability 0.1. If a collision with a wall happens, the agent stays in the same state.

1. Write down the optimal policy for this grid. (For example, $\pi(1,1) = down, \pi(1,2) = up, \pi(2,1) = left, \pi(2,2) = right$, this is definitely NOT an optimal policy.)

2. Suppose the agent knows the transition probabilities. Give the first two rounds of (synchronous) *value iteration* updates for state (1,2) and (2,1), with a discount of 0.9. (Assume V_0 is 0 everywhere and compute V_i for times i = 1,2. Also, we assume the values of terminal states $V(1,3) = V(2,3) = 0$ for all iterations). Hint: *Value iteration* uses the update equation $v_{k+1}(s) = \max_a \sum_{s',r} p(s',r|s,a)[r + \gamma v_k(s')]$.

3. The agent starts with the policy that always chooses to go right, and executes the following three trials: 1) (1,1)-(1,2)-(1,3), 2) (1,1)-(1,2)-(2,2)-(2,3), and 3) (1,1)-(2,1)-(2,2)-(2,3). What are the Monte Carlo (direct utility) estimates for states (1,1) and (2,2), given these traces?

4. Using a learning rate of $\alpha = 0.1$, a discount of $\gamma = 0.9$, and assuming initial V values of 0, what updates does the TD(0)-learning agent make after trials 1 and 2, above? Hint: TD(0) update equation is $v(s) = v(s) + \alpha(r + \gamma v(s') - v(s))$.

5.11. (*n*-Step Return) The expected value of all *n*-step returns is guaranteed to improve in a certain way over the current value function as an approximation to the true value function. Prove the following *error reduction property* of n-step returns

$$\max_s \left| E_\pi \left\{ R_t^{(n)} | s_t = s \right\} - V^\pi(s) \right| \leq \gamma^n \max_s \left| V(s) - V^\pi(s) \right|,$$

where $R_t^{(n)}$ is *n*-step return at time t.

The following exercise requires you to explore and synthesize the knowledge of "eligibility trace" beyond this textbook.

5.12. (Value-Based RL) Consider the small corridor gridworld shown in Fig. 5.11 below. S and G represents the start and goal (terminal) states, respectively. In each of the two non-terminal states there are only two actions, *right* and *left*. These actions have their usual consequences in the start state (left causes no movement in the first state), but in the second state they are reversed, so that *right* moves to the left and *left* moves to the right. The reward is -1 per step as usual. We approximate the action-value function using two features $\mathbf{x}_1(s,a) = \mathbf{1}\{a = right\}$ and $\mathbf{x}_2(s,a) = \mathbf{1}\{a = left\}$ for all states s. We sample an episode till the goal by sequentially taking actions *right, right, right, left*. Assume the experiment is undiscounted.

(1) Approximate the action-value function by a linear combination of these features with two parameters: $\hat{Q}(s, a, \mathbf{w}) = \mathbf{x}_1(s,a)w_1 + \mathbf{x}_2(s,a)w_2$. If $w_1 = w_2 = 1$, calculate the λ-return q_t^λ corresponding to this episode for $\lambda = 0.5$.

(2) Using the forward-view TD(λ) algorithm and our linear function approximator, what are the sequence of updates to weight w_1? What is the total update to weight w_1? Use $\lambda = 0.5, \gamma = 1, \alpha = 0.5$ and start with $w_1 = w_2 = 1$.

(3) Define the TD(λ) accumulating eligibility trace $\mathbf{e}_t$ when using linear value function approximation. Write down the sequence of eligibility traces corresponding to *right* action, using $\lambda = 0.5, \gamma = 1$.

(4) Using the backward-view TD(λ) algorithm and our linear function approximator, what are the sequence of updates to weight w_1? (Use offline updates, i.e., do not actually change your weights, just accumulate your updates). What is the total update to weight w_1? Use $\lambda = 0.5, \gamma = 1, \alpha = 0.5$ and start with $w_1 = w_2 = 1$.

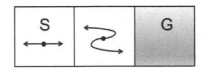

Figure 5.11: Small corridor gridworld.

5.13. (Gaussian Policy) Assume Gaussian policy is used in the policy gradient reinforcement learning. The Gaussian mean is a linear combination of state features

$$\mu(s) = \phi(s)^T w = \sum_i \phi_i(s)w_i,$$

where $\phi(\cdot)$ represents the vector of feature functions and w represents the weight vector. Also, assume a fixed variance σ^2. Show that that the score function $\nabla_w \log \pi_w(a|s, w)$ of Gaussian policy is given by

$$\nabla_w \log \pi_w(a|s, w) = \frac{(a - \mu(s))\phi(s)}{\sigma^2}.$$

5.14. (Policy-Based RL) Consider the small corridor gridworld shown in Fig. 5.11.

(1) Explain why an action-value method with ϵ-greedy action selection will not generate the optimal policy.

(2) We use two features: $\phi_1(s, a) = \mathbf{1}\{a = right\}$ and $\phi_2(s, a) = \mathbf{1}\{a = left\}$ for all states s. Our approximated policy is the softmax policy, i.e., $\pi_\theta(s, a) \propto e^{\phi^T \theta}$. We sample an episode till the goal by sequentially taking actions *right, right, right, left*. Using Monte-Carlo policy gradient method (REINFORCE), what are the sequence of offline updates to parameter θ? What is the probability of selecting the *right* action after this episode? Use $\alpha = 0.01, \gamma = 1$ and start with $\theta_1 = \theta_2 = 1$.

CHAPTER 6

Deep Reinforcement Learning

CONTENTS

6.1 INTRODUCTION TO DEEP RL

Deep learning is one strategy for generating feature representation. It maps input to output with multiple layers. This structure allows the model to learn the representation of complicated input as hierarchical concepts, building each concept upon each other from low-level features to more abstract representations. Thanks to the increase of the number of training examples and the improvement of computer hardware and software, deep learning has become more useful and powerful. In recent years, deep learning has demonstrated significant success in the field of computer vision, speech recognition, and natural language processing.

As introduced in the previous chapters, the goal of reinforcement learning is to create an agent to maximize the total reward from decision making. In the context of reinforcement learning, the agent interacts with the environment, observes the change of states influenced by actions, and receives the reward signals. By the process of trial and error, the agent learns to take a sequence of actions that lead to the goal.

In general, the RL system shall be generalizable so as to solve a more complicated task that reaches human-level performance. That is the recent advance in deep reinforcement learning (DRL). DRL is the integration of reinforcement learning with deep learning, where the deep neural network (DNN) is used as function approximations in the RL framework, optimizing the loss function (with respect to the weights of neural network) with gradient descent. DRL allows the agent to learn the meaningful representation directly from the raw inputs, reducing the need for domain knowledge and handcraft features. It also helps scale up the dimensionality of RL problems.

Different kinds of DRL algorithms apply approximations to different components of RL. One choice is to use a neural network to approximate the value function, which is to estimate how good the state or the state-action pair is. Another choice is to use a neural network to approximate the policy, which is how the agent chooses an action in a given state. The other choice is to learn model dynamics with the neural network. Since the components of RL are parametrized by the neural network, the frameworks can be trained using backpropagation and stochastic gradient descent to update the parameters, i.e., the weights of the neural network. In this chapter, we discuss several typical DRL algorithms that apply DNN to approximate value functions, policy functions and RL models, respectively.

6.2 DEEP NEURAL NETWORKS

In this section, we recap the basic theory of deep neural networks. Readers who are familiar with neural networks can quickly walk through this section to refresh themselves. Other readers, however, can use this section as a pilot for a comprehensive study of neural networks. One can easily find tutorials on deep neural networks in the literature.

In general, an artificial neural network (ANN) is a computational model to mimic the mechanism of processing the incoming information by the biological neural networks in the human brain. The basic

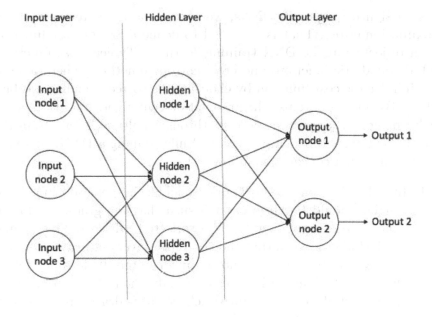

Figure 6.1: A feed-forward neural network.

element of ANN is the *neuron*, which receives input from some other neurons, or from an external source and then computes an output. In ANN, a neuron performs a function of the sum of the weighted inputs, i.e.,

$$y = f(w_0 + w_1 x_1 + w_2 x_2),$$

where x_1, x_2 are the inputs from two other neurons or external sources, and w_0, w_1, w_2 are the assigned weights (w_0 is a bias term). The function f is typically chosen as

$$\text{Sigmoid:} \quad f(x) = \frac{1}{1 + e^{-x}},$$

$$\text{ReLU:} \quad f(x) = \max\{0, x\}.$$

Other functions such as *perceptrons* and *tanh* are also possible choices.

Then an ANN is defined as a set of connected neurons. One example is the feed-forward neural network as shown in Fig. 6.1, the first and simplest ANN with a well-defined input layer, hidden layer and output layer. If an ANN has multiple hidden layers between the input and output layers, we call this ANN a deep neural network (DNN). In general, DNNs can model complex non-linear relationships. To learn these assigned weights in DNNs, we need some measurements of approximation errors. That is, we need to define a loss or cost function as an objective in the DNN training/learning. Typical cost functions include quadratic functions and cross entropy functions. Then we need to minimize the cost function by choosing the correct weights and bias values. By doing so, we use the gradient descent algorithm in which we backpropagate the gradient descent through multiple layers, from the output layer back to the input layer. While training a DNN, there are some engineering concerns as follows:

1. Initialization on the network weights: in general, initialized weights should be large enough such that the gradients do not decay to zero through a deep network (to be discussed later), and not be too large such that the non-linear layers saturate. Random initialization is always a choice but definitely it does not follow the aforementioned principles of initialization. A better choice is Xavier initialization in which each weight is drawn from a distribution with zero mean and a specific variance

$$Var(w_j) = \frac{1}{n_j},$$

where n_j is the number of inputs to the neuron j.

2. Batch size on data inputs: Batches allow us to use stochastic gradient descent to minimize the cost function. However, there is a tradeoff on determining the batch size. If the size is small, the batch is less representative of data. If the size is large, however, the training time can be long. Experience on specific applications is required to choose a suitable batch size.

3. Learning rate: This defines the step size during gradient descent. If the step size is small, the convergence can be very slow. If the step size is large, however, the algorithm might not be converging to the optimum, and instead, one may observe oscillations around the optimum. This fact implies that we shall start with a large step size and then reduce the size gradually as the solutions become close to the optimal values. Thus motivated, some popular algorithms such as AdaGrad, RMSProp and Adam have been proposed in the literature, which can adjust the learning rate based on the rate of descent.

4. Overfitting: An overfitted model is a statistical model that contains more parameters than can be justified by the data. Such a model can be poorly extended to other datasets. Thus far, there are several approaches to mitigate this issue. *L1/L2 regularization* is a widely used approach by adding a penalty for larger weights in the model. *Dropout* is a technique unique to neural networks in which neurons are randomly removed during training such that the network does not over rely on any particular neuron. Another approach is to *expand the dataset* by tilting images, adding low white noise to sound data, and so forth. Then the expanded dataset is used for training.

Overall, the well-known DNN includes convolutional neural networks (CNNs) used in computer vision and automatic speech recognition (ASR) and recurrent neural networks (RNNs) used in language modeling. In what follows, we provide a high-level idea of these two networks. A comprehensive tutorial on DNN can be found in [62, 118, 44].

6.2.1 Convolutional Neural Networks

Like the simple perceptron as an activation function in the neural network, CNNs also stemmed from biological research. Hubel and Wiesel studied the structure of the visual cortex in mammals, revealing that neurons in the visual cortex only have a small local receptive field. Due to this groundbreaking discovery, they won the Nobel Prize in 1981. Inspired by this result, Yann LeCun *et al.* in [80] described the famous LeNet-5 architecture in Fig. 6.2, the first CNN used for digit recognition. Typically, CNNs consist of several technical aspects in their architecture: convolutions, filtering and subsampling.

We next describe in more detail these technical aspects in LeNet-5. LeNet-5 comprises 7 layers, each containing trainable weights. The input is a 32×32 image. The convolutional layers are labeled Cx, subsampling layers are labeled Sx, and fully connected layers are labeled Fx, where x is the layer index. In the convolutional layer, filters are used to perform convolutional computing on the input data. Such filters are commonly visualized as grids that slide over the width and height of the input volume. One convolutional filter of a 3×3 grid with assigned weights is illustrated in Fig. 6.3. In LeNet-5, layer C1 has 6 feature maps using 6 different convolutional filters. Each unit in each feature map is a result of performing a 5×5 convolutional filtering on the input image pixels. These filters slide one unit at a time (i.e., stride $= 1$) over

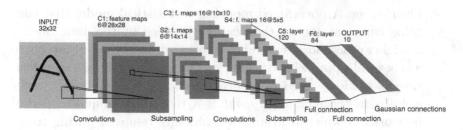

Figure 6.2: Architecture of LeNet-5, a convolutional neural network, here for digits recognition [80].

the width and height of the image. Then the size of the feature maps is 28×28 which prevents the sliding from falling off the boundary. The subsampling layers, also known as pooling layers, will subsample the feature maps, which reduces the memory use and computer load as well as reducing the number of parameters. For instance, the subsampling can be done by taking the maximum, or addition of values in a neighborhood in the feature map. In LeNet-5 layer S2, each unit in each feature map is connected to a 2×2 neighborhood in the corresponding feature map in C1. The four inputs to a unit in S2 are added, then multiplied by a weight, and added to a bias value. Then the result is passed through a sigmoidal function. Note that this pooling layer with non-overlapping 2×2 receptive fields removes 75% information. Similarly, the other layers Cx and Sx in LeNet-5 follows that in C1 and S2, respectively. Finally, in LeNet-5, the output layer is composed of Euclidean radial basis function units, which can be interpreted as the unnormalized negative log-likelihood of a Gaussian distribution in the space of configurations of layer F6.

We remark that the *dropout* technique is also commonly deployed with CNN to prevent overfitting. Beside LeNet-5, there exist some other famous CNN architectures such as AlexNet, GooglLeNet and ResNet. We refer the interested readers to the given reference for details.

6.2.2   Recurrent Neural Networks

In the real world, not all problems like digit recognition in CNN can be converted into one with fixed length inputs and outputs. For instance, consider a problem in which the neural network outputs *true* if the input binary sequence (e.g., 10101110) has even number of 1s and outputs *false* otherwise. Since the length of the input sequence is

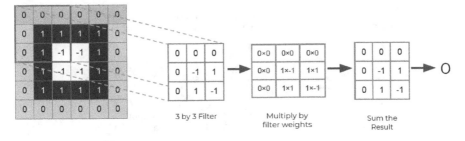

Figure 6.3: Convolutional filtering.

not fixed, this problem requires the neural network to store and use context information over the time domain. Thus motivated, a neuron in the neural network should take the previous output or hidden states as input to itself at time t. One example is shown in Fig. 6.4. By doing so, this recurrent neuron takes advantage of its historical information about the happenings before time t. In other words, this neuron is given a certain amount of memory. A network with such recurrent neurons is called a recurrent neural network (RNN).

The RNN is very flexible in its inputs and outputs for both sequences and single vector values. On the one hand, the mapping can be "sequence to vector" or "sequence to sequence." Take the *sentiment classification* (e.g., classify a movie review from IMDB) as an example. The inputs are comments with one or more words and the output is "positive" or "negative" based on the comments. Fig. 6.5 illustrates the two RNN mappings for the sentiment classification. On the other hand, the mapping can be "single vector" to "sequence." One popular example is *image captioning*. That is, as shown in Fig. 6.6, given an image as an input, the system will produce a sentence describing its contents.

To train an RNN, the backpropagation algorithm can be used. Recall that backpropagation propagates the error gradient from the output layer to the input layer. However, for deeper networks, one key issue for backpropagation is the vanishing and exploding gradients. Specifically, the gradients can get smaller and smaller as the error gradient is backward propagated to the lower layers (i.e., layers close to input layer). Eventually the weights can never change at lower levels. The opposite in which the gradients explode on the way backward can also occur. To resolve this issue, one can shorten the time steps used for prediction in the recurrent neuron, but this makes the model worse

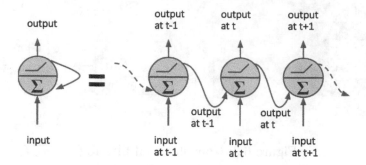

Figure 6.4: The behavior of a recurrent neuron (left) over time: the output at time t-1 and the input at time t are aggregated and then fed into the activation function to generate the output at time t.

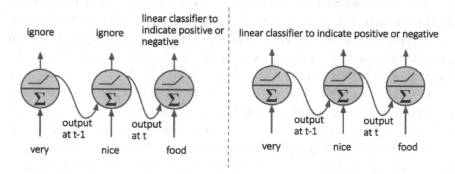

Figure 6.5: Sentiment classification. Left: RNN mapping from sequence to single vector; Right: RNN mapping from sequence to sequence.

at predicting longer trends. Furthermore, RNN will begin to "forget" the first inputs as time goes by because the information is lost at each step going through the recurrent neuron. As a result, the long short-term memory (LSTM) neuron was created to address these issues. The detailed structure of the LSTM neuron can be found in [57].

6.3 DEEP LEARNING TO VALUE FUNCTIONS

Recall that value function is a prediction of future reward. It represents how good it is for an agent to be in a given state or how good it is for an agent to perform the action in a given state. A value function can be represented as a lookup table, where each state in the state space has a separate value. When using RL to solve large real-world problems, such

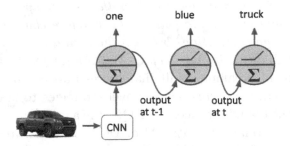

Figure 6.6: Image captioning via RNN.

as robot navigation in continuous state space, it becomes impractical to represent all the entries in a table because the state space is continuous or too large. In such cases, value function approximation can be used to estimate the true value function regardless of the size of the state space.

In this chapter, the value function approximation is written as

$$V(s; w) \approx V_\pi(s),$$

where V_π is the true state value function for a given policy π. $V(s; w)$ is the function approximator, parameterized by the weight vector w. Given an input state s, where s can be any state in the state space, by feeding it to the function approximator, the function approximator should fit the true value function as much as possible. The value-based DRL then uses the deep learning (i.e., deep neural network) to represent the value function.

Similarly, we can use the same paradigm for the approximation of the action-value function

$$Q(s, a; \theta) \approx Q_\pi(s, a),$$

where $a \in \mathcal{A}$ is the action. Recall that in Q-learning, the Q value is updated as

$$Q(s, a) \leftarrow Q(s, a) + \alpha[r + \gamma \max_{a'} Q(s', a') - Q(s, a)]. \qquad (6.1)$$

In general, the Q value can converge to an optimal value when using the tabular method. However, when combining the Q-learning with the non-linear approximator such as neural network, it would cause the Q-network to diverge. This is because of *"the correlations presenting in the sequence of observations, the fact that small updates to Q value may significantly change the policy and therefore change the data distribution, and the correlations between the action-values and the target values"* [109]. Along this line, *deep Q-Network* (DQN) by Google Deep-Mind is a ground-breaking result that successfully combines Q-learning with a deep neural network using novel strategies to stabilize the Q-learning. In the training process of DQN, the agent learns directly from the high-dimensional raw data. Also, DQN demonstrates that its RL agent is capable of playing 2600 Atari games at the same or beyond the level of professional human players. In what follows, we will introduce DQN with a certain level of detail.

6.3.1 DQN

In general, DQN utilizes two primary techniques for stabilizing the Q-learning: *fixed target Q-network* and *experience replay*. Recall that our goal is to find the best parameter θ in the deep neural network such that

$$Q(s, a; \theta) \approx Q_\pi(s, a).$$

In DQN, optimizing θ can be done sequentially by minimizing a sequence of loss functions $\mathcal{L}_i(\theta_i)$ that is optimized at each iteration,

$$\mathcal{L}_i(\theta_i) = E_{s,a,r,s' \sim \rho} \left[\left(r + \gamma \max_{a'} Q(s', a'; \theta_i) - Q(s, a; \theta_i) \right)^2 \right],$$
(6.2)

where ρ is a joint probability distribution over states s, s', reward r and action a. Note that this loss function is the one used by the Q-learning update (6.1) at iteration i.

DQN adopts the *fixed target Q-network*, which uses an older set of the parameters θ^- for the Q learning target y_i, i.e.,

$$y_i = r + \gamma \max_{a'} \hat{Q}(s', a'; \theta^-),$$
(6.3)

where $\hat{Q}$ denotes the target Q-network. That is, DQN maintains a separate Q-network for the Q learning target and updates it periodically. After a number of C updates, the current parameter θ of the Q network clones to the target Q-network $\hat{Q}$, and then fixes the $\hat{Q}$ in the following C updates. This method increases the stability. This is because the delay of updating the Q learning target is like the supervised learning where the target does not depend on the parameters being updated. It keeps the target function from changing too fast and thus reduces the chance of oscillation and divergence. Using the fixed target Q-network, the loss function can be rewritten as

$$\mathcal{L}_i(\theta_i) = E_{s,a,r,s'\sim\rho}\left[(r + \gamma \max_{a'} \hat{Q}(s',a';\theta^-) - Q(s,a;\theta_i))^2\right].$$
(6.4)

Then, to optimize the weights θ_i of the deep neural network at iteration i, we differentiate the loss function with respect to θ and arrive at the following:

$$\nabla_{\theta_i}\mathcal{L}_i(\theta_i) =$$
$$2E_{s,a,r,s'\sim\rho}\left[(r + \gamma \max_{a'} \hat{Q}(s',a';\theta^-) - Q(s,a;\theta_i))\nabla_{\theta_i}Q(s,a;\theta_i)\right].$$
(6.5)

One can see that it is nontrivial to compute the full expectations in the above gradient. However, the method of stochastic gradient descent (SGD), which is a stochastic approximation of the gradient descent optimization and tries to find minima or maxima by iteration, has been widely used for such optimizations in the literature. Therefore, using SGD, the expectation in $\nabla_{\theta_i}\mathcal{L}_i(\theta_i)$ is replaced by one sampled value and the neural network weights θ can be updated iteratively as follows,

$$\theta_{i+1} = \theta_i + \alpha\nabla_{\theta_i}\mathcal{L}_i(\theta_i).$$
(6.6)

On the other hand, in order to ensure the learning stability, DQN adopts another novel technique—*experience replay*. Experience replay builds a dataset from the experiences that the agent has seen at each time step. In particular, at time step t, the agent observes the state s_t, takes an action a_t, receives the reward r_t and moves to the next state s_{t+1}. The agent then appends the experience tuple $e_t = (s_t, a_t, r_t, s_{t+1})$ into the replay buffer $D = \{e_1, e_2, ...e_t\}$. When performing the Q-learning update, instead of selecting the online samples, it draws samples randomly from the replay buffer D. Compared to the conventional Q-learning, the experience replay has several advantages. First, the agent learns more efficiently from data because each experience is used in many weight updates. Second, it reduces the variance in the Q-learning update. In the standard Q-learning, the consecutive samples are highly correlated (e.g., considering a video game, we can imagine that screenshots taken one step after another are highly correlated). The random sampling in experience replay breaks such correlations.

Note that DQN is a model-free and off-policy algorithm, in which only samples from the emulator are used for solving the task. Putting the above together, the DQN pseudocode is presented in Algorithm 19. In the algorithm, ϵ-greedy policy is employed for the agent to select and execute actions. Also, a function ϕ can be used to produce a fixed length representation of histories, which is fed as inputs to the neural network.

Algorithm 19 DQN Algorithm

1: Initialize replay memory D to capacity N
2: Initialize action-value function Q with random weights θ
3: Initialize target action-value function $\hat{Q}$ with weights $\theta^- = \theta$
4: **for** episode $= 1, 2, \cdots, M$ **do**
5:     Initialize sequence $s_1 = \{x_1\}$ (x_i is the raw data from the environment) and preprocess the sequence $\phi_1 = \phi(s_1)$
6:     **for** $t = 1, 2, \cdots, T$ **do**
7:         Select a random action a_t using ϵ greedy policy
8:         Execute action a_t and observe reward r_t and the new data input x_{t+1} from the environment
9:         Set $s_{t+1} = s_t, a_t, x_{t+1}$ and preprocess $\phi_{t+1} = \phi(s_{t+1})$
10:         Store transition $(\phi_t, a_t, r_t, \phi_{t+1})$ in D
11:         Sample random minibatch of transitions $(\phi_j, a_j, r_j, \phi_{j+1})$ from D
12:         Set $y_j = \begin{cases} r_j, \text{if episode terminates at step } j+1 \\ r_j + \gamma max_{a'} \hat{Q}(\phi_{j+1}, a'; \theta^-), \text{otherwise} \end{cases}$
13:         Preform a gradient descent step on $(y_j - Q(\phi_j, a_j; \theta))^2$ with respect to the network parameters θ, i.e., update in (6.6)
14:         Every C steps reset $\hat{Q} = Q$
15:     **end for**
16: **end for**

6.3.1.1 Example

Example (*Autonomous Braking System* [26])

Nowadays, autonomous driving is envisioned to become prevalent in the near future. Among the challenging safety designs required by autonomous driving, autonomous braking systems owns the top priority. Specifically, this braking system automatically reduces the velocity of the vehicle when a threatening obstacle is detected. Given various and unpredictable situations on real roads, any pre-designated brake control protocol cannot be adopted for autonomous driving. Thus motivated, a DQN-based intelligent braking system has been developed. We herein consider the threat from pedestrians as an example, and the RL model is described below (see Fig. 6.7).

States: The states are the velocity of the vehicle and the relative position of the pedestrian to the moving vehicle. Obviously the state space is continuous, a fact that requires the use of DNN to approximate the continuous space functions.

Actions: There are four actions with different intensities in the proposed braking system: no braking, weak braking, medium braking and strong braking. Definitely, more refined braking actions can be considered as well.

Reward: One intuitive reward function at instance t can be designed as

$$r_t = -(\alpha d_t + \beta)\delta_t - (\eta v_t^2 + \lambda)1_{ac},$$

where d_t represents the relative distance between the vehicle and the pedestrian, and δ_t represents the difference between the vehicle velocities v_t and v_{t-1}. The first term $(\alpha d_t + \beta)\delta_t$ prevents the vehicle from braking too early. On the other hand, the term $(\eta v_t^2 + \lambda)1_{ac}$ (1_x is the indication function on event x) indicates the penalty that the agent receives when the accident occurs (i.e., the higher the velocity, the higher the penalty). The tuning parameters $\alpha, \beta, \eta, \lambda$ are the weights that balance the trade-off between the two terms.

In the experiments, leaky ReLU [115] is used as the nonlinear function of each neuron in DNN. In addition, the RMSProp algorithm is applied to optimize the neural network. As shown in Fig. 6.8, for 1000 trials with different initial position of the pedestrian the vehicle stops around $5m$ away from the pedestrian for most of trials. Given $3m$ is the typical safe distance, this DQN-based braking system performs reasonably well.

6.4 DEEP LEARNING TO POLICY FUNCTIONS

In the previous section, we introduced the value-based DRL, where the action is selected according to the estimated state-action value, e.g., ϵ greedy policy. However, value-based DRL has limitations in continuous actions and often requires large memory experience replay buffer. In this section, we will discuss another approach, named *policy-based* DRL, which addresses the limitations of value-based DRL.

In Section 5.3.3, we have introduced the policy gradient approach.

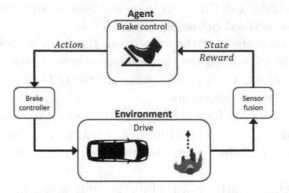

Figure 6.7: DQN-based autonomous braking systems [26].

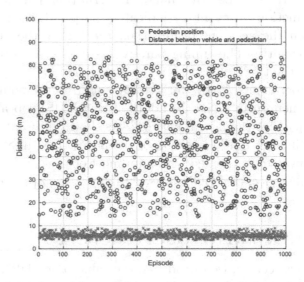

Figure 6.8: Initial position of the pedestrian and the relative distance between the pedestrian and vehicle after the episode ends for 1000 trials [26].

That is, we directly parameterize the policy with parameter w, where we use $\mu_w(s)$ (or $\mu(s|w)$) and $\pi_w(a|s)$ (or $\pi(a|s,w)$), the probability distribution over actions, to respectively represent the deterministic and stochastic policy. One can see that policy gradient has several advantages over value-based learning. On the one hand, policy gradient methods are popular in RL with continuous action spaces. On the other hand, policy gradient can learn stochastic policy while value-based learning only leads to deterministic policy, e.g., greedy strategy. For completeness, below we briefly review the main steps of policy gradient method.

To optimize the parameter w, an objective $J(w)$, a function of the policy parameter, is defined as

$$J(w) = v_{\pi_w}(s_0) = E[r_1 + \gamma r_2 + \gamma^2 r_3 + ...|s_0, \pi(:, w)],$$

with its gradient over the parameter w (*gradient policy theorem* [160]) given by

$$
\begin{aligned}
\nabla_w J(w) &= \sum_s p_\pi(s|w) \left[\sum_a Q^{\pi_w}(s,a) \nabla_w \pi(a|s,w) \right] \\
&= E_\pi \left[Q^{\pi_w}(s,a) \nabla_w \log \pi(a|s,w) \right],
\end{aligned}
\tag{6.7}
$$

where $p_\pi(s|w) = \lim_{t\to\infty} Pr(S_t = s|s_0, w)$ is the stationary distribution of states under π, which we assume exists and is independent of s_0 for all policies. To maximize the expected return $J(w)$ with the optimized w, stochastic gradient descent can be used to iteratively update parameter w,

$$w_{t+1} = w_t + \alpha \nabla_{w_t} J(w_t),$$

where $\nabla_{w_t} J(w_t)$ is the gradient of the performance measure with respect to its argument w_t at iteration t. Recall that we name any method that follows this general iterative scheme to find the optimal policy as a *policy gradient method*.

The first policy gradient algorithm, REINFORCE, is also introduced in Section 5.3.3, where $Q^{\pi_w}(s,a)$ in (6.7) is estimated by the return G_t received starting from time step t. That is,

$$w_{t+1} = w_t + \alpha \gamma^t G_t \frac{\nabla_{w_t} \pi(a|s, w_t)}{\pi(a|s, w_t)}.$$

However, REINFORCE often suffers from high variance due to the nature of Monte Carlo sampling. One approach to reduce such high variance is to subtract a baseline function $B(s) = V_{\pi_w}(s)$ (state value function) from the policy gradient (6.7), i.e.,

$$
\nabla_w J(w) = \sum_s p_\pi(s|w) \left[\sum_a (Q^{\pi_w}(s,a) - V_{\pi_w}(s)) \nabla_w \pi(a|s,w) \right]
$$
$$
= E_\pi \left[(Q^{\pi_w}(s,a) - V_{\pi_w}(s)) \nabla_w \log \pi(a|s,w) \right]. \tag{6.8}
$$

To further reduce the high variance in the learning process, one can also employ the actor-critic algorithm to approximate both policy and value by taking advantage of bootstrapping like TD method. The actor refers to the learned policy π_w and critic refers to the action-value function approximator $Q(s,a|\theta) \approx Q^{\pi_w}(s,a)$, where θ is the parameter of critic. The methods of using this idea to reduce the variance include *asynchronous advantage actor-critic* (A3C) [108], *generalized advantage estimation* (GAE) [144], etc. Along this line, Silver *et al.* [151] introduced the *deterministic policy gradient* (DPG) algorithm. DPG is an off-policy actor-critic algorithm. The difference between DPG and stochastic policy gradient is that DPG is the expected gradient of the action-value function which integrates over the state space, while the stochastic policy gradient integrates over the state and action space. Compared with the stochastic policy gradient, it is proved that DPG can be estimated much more efficiently and performs better in a high-dimensional task.

As deep learning is successfully applied to value-based RL such as DQN, it also becomes an important role in policy-based RL. One direction is that in the policy gradient methods, the policy is now parameterized by DNN. On the other hand, the aforementioned actor-critic algorithms can also be integrated with deep learning (by using DNN to approximate both policy and value functions). In what follows, we introduce two basic policy-base DRL algorithms, the *deep DPG* (DDPG) [90] and the *asynchronous advantage actor-critic* (A3C) [108].

6.4.1 DDPG

We first briefly introduce the *deterministic policy gradient* (DPG) algorithm. Essentially, DPG can be viewed as the deterministic analogue to the policy gradient theorem in (6.7). That is, using the parameterized deterministic policy $\mu_w(s)$, it yields

$$\nabla_w J(w) = \mathbb{E}_s[\nabla_w \mu_w(s) \nabla_a Q^{\mu_w}(s, a)|_{a=\mu_w(s)}]. \qquad (6.9)$$

One may notice that the above formula does not look like the stochastic version (6.7). However, Silver *et al.* [151] showed that for a wide class of stochastic policies the DPG is in fact a limiting case of the stochastic policy gradient.

Now we leverage DPG to introduce a deterministic actor-critic algorithm—DDPG. Recall that DQN is able to stabilize the process of using deep learning for value function approximation, which was believed to be unstable. When it comes to the continuous action space, it is not straightforward to apply DQN directly. One naive approach is to discretize the continuous action space. However, it has many limitations. First, it would cause the curse of dimensionality. In DQN, we need to choose the action that maximizes the Q value at every time step. But maximizing the Q value over each action is computationally expensive when the action space is too large. Mostly this maximization is too complicated to achieve. To handle the problem, DDPG combines DPG with DQN. DDPG is a model-free, off-policy actor-critic algorithm using deep learning for function approximations and thus is capable of learning continuous actions. It has been proved in [90] that DDPG can achieve the robust stability and performance over 20 simulated physics tasks using the same network architectures and hyperparameters, and can learn policies from raw pixel observation. Fig. 6.9 shows renderings of some of the environments used in the task.

Concretely, DDPG has an actor network $\mu(s|w)$ that estimates the deterministic policy and a critic network $Q(s, a|\theta)$ that estimates the value function. Similar to DQN, DDPG uses the idea of *fixed target network* to reduce the variation of value functions and *experience replay* to break the correlation of sampling data during training. Furthermore, instead of directly replicating all target parameters periodically, DDPG uses the "soft" target update:

$$w' \leftarrow \tau w + (1 - \tau)w', \quad \tau \ll 1. \qquad (6.10)$$

DDPG maintains both target networks for actor μ' and critic Q'. This technique allows the target network to change slowly and increase the stability for training.

One observation in low-dimensional features is that the difference

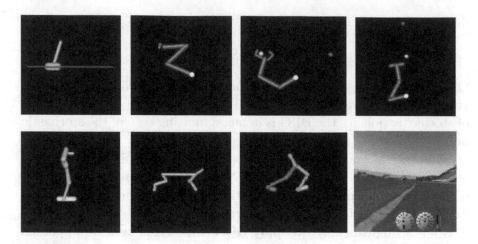

Figure 6.9: Example screenshots of a sample of environments solved with DDPG. In order from the upper left: the cartpole swing-up task, a reaching task, a grasp and move task, a puck-hitting task, a monoped balancing task, two locomotion tasks and Torcs (driving simulator) [90].

of physical units in different components results in the difficulty of finding generalized hyperparameters. DDPG uses batch normalization to learn in different environments effectively. In addition, to address the problem of the lack of exploration of deterministic policy in the continuous action space, DDPG introduces the exploration policy by adding a noise sample to the actor:

$$\mu'(s_t) = \mu(s_t|w_t) + \mathcal{N}, \tag{6.11}$$

where $\mathcal{N}$ is a noise process. The DDPG algorithm is summarized in Algorithm 20.

6.4.2 A3C

A3C is an algorithm that combines the actor-critic algorithm (introduced in Section 5.3.4) with the idea of asynchronous parallel actor-learners. Similar to the actor-critic algorithm, the algorithm maintains a policy network (actor) and value network (critic) by DNN, where the policy network is to predict the action probability, and the value network is to estimate how good the policy is. The update performed by the algorithm uses the state value function as the baseline bias function (i.e., advantage function). However, A3C uses a global network

---

Algorithm 20 DDPG Algorithm

1: Randomly initialize critic network $Q(s, a|\theta)$ and actor $\mu(s|w)$ with weights θ and w

2: Initialize target network Q' and μ' with weights $\theta' \leftarrow \theta$, $w' \leftarrow w$

3: Initialize replay buffer D

4: **for** episode $=1, 2, \cdots, M$ **do**

5:     Initialize a random process $\mathcal{N}$ for action exploration

6:     Receive initial observation state s_1

7:     **for** t$=1, 2, \cdots, T$ **do**

8:         Select action $a_t = \mu(s_t|w) + \mathcal{N}_t$ according to the current policy and exploration noise

9:         Execute action a_t and observe reward r_t and observe new state s_{t+1}

10:         Store transition (s_t, a_t, r_t, s_{t+1}) in D

11:         Sample a random minibatch of N transitions (s_i, a_i, r_i, s_{i+1}) from D

12:         Set $y_i = r_i + \gamma Q'(s_{i+1}, \mu'(s_{i+1}|w')|\theta')$

13:         Update critic (i.e., parameter θ) by minimizing the loss:

$$L = \frac{1}{N} \sum_{i=1}^{N} (y_i - Q(s_i, a_i|\theta))^2$$

14:         Update the actor policy (i.e., parameter w) using the sampled policy gradient:

$$\nabla_w J(w) \approx \frac{1}{N} \sum_{i=1}^{N} \nabla_a Q(s, a|\theta)|_{s=s_i, a=\mu(s_i|w)} \nabla_w \mu(s|w)|_{s=s_i}$$

15:         Update the target networks:

$$\theta' \leftarrow \tau\theta + (1-\tau)\theta'$$
$$w' \leftarrow \tau w + (1-\tau)w'$$

16:     **end for**

17: **end for**

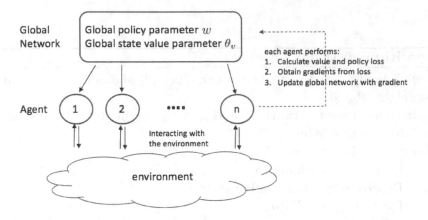

Figure 6.10: A3C architecture.

with shared parameters and multiple agent threads that have their own setting of parameters for learning. Each agent thread runs at the same time in their copies of the environment, accumulating the gradients and then asynchronously updates the global network parameters periodically. The A3C architecture is shown in Fig. 6.10.

The use of multiple agents has several advantages. First, it helps to stabilize the training. Since each agent has its own copy of the environment, agents are allowed to explore different parts of the environment as well as to use different policies at the same time. In other words, different agents will likely experience different states and transitions. Therefore, when agents update the global parameters with their local parameters in an asynchronous manner, the global parameters update will be less correlated than using a single agent. Second, the nature of multi-threads in A3C indicates that A3C needs much less memory to store experience, i.e., no need to store the samples for experience replay as that used in DQN. Furthermore, the practical advantages of A3C is that it allows training on a multi-core CPU rather than GPU. When applied to a variety of Atari games, for instance, agents achieve a better result with asynchronous methods, while using far less resource than these needed on GPU. The A3C algorithm for one actor-learner thread is given in Algorithm 21.

Notice that the update to both the policy and the value-function involves the mix of n-step returns. That is, the policy and the value function are updated after every $t_{\max}$ action or when a terminal state is reached. Essentially, this update is an iterative implementation of

---

Algorithm 21 A3C Algorithm - each actor-learner thread

1: Initialize global shared parameter vectors w and θ_v and set global shared counter $T = 0$
2: Initialize thread-specific parameter vectors w' and θ_v'
3: Initialize thread step counter $t \leftarrow 1$
4: **repeat**
5:    Reset gradients: $dw \leftarrow 0$ and $d\theta_v \leftarrow 0$
6:    Synchronize thread-specific parameters $w' = w$ and $\theta_v' = \theta_v$
7:    Set $t_{start} = t$, get state s_t
8:    **repeat**
9:       Perform a_t according to policy $\pi(a_t|s_t; w')$
10:       Receive reward r_t and new state s_{t+1}
11:       $t \leftarrow t + 1$
12:       $T \leftarrow T + 1$
13:    **until** terminal s_t or $t - t_{start} == t_{max}$
14:    $R = \begin{cases} 0, & \text{for terminal } s_t \\ V(s_t; \theta_v'), & \text{for non-terminal } s_t \text{ //Bootstrap from last state} \end{cases}$
15:    **for** $i \in \{t - 1, ..., t_{start}\}$ **do**
16:       $R \leftarrow r_i + \gamma R$
17:       Accumulate gradients with respect to global shared w:

$$dw \leftarrow dw + \nabla_{w'} \log \pi(a_i|s_i; w')(R - V(s_i; \theta_v'))$$

18:       Accumulate gradients with respect to global shared θ_v:

$$d\theta_v \leftarrow d\theta_v + \nabla_{\theta_v'}(R - V(s_i; \theta_v'))^2$$

19:    **end for**
20:    Perform asynchronous update of w using dw and of θ_v using $d\theta_v$
21: **until** $T > T_{max}$

---

the gradient

$$\nabla_{w'} \log \pi(a_t|s_t; w')(\sum_{i=0}^{k-1} \gamma^i r_{t+i} + \gamma^k V(s_{t+k}; \theta'_v) - V(s_t; \theta'_v)),$$

where k can vary from state to state and is upper bounded by $t_{\max}$. As discussed above, in order to improve the stability of learning, the A3C algorithm applies parallel actor-learners and accumulated updates. Namely, the asynchronous update and the different experience from each actor-learner breaks the correlation of environment inputs to the system. In practice, some parameters of the neural network are typically shared by both the policy and the value function. In [108], a convolutional neural network is used for both networks, where it has one softmax output for the policy $\pi(a_t|s_t; w)$ and one linear output for the value function $V(s_t; \theta_v)$, with all non-output layers shared.

Entropy is a measure of the uncertainty of a random variable [31]. Let X be a discrete random variable with alphabet $\mathcal{X}$ and probability mass function $p(x) = Pr\{X = x\}, x \in \mathcal{X}$. Then the entropy of X is defined by

$$H(X) = -\sum_{x \in \mathcal{X}} p(x) \log p(x).$$

For example, let $X = a, b, c, d$ with probability $\frac{1}{2}, \frac{1}{4}, \frac{1}{8}$ and $\frac{1}{8}$. Then

$$H(X) = -\frac{1}{2} \log \frac{1}{2} - \frac{1}{4} \log \frac{1}{4} - \frac{1}{8} \log \frac{1}{8} - \frac{1}{8} \log \frac{1}{8} = \frac{7}{4}.$$

Similarly, if X is a random continuous variable with the probability density function $f(x) > 0$, the (differential) entropy $H(X)$ is defined as

$$H(X) = -\int_S f(x) \log f(x) dx,$$

where S is the support set of the random variable. For example, consider a random variable distributed uniformly in the closed set $[0, a]$, i.e., its density is $\frac{1}{a}$ in $[0, a]$ and 0 elsewhere. Then

$$H(X) = -\int_0^a \frac{1}{a} \log \frac{1}{a} = \log a.$$

Also, as stated in [108], adding the *entropy* of the policy π to the objective function can improve exploration by discouraging premature convergence to suboptimal deterministic policies. By doing so, the new objective function with respect to the policy parameters is given by

$$\nabla_{w'} \log \pi(a_t|s_t; w')(R - V(s_t; \theta'_v)) + \beta H(\pi(s_t; w')),$$

where H is the (differential) entropy and β is the weight for the entropy regularization.

6.4.2.1 Example

Example (*Virtual-to-Real Reinforcement Learning for Autonomous Driving* [122]):

Autonomous driving requires the agent to learn the driving policy that automatically outputs control signals for steering wheel, throttle, brake, etc., based on the observed surroundings. Compared with the straightforward idea of using supervised learning, which requires a huge amount of data that needs to capture most on-road situations, reinforcement learning is more promising due to its trial-and-learn nature. However, training an autonomous vehicle in the real world is prohibited because of the unaffordable cost of damages to vehicles and the surroundings. Therefore, training the agent in the virtual world to achieve a human-level driving performance is highly desirable in industry and academia.

In general, the visual appearances between the virtual and the real driving scenes are different to some extent. But they always share similar scene parsing structure. This motivates the approach of constructing a simulation environment (by translating virtual images to their realistic counterparts) that looks very similar to the real world in terms of both scene parsing structure and object appearance. Then the A3C algorithm can be used to train such an autonomous driving system. In particular, the state input to the algorithm is the realistic images, which are obtained by filtering the virtual images. The actor network is a 4-layer convolutional network with ReLU activation functions in-between. The network takes in 4 consecutive RGB frames as state input and outputs 9 discrete actions corresponding to "go straight with acceleration," "go left with acceleration," "go right with acceleration," "go straight and brake," "go left and brake," "go right and brake," "go straight," "go left," and "go right." The reward at time step t is designed as

$$r_t = \begin{cases} (v_t \cos(\alpha) - dist^{(t)}_{\text{center}})\beta, & \text{if no collision,} \\ \gamma, & \text{if collision,} \end{cases}$$

where v_t is the speed (in m/s) of the vehicle at time step t, α is the angle between the vehicle's speed and the tangent line of the track, and $dist^{(t)}_{\text{center}}$ is the distance between the center of the vehicle and the middle of the track. β and γ are constants and are determined at the beginning of training. The agent is trained with 12 asynchronous threads, and with the RMSProp optimizer. The resulting performance under such training assumptions proves that the driving policy trained by A3C can nicely adapt to the complicated real-world situations. Detailed evaluation results can be found in [122].

6.5 DEEP LEARNING TO RL MODEL

Recall that when an MDP model including the state and reward transition probabilities is known in advance the optimal policy can be directly obtained following the model-based RL algorithms in Chapter 4. If the environment is unknown or model-free, the agent can always learn the model first and then search for the optimal policy. In the process of learning a model, if the state space is continuous or prohibitively large, one can also use DNN to approximate the transition probabilities. An objective function of measuring the goodness of the model can be defined to optimize the parameters or weights in DNN. As used in the DRL algorithms in the previous sections, rather than computing the full expectation in the gradient of the objective function, stochastic gradient descent can be employed to efficiently solve the optimization in a sequential manner. Although the basic idea and the route of achieving solutions are quite straightforward, the model-based DRL has not been commonly used due to many challenges. For instance, initial observations show that the approximation errors in the transition model can be compounded over the trajectory in an episode. In this case, the rewards can be totally wrong by the end of a long trajectory.

In the literature, several approaches have been proposed to learn the RL model using raw data, e.g., pixel information [121, 99, 120, 119]. The basic idea is to embed high-dimensional observations into a low-dimensional space using autoencoders. By doing so, if the model of the environment can be learned accurately, most of the simple off-the-shelf model-based RL algorithms can be used for solving such tasks. For instance, [29] showed that even very simple controllers can control a robot directly from the camera images. Furthermore, the learned model can also help performance explorations only based on simulations of the DNN model-based environment, a model that can handle high-dimensional raw data [131].

One compelling feature of using DNN to model the environment is that such models can to a certain extent overcome the aforementioned compounded errors induced by planning based on imperfect models. In particular, the agent can choose to discard or downplay the outputs of DNN if it believes that the model is inaccurate for the time being [131]. There exist many other ways to make use of the flexibility of the DNN-based models. For example, based on its estimate of the model accuracy, the agent can decide to run over a long trajectory or a short trajectory or simply take some actions [124].

In summary, the model accuracy is imperative in model-based DRL. It is necessary to find efficient and effective strategies of using raw data to improve the model accuracy. Therefore, model-based DRL remains a very active research area.

6.6 DRL COMPUTATION EFFICIENCY

Although DRL has achieved many astonishing successes, the experiment cost remains a key bottleneck for implementing DRL in research and industrial applications. For instance, the training time of DQN or A3C using only a central processing unit (CPU) could be prohibitively longer than several weeks. Note that in DRL the neural network is employed in both learning/optimizing the weights and in executing the agent's current policy. Due to the particular structure advantage for matrix multiplications, graphics processing units (GPU) are now widely used to accelerate DRL computations. This is because both forward and backward computation of neural networks are essentially matrix multiplications. One GPU with hundreds of simpler cores and thousands of concurrent hardware threads can significantly accelerate matrix multiplications. Also, the cost of using GPU can be reduced in the order of magnitude. For example, a GPU with 6000 cores has a cost of $11,000 but we need hundreds of CPUs to own 6000 cores and the cost could be millions of dollars.

On the other hand, the investigation on parallel computing for DRL has been underway for quite a few years. For instance, parallelized DQN using the parameter-server-based distributed computing architecture has been proved to achieve sub-linear speedups in learning process [114]. Furthermore, using a distributed, prioritized reply buffer can support even faster learning in DQN while using a single GPU for training and hundreds of CPU cores for simulation [59]. As for the policy gradient method A3C, a parallelized algorithm itself, using a GPU can also speed up the learning process over CPU-only A3C [11].

However, one should be advised that some issues may also arise from using GPU when the neural network is large (billion-plus connections between neurons). For example, a neural network with 5.6 billion connections has a size of 20 gigabytes. Such a network cannot be trained over a typical GPU with 5 gigabytes of memory. For such a case, a mixed use of GPUs and CPUs can be a solution in which a CPU with larger memory holds most of the parameters. We refer the interested readers to [32] for the detailed implementation of such a solution.

6.7 REMARKS

DRL has been evolving exponentially fast in recent years. The survey paper [6] is a good reference to walk through. This section was only intended to provide some fundamental DRL algorithms, upon which more advanced algorithms can be developed. In the section of deep learning to policy functions, we presented the actor-critic based method including DDPG and A3C. In fact, when the neural network is large, e.g., a large number of parameters to optimize, searching directly for a policy can be cumbersome and suffer from severe local minima. Thus motivated, methods including guided policy search (GPS) [83] and trust region policy optimization (TRPO) [65] have been devised recently. In particular, GPS takes a few sequences of actions from another controller and, after learning from these actions, can successfully bias the search toward a good (local) optimum. On the other hand, TRPO restricts the optimization steps to lie within a region such that the updated policy cannot deviate too widely from previous policies.

As we have claimed, DRL algorithms can handle high-dimensional inputs from real-world applications. However, when samples are not cheap to collect, or the learning speed of DRL is slow due to the extremely large number of samples, exploiting previously acquired knowledge from related tasks is of importance to speed up DRL training. In this context, transfer learning [166], curriculum learning [203] and some other architectures have drawn quite a lot of attention and have become active research areas.

In most reinforcement learning algorithms such as SARSA, Q-learning, DQN and DDPG, only simple exploration strategies (e.g., ϵ-greedy or softmax) are employed for exploration. In Chapter 3. we have introduced the upper confidence bound (UCB) algorithm which could perform much better. This algorithm is one of the main principled exploration strategies for trading off between exploration and exploitation in the context of Bayesian optimization [146]. However, an issue may arise from sample inefficiency or sparse rewards, implying that the rewards could be more obsolete. This remains an open problem in the RL community. Along this line, one good work using *intrinsic motivation* can be found in [143], which essentially advocates decreasing uncertainty in the environment-learning process. As also pointed out in [6], there exists some early work on deep reinforcement learning that tried to implement intrinsic motivation via maximizing information gain [111, 60] or minimizing model prediction error [155, 125].

6.8 EXERCISES

6.1. Explain why neural networks with only linear activation functions are uninteresting (that is, networks of neurons where, for each neuron, the output is some constant times the weighted sum of the inputs). Use equations if necessary.

6.2. Backpropagation can be used to find an image that activates a particular neuron. "Guided backpropagation" is a refined approach which generates more informative images. Review the paper "Striving for Simplicity: The All Convolutional Net" by J. T. Springenberg, *et al.*, and then describe how the guided backpropagation works.

6.3. Describe the role of the pooling layer in a CNN.

6.4. A convolutional neural network has 4 consecutive 3×3 convolutional layers with stride 1 and no pooling. How large is the support of (the set of image pixels which activate) a neuron in the 4th non-image layer of this network?

6.5. Consider the three-node RNN in Fig. 6.11. Mathematically, it is

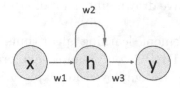

Figure 6.11: Three-node RNN.

given by

$$y_t = w_3 h_t,$$

$$h_t = \sigma(w_2 h_{t-1} + w_1 x_t),$$

where x_t, h_t and y_t, respectively, denote the input, hidden unit and output at time t. Here $\sigma(\cdot)$ represents the sigmoid function. Suppose you wish to train this network using gradient descent to fit the input/output time series

$$\Big((x_1, y_1), (x_2, y_2), \cdots, (x_T, y_T)\Big).$$

Derive the gradient descent rule for training this network. That is, calculate the gradient including each network parameter, and give the training algorithm. Derive your algorithm to minimize the sum of squared errors

$$\sum_{t=1}^{T} (\hat{y}_t - y_t)^2,$$

where $\hat{y}_t$ is the estimated output. Assume when calculating y_1, that $x_0 = 1$.

6.6. Explain why we need to use "experience replay" and "fixed Q-targets" in DQN.

6.7. Describe the difference between deterministic policy gradient (DPG) and deep deterministic policy gradient (DDPG).

6.8. What is the benefit of using multiple agents in an asynchronous manner in A3C?

III

Case Studies

CHAPTER 7

Reinforcement Learning for Cybersecurity

CONTENTS

With the widespread deployment of Internet technology in modern businesses, cybersecurity has become an emerging serious issue that needs to be addressed. Numerous approaches have been proposed to defend computer systems from cyberattacks. In Chapter 2, we have introduced the definition, objectives and types of cybersecurity, and also provided a few problems of cybersecurity in cyber-physical systems. As introduced in Part II of this book, the nature of reinforcement learning enables this machine learning technique to be a promising tool for tackling various cyber-security issues. Concretely, compared with the traditional learning methods, such as supervised learning, reinforcement learning does not require predesigned or classified data. Furthermore, it can adapt itself online to the changing learning environment. This fact makes it ideal for identifying cyber attacks, as they are becoming more and more idiosyncratic. In this chapter, we will first briefly summarize the contemporary challenges of cybersecurity and then survey the applications of reinforcement learning on cybersecurity protection.

7.1 TRADITIONAL CYBERSECURITY METHODS

With the rapid development and widespread popularization of computer and network technology, more and more enterprises have set up different types of business in the Internet/Intranet environment. As a result, E-mail, file sharing, instant messaging and collaboration servers have become the most important IT infrastructure in today's business society. However, most enterprises are not well aware of the risks associated with Internet interconnection when they enjoy the benefits of the Internet.

7.1.1 Traditional Cybersecurity Technologies

In Chapter 2, we have introduced some common threats that contemporary network systems face. In what follows, we present some traditional security technologies, and explain why they are inadequate in the modern Internet era.

Antivirus software: Antivirus software uses signature matching to detect existing viruses and malwares on the hard disk [163]. However, virus scanning is an expensive operation, since it requires reading the whole hard disk. Furthermore, antivirus software requires frequent update to its virus database, to ensure new viruses are detected. These disadvantages make antivirus software unsuitable for lightweight devices, such as wireless sensors. More importantly, many types of cyber attacks are not launched through viruses. For instance, none of the common attacks introduced in Chapter 2 explicitly requires the launch of a virus. For such attacks, antivirus software is useless.

Firewalls: The firewall is a protective barrier formed by a combination of software and hardware equipment, between the internal and external networks. Firewall works by following predetermined rules to block suspicious Internet connections. However, since the rules are prescribed by humans, they are highly error-prone [27]. Also, it is not a trivial task to decide the rules for suspicious connections. The attacker may forge his IP address to make the connection seem as innocent as possible. This significantly reduces the effectiveness of firewalls [36].

IDS and IPS: IDS (Intrusion Detection System) and IPS (Intrusion Prevention System) are security systems which detect and block malicious programs and operations. They differ from antivirus software in that they do not depend on specific fingerprints of the malwares, but deduce malicious intents from the programs' behaviors. But similar to firewalls, IDS suffers from many limitations. Recently considerable attention has been paid to augment IDS with machine learning techniques [4, 69]. Readers will find such an example in the following case-study chapters.

Encryption technology: Encryption is a way for encoding messages such that only relevant parties can decode the text. Encrypted messages can be safely transmitted. However, they must be decoded before we can do computations on the data [136]. As discussed in Chapter 2, a recent breakthrough in cryptography is the so-called *homomorphic encryption,* where calculations can be done on data without decrypting it [45]. However, the efficiency of homomorphic encryption is still limited.

Authentication technology: Authentication means verifying the identity of the user before allowing one to access sensitive data in a network. An enhanced authentication mechanism can reduce the possibility of successful attacks to a network environment. Username plus password is the most widely implemented authentication method. But it is subject to various cracking techniques [56]. Furthermore, authentication cannot differentiate between a normal user and a hijacked user, or even an attacker who has obtained the password otherwise.

7.1.2 Emerging Cybersecurity Threats

In addition to the lack of end-to-end solutions to the traditional cybersecurity problems, new cybersecurity threats are emerging from the use of the advanced technology and the change of people's daily behavior and the surroundings. The emerging threats include but are not limited to the following:

Data wars: Both businesses and cyber criminals began paying close attention to valuable data, which are viewed by some as potential currencies [167]. The key assets that criminals covet are divided into two categories: the dataset itself, and the individuals associated with data sets.

Artificial intelligence (AI): New cybersecurity vulnerabilities will continue to emerge. A contributing factor is our growing ability to predict human behavior accurately, and exploit security policy flaws accordingly. Although the current debate is still at an abstract level, it is predicted that this powerful predictive capability will reveal new security vulnerabilities which easily overshadow the existing defense concepts and control practices [202].

Internet of things (IoT): It is foreseeable that IoT will become an important part of our daily life. But this also means that hackers will have more new opportunities to manipulate and exploit all kinds of network devices, and the specific means will be more cryptic and undetectable. Unsurprisingly, there has been considerable effort in strengthening the network security of IoT [200].

Emotional analysis: Smartphones and wearable devices can expose intimacy among users, leading to unexpected tracking of such relationships by malicious people. Such data are extremely valuable in social engineering. A notorious recent example is the illegal exploitation of Facebook user privacy by Cambridge Analytica, which allegedly used such data to manipulate the U.S. presidential election [138].

In the near future, information and network security will be of utmost importance in the IT industry, and the most important issues that need to be addressed will be concentrated in the following three areas. The first one is to protect the privacy of user data. In the traditional data centers, the system manager can utilize the data arbitrarily, thus leading to the Facebook privacy leakage incident. An emerging solution to this problem is the blockchain. It is decentralized, and all data transfers are strictly encrypted. Therefore, user privacy will be safer. The second one is to differentiate legitimate network nodes from spoofing attackers. The verification mechanism of the system must be able to identify illegal or even malicious node accesses of the network. This is also the key to the various kinds of information security technology against system loopholes [97]. The third one is to establish secure communication protocols between the nodes of the network. The Internet users or entities must be able to ensure real-time secure transmission including data security. In summary, as long as data is associated with its economic lure, which will be even truer in the future, the battle between businesses and cyber attacks will never end.

7.2 EXAMPLES OF RL TO CYBERSECURITY APPLICATIONS

In this section, we present a few examples of using reinforcement learning to resolve the emerging cybersecurity threats, which cannot be directly handled by the traditional anti-attack technologies. These examples are the representations of applications of significant advanced technologies, including mobile crowdsensing, cognitive radio network and edge computing. The following presentation is intended to help readers identify a few reinforcement learning research directions related to cybersecurity, rather than introduce the complete work. If interested, readers can find the details of these results in the references.

7.2.1 Faked Sensing Attacks in Mobile Crowdsensing

A typical mobile crowdsensing (MCS) problem is described as follows: As more and more mobile devices are equipped with sensors such as accelerometers and global positioning systems, it is increasingly prevalent for mobile devices to provide location-based services. To utilize this kind of resource, a platform or server recruits mobile users to monitor the environment and send information back, then rewards them according to the importance and the accuracy of their sensing data. In this case, selfish users can choose to maximize their profits by providing faked sensing results to save their sensing costs and avoid privacy leakage. This kind of behavior pattern is called faked sensing attacks. We remark that the payment and reward method has been widely used to stimulate mobile sensing, data acquisition and distributed computing. Such examples can be found in [34, 39, 40, 177, 86].

In essence, this situation can be modeled as a Stackelberg game, in which the leader moves first and then the follower moves sequentially. In this game, the leader and the follower compete on quality/profit. In mobile crowdsensing as shown in Fig. 7.1, the MCS server as the leader of a Stackelberg game first determines a payment policy and broadcasts it to all users. Each user then devises its own policy to decide his or her sensing effort, e.g., how many resources should be allocated for the sensing task. An over-payment policy stimulates more mobile users to contribute to the MCS application and suppresses faked sensing attacks. However, it will result in network congestion and thus decrease the utility of the MCS server. On the other hand, less payment stimulates less potential users to participate and contribute. Therefore, it is nontrivial to find an appropriate payment policy for mobile users.

In [190], the payment process is formulated as a finite MDP based on the fact that the current reward stimulates future sensing efforts. The goal of the system is to find an optimal payment policy to reward users reporting valuable and high-quality sensing data and punish the faked sensing attacks. In real-world applications, sensing models of smartphones are not available. As a result, Q-learning is applied to

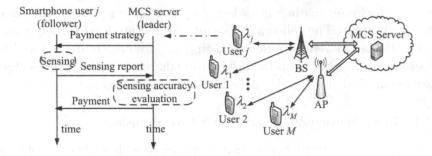

Figure 7.1: Mobile crowdsensing system overview, where λ_j represents the importance of sensing data from user j and reflects the dynamism of the contribution of the user due to the difference in the sensing location and response time.

find the payment policy due to its model-free nature. Specifically, the payment strategy is determined based on the observed state of the previous sensing report quality and payment policy and a quality function or Q-function that describes the discounted long-term reward for each state-action pair. Furthermore, in order to address the problem of slow learning rate in a large state space for Q-learning, a deep Q-network is applied to accelerate the learning process and enhance the sensing performance against the faked sensing attacks. Extensive simulation results in [190] showed that a DQN-based MCS system significantly outperforms the Q-learning strategy and the random payment strategy.

7.2.2 Security Enhancement in Cognitive Radio Networks

A cognitive radio network (CRN) [91] enables unlicensed users (or secondary users, SUs) to sense for and opportunistically operate in underutilized licensed channels, which are owned by the licensed users (or primary users, PUs). CRN has been regarded as the next-generation wireless network centered on the application of artificial intelligence, which helps the SUs to learn about, as well as to adaptively and dynamically reconfigure its operating parameters, including the sensing and transmission channels, for the network performance enhancement. This motivates the use of artificial intelligence to enhance security schemes for CRNs. Provisioning security in CRNs is challenging since existing techniques, such as entity authentication, are not feasible in the dynamic environment that CRN presents since they require pre-registration. In addition, these techniques cannot prevent an authenticated node from acting maliciously. Now, we discuss some advantages of using RL for the security enhancement in CRNs:

1. RL enables SUs to learn from experience without using an accurate model of the operating environment, and even without using any model, allowing the nodes to adapt themselves to their dynamic and uncertain operating environment. Thanks to the nature of adaptation, RL is useful in identifying the SU behavior, such as the change from an honest SU to a malicious SU.

2. RL enables SUs to make decisions based on a series of chosen actions, with the notion of maximizing the long-term reward, rather than following the decisions made by the base station.

3. RL enables SUs to explore new operating environments and exploit the knowledge gained so far.

Therefore, RL-based security enhancement schemes in CRNs are capable of learning new security attacks and detecting previously learned ones. Until now, RL-based security enhancement schemes have been successfully applied in a number of diverse problems, such as channel sensing, channel access, routing and data sensing/reporting. In what follows, we present a sample case study of the anti-jamming defense in [174] to show the guidelines for the application of RL to CRNs.

Radio jamming is a Denial of Service (DoS) attack which targets at disrupting communications at the physical and link layers of a wireless network. On one type of jamming, a jamming attacker can prevent legitimate users from accessing an open spectrum band by constantly injecting packets into this spectrum [116]. Another type of jamming is to inject high interference power around the vicinity of a victim, so that the signal-to-noise ratio (SNR) deteriorates heavily and no data can be received correctly [187, 196]. In some cases, we can assume that the attackers will only jam the secondary users transmission, not jam the licensed bands when the primary users are active. As discussed in [116], this is either "because there may be a very heavy penalty on the attackers if their identities are known by the primary users, or because the attackers cannot get close to the primary users." Therefore, secondary users need to perform dynamic channel access in order to maximize channel utilization in CRNs because a fixed channel access

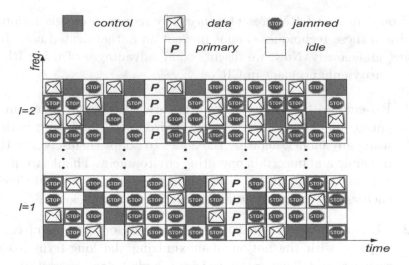

Figure 7.2: Illustration of the anti-jamming defense. Radio resource is represented in frequency and time domain. The jamming attack pattern is changing from time index $I = 1$ to $I = 2$.

schedule can be easily detected and jammed by attackers. In [174], RL with minimax Q-learning is applied to find an optimal channel access strategy. The state of RL is defined as a tuple of the presence of PU in spectrum j, node i throughput, the number of jammed control channels in spectrum j and the number of jammed data channels in spectrum j. The action space is then defined as the choice of the available control and data channels to transmit. The reward is the spectrum gain when the agent selects an unjammed channel. The main objective is to help SUs to learn the dynamic attack strategies from malicious SUs, who tend to optimize their attacks. This implies that SUs must learn to take optimal actions in the presence of worst-case attacks from malicious SUs. Hence, a minimax Q-learning algorithm is chosen.

7.2.3 Security in Mobile Edge Computing

Mobile edge computing (MEC) provides data storage, computing and application services with edge devices such as Access Points (APs), laptops, base stations, switches and IP video cameras at the network edge. Being closer to customers than the cloud, mobile edge computing can provide the Internet of Things (IoT), cyber-physical systems, vehicular networks, smart grids and embedded AI with low latency, location

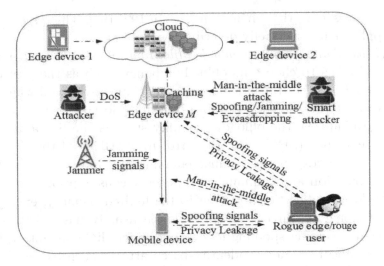

Figure 7.3: Threats in mobile edge caching.

awareness and mobility support. Mobile edge caching reduces the duplicated transmissions and backhaul traffic, improves the communication efficiency, and provides quality of services for caching users. From the security perspective, however, due to the limited computation, energy, communication and memory resources, the edge devices are protected by different types of security protocols, which are in general less secure compared with cloud servers and data centers. In addition, mobile edge caching systems consist of distributed edge devices that are controlled by selfish and autonomous people. The edge device owners might be curious about the data contents stored on their cache and sometimes even launch insider attacks to analyze and sell the privacy information of the customers. Therefore, MEC systems are more vulnerable to security threats such as wireless jamming, Distributed Denial of Service attacks (DDoS), spoofing attacks including rogue edge and rogue mobile devices, man-in-the-middle attacks, and smart attacks. Fig. 7.3 illustrates the possible attacks during the mobile offloading procedure and the cashing perspective.

As motivated by the aforementioned security threats in MEC, recently RL techniques have been used to study dynamic security games. The proposed RL-based security schemes, such as the anti-jamming channel access scheme, the authentication scheme and the malware detection scheme, have been proved to exceed the benchmark deterministic schemes, e.g., the schemes in [191, 5, 192, 194]. These scenarios of RL applications are briefly described as follows:

RL-based anti-jamming mobile offloading: In a MEC system, a mobile device has to choose its offloading policy, such as the part of the data to offload, the transmit power, channel and time, and which edge nodes to connect to, each from a given finite feasible action set. The goal is to improve the offloading quality such as the Signal-to-Noise-plus-Interference (SINR) and Bit Error Rate (BER) of the signals received by the edge nodes against jamming and interference and save the computation and communication energy consumption.

RL-based authentication: Due to the limited memory, energy and computational resources, a mobile device usually has difficulty estimating the ongoing spoofing model and prefers light-weight authentication protocols to detect identity-based attacks such as spoofing attacks, Sybil attacks and rogue edge attacks. Each edge node also needs fast detection of a large number of spoofing messages and rogue users. To this end, PHY-authentication techniques that reuse the existing channel estimates of the source node and/or the ambient radio signals provide light-weight protection against identity-based attacks without leaking user privacy such as their locations.

RL-based friendly jamming: Secure collaborative caching in MEC has to protect data privacy and resist eavesdropping. For example, an edge node can send friendly jamming signals according to the data stored in the caching system to prevent the eavesdropping attacker from understanding the information sent from a mobile node or another edge node. In this way, each edge node has to determine whether to attend the friendly jamming according to the network topology, the channel models and the presence of the attackers. An edge node has to decide whether to compute the data or to forward the data received from the mobile device to the cloud, and whether to store the "popular" data in the edge against privacy leakage and DoS attacks.

One good example of applying RL to provide secure offloading to the edge nodes against jamming attacks can be found in [193].

7.2.4 Dynamic Scheduling of Cybersecurity Analysts

The task of a cybersecurity analyst includes examining the alerts generated by an Intrusion Detection System (IDS), such as SNORT or a Security Information and Event Management (SIEM) tool, and then identifying those alerts that are considered significant. In this domain, dynamic scheduling to manage cybersecurity analysts to minimize risk is a critical infrastructure problem that poses several operational challenges and garners importance at the level of national security [48]. The cybersecurity analysts can be viewed as a resource that must be allocated to the process of examining alerts in an optimal way to minimize risk while satisfying the resource constraints. Such resource constraints include the number of sensors on which an analyst can be trained or assigned, the expertise mix that the cybersecurity defense organization wishes to own, the expected utilization of the analysts, the time taken by an analyst to investigate an alert (translates to analyst workload), and the preferences such as shift hours and days off in a week for the analysts. Given such a highly dynamic environment and conditions, the existing static or adaptive scheduling solutions in manufacturing and service applications cannot be directly applied to address the problem of scheduling cybersecurity analysts. However, if the problem is modeled as a dynamic programming problem and then solved using reinforcement learning with the objective to minimize the number of analysts and optimize the sensor-to-analyst allocation, it is proved that the overall risk can be minimized or reduced under a threshold.

7.3 REMARKS

The future of cybersecurity is sophisticated: It is conducted via the interaction of man and machine. Machines can perform the heavy lifting such as data aggregation, data classification and pattern recognition, and then help to obtain actionable insight and make optimized decisions. Definitely, these powerful machines can be employed by attackers such that most traditional methods for cybersecurity will be out-of-date. This points us to the fact that machine learning is necessary and imperative to prevent smart attacks that might be currently happening.

In this chapter, we have reviewed traditional methods for cybersecurity and identified a few emerging cyber threats leveraging the advanced technologies. In the literature, RL has been proved useful to deal with these new threats. We have provided some RL examples, in which readers may obtain some hint on how to apply RL to cybersecurity applications. These examples can be treated as a starting point for readers who wish to begin research in this field. In the following chapters, we dive into two case studies on RL-based cybersecurity.

7.4 EXERCISES

7.1. Explain the following terms:
  a) Intrusion Prevention System
  b) Data war
  c) Stackelberg game
  d) Cognitive radio network
  e) Radio jamming and friendly jamming

7.2. Why are traditional cybersecurity strategies insufficient in face of emerging threats?

7.3. How does crowd-sensing payment policy affect businesses and users?

7.4. What are some applications of RL in mobile edge computing?

The following problems require readers to explore beyond the text.

7.5. In the text, we saw that the quality of mobile crowd-sensing could be controlled by adjusting the payment policy. This technique depends on the server actually knowing the quality of the submitted data. This is usually done by introducing a classification algorithm, which gives a quality estimation. To design a fair reward scheme, we need to know the error distribution of the estimation. Discuss how Q-learning can automatically adapt to an unknown error distribution. This demonstrates one of the fundamental advantages of reinforcement learning, that of model-independence. Hint: see reference [190] ("A Secure Mobile Crowdsensing Game with Deep Reinforcement Learning" by Liang Xiao *et al.*) for a possible implementation.

7.6. We discussed how reinforcement learning can be used to help mobile devices choose the edge node to offload its data, in a MEC system. One of the defining characteristics of a mobile network environment is its fluctuating channel quality. Implement an RL algorithm that chooses an edge node with penalty based on the bit error rate. Then increase the penalty of some edge nodes to simulate users moving away from those nodes. Observe how the algorithm gradually moves to other nodes. This demonstrates how RL algorithms can adapt to evolving environments. Hint: see reference [174] ("An Anti-jamming Stochastic Game for Cognitive Radio Networks" by B. Wang *et al.*) for a possible implementation.

CHAPTER 8

Case Study: Online Cyber-Attack Detection in Smart Grid

CONTENTS

8.1 INTRODUCTION

The next-generation power grid, i.e., the smart grid, relies on advanced control and communication technologies. This critical cyber infrastructure makes the smart grid vulnerable to hostile cyber-attacks [89, 178, 199]. The main objective of attackers is to damage or mislead the state estimation mechanism in the smart grid to cause wide-area power blackouts or to manipulate electricity market prices [195]. There are many types of cyber-attacks, among them *false data injection* (FDI), jamming, and *denial of service* (DoS) attacks are well known. FDI attacks add malicious fake data to meter measurements [93, 18, 88, 75], jamming attacks corrupt meter measurements via additive noise [74], and DoS attacks block the access of the system to meter measurements [8, 206, 75].

The smart grid is a complex network and any failure or anomaly in a part of the system may lead to huge damages on the overall system in a short period of time. Hence, early detection of cyber-attacks is critical for a timely and effective response. In this context, the framework of quickest change detection [130, 15, 169, 128] is quite useful. In the quickest change detection problems, a change occurs in the sensing environment at an unknown time and the aim is to detect the change as soon as possible with the minimal level of false alarms based on the measurements that become available sequentially over time. After obtaining measurements at a given time, the decision maker either declares a change or waits for the next time interval to have further measurements. In general, as the desired detection accuracy increases, detection speed decreases. Hence, the stopping time, at which a change is declared, should be chosen to optimally balance the tradeoff between the detection speed and the detection accuracy.

If the *probability density functions* (PDFs) of meter measurements for the pre-change, i.e., normal system operation, and the post-change, i.e., after an attack/anomaly, cases can be modeled sufficiently accurately, the well-known *cumulative sum* (CUSUM) test is the optimal online detector [112] based on Lorden's criterion [95]. Moreover, if the PDFs can be modeled with some unknown parameters, the generalized CUSUM test, which makes use of the estimates of unknown parameters, has asymptotic optimality properties [15]. However, CUSUM-based detection schemes require perfect models for both the pre- and post-change cases. In practice, capabilities of an attacker and correspondingly attack types and strategies can be totally unknown. For instance, an attacker can arbitrarily combine and launch multiple attacks simultaneously or it can launch a new unknown type of attack. Then, it may not always be possible to know the attacking strategies ahead of time and to accurately model the post-change case. Hence, universal detectors, not requiring any attack model, are needed in general. Moreover, the generalized CUSUM algorithm has optimality properties in minimizing a least favorable (worst-case) detection delay subject to false alarm constraints [112, 15]. Since the worst case detection delay is a pessimistic metric, it is, in general, possible to obtain algorithms performing better than the generalized CUSUM algorithm.

Considering the pre-change and the post-change cases as hidden states due to the unknown change-point, a quickest change detection problem can be formulated as a partially observable *Markov decision process* (POMDP) problem. For the problem of online attack detection in the smart grid, in the pre-change state, the system is operated under normal conditions and using the system model, the pre-change measurement pdfs can be specified highly accurately. On the other hand, the post-change measurement pdfs can take different unknown forms depending on the attacker's strategy. Furthermore, the transition probability between the hidden states is unknown in general. Hence, the exact model of the POMDP is unknown.

Reinforcement learning (RL) algorithms are known to be effective in controlling uncertain environments. Hence, the described POMDP problem can be effectively solved using RL. In particular, as a solution, either the underlying POMDP model can be learned and then a model-based RL algorithm for POMDPs [139, 38] can be used or a model-free RL algorithm [66, 126, 94, 79, 127] can be used without learning the underlying model. Since the model-based approach requires a two-step solution that is computationally more demanding and only an approximate model can be learned in general, we prefer to use the model-free RL approach.

Outlier detection schemes such as the Euclidean detector [98] and the cosine-similarity metric-based detector [134] are universal as they do not require any attack model. They mainly compute a dissimilarity metric between actual meter measurements and predicted measurements by the Kalman filter and declare an attack/anomaly if the amount of dissimilarity exceeds a certain predefined threshold. However, such detectors do not consider the temporal relation between attacked/anomalous measurements and make sample-by-sample decisions. Hence, they are unable to distinguish instantaneous high-level random noise realizations from long-term or persistent anomalies caused by an unfriendly intervention to the system. Hence, compared to the outlier detection schemes, more reliable universal attack detection schemes are needed.

In this chapter, we consider the smart grid security problem from a defender's perspective and seek an effective detection scheme using RL techniques. Note that the problem can be considered from an attacker's perspective as well, where the objective would be to determine the attacking strategies leading to the maximum possible damage on the system. Such a problem can be particularly useful in vulnerability analysis, i.e., to identify the worst possible damage an attacker may introduce to the system and accordingly to take necessary precautions.

In the literature, several studies investigate vulnerability analyses using RL, such as [30] for FDI attacks and [198] for sequential network topology attacks. We further note that the problem can also be considered from both the defender's and attacker's perspectives simultaneously, which corresponds to a game-theoretic setting.

In this chapter, we present an online cyber-attack detection algorithm using the framework of model-free RL for POMDPs [1]. The presented algorithm is universal, i.e., it does not require attack models. This makes the presented scheme widely applicable and also proactive in the sense that new unknown attack types can be detected. Since we follow a model-free RL approach, the defender learns a direct mapping from observations to actions, *stop* or *continue*, by trial and error. In the training phase, although it is possible to obtain/generate observation data for the pre-change case using the system model under normal operating conditions, it is generally difficult to obtain real attack data. For this reason, we follow a robust detection approach by training the defender with low-magnitude attacks that correspond to the worst-case scenarios from a defender's perspective since such attacks are quite difficult to detect. Then, the trained defender becomes sensitive to detecting even slight deviations of meter measurements from the normal system operation. The robust detection approach significantly limits the action space of an attacker as well. That is, to prevent the detection, an attacker can only exploit very low attack magnitudes that are practically not much of interest due to their minimal damage on the system.

8.2 SYSTEM MODEL AND STATE ESTIMATION

8.2.1 System Model

Suppose that there are K meters in a power grid consisting of $N + 1$ buses, where usually $K > N$ to have the necessary measurement redundancy against noise [1]. One of the buses is considered as a reference bus and the system state at time t is denoted with $\mathbf{x}_t = [x_{1,t}, \ldots, x_{N,t}]^{\mathrm{T}}$ where $x_{n,t}$ denotes the phase angle at bus n at time t. Let the measurement taken at meter k at time t be denoted with $y_{k,t}$ and the measurement vector be denoted with $\mathbf{y}_t = [y_{1,t}, \ldots, y_{K,t}]^{\mathrm{T}}$. Based on the widely used linear DC model [1], we model the smart grid with the

---

[1] A full presentation of this case study can be found in [73].

following state-space equations:

$$\mathbf{x}_t = \mathbf{A}\mathbf{x}_{t-1} + \mathbf{v}_t, \tag{8.1}$$

$$\mathbf{y}_t = \mathbf{H}\mathbf{x}_t + \mathbf{w}_t, \tag{8.2}$$

where $\mathbf{A} \in \mathbb{R}^{N \times N}$ is the system (state transition) matrix, $\mathbf{H} \in \mathbb{R}^{K \times N}$ is the measurement matrix determined based on the network topology, $\mathbf{v}_t = [v_{1,t}, \ldots, v_{N,t}]^{\mathrm{T}}$ is the process noise vector, and $\mathbf{w}_t = [w_{1,t}, \ldots, w_{K,t}]^{\mathrm{T}}$ is the measurement noise vector. We assume that $\mathbf{v}_t$ and $\mathbf{w}_t$ are independent additive white Gaussian random processes where $\mathbf{v}_t \sim \mathcal{N}(\mathbf{0}, \sigma_v^2 \mathbf{I}_N)$, $\mathbf{w}_t \sim \mathcal{N}(\mathbf{0}, \sigma_w^2 \mathbf{I}_K)$, and $\mathbf{I}_K \in \mathbb{R}^{K \times K}$ is an identity matrix. Moreover, we assume that the system is observable, i.e., the observability matrix

$$\mathbf{O} \triangleq \begin{bmatrix} \mathbf{H} \\ \mathbf{HA} \\ \vdots \\ \mathbf{HA}^{N-1} \end{bmatrix}$$

has rank N.

The system model given in (8.1) and (8.2) corresponds to the normal system operation. In the case of a cyber-attack, however, the measurement model in (8.2) is no longer true. For instance:

1. In the case of an FDI attack launched at time τ, the measurement model can be written as

$$\mathbf{y}_t = \mathbf{H}\mathbf{x}_t + \mathbf{w}_t + \mathbf{b}_t \mathbb{1}\{t \geq \tau\},$$

where $\mathbb{1}$ is an indicator function and $\mathbf{b}_t \neq \mathbf{0}$ denotes the injected malicious data at time $t \geq \tau$.

2. In the case of a jamming attack with additive noise, the measurement model can be written as

$$\mathbf{y}_t = \mathbf{H}\mathbf{x}_t + \mathbf{w}_t + \mathbf{u}_t \mathbb{1}\{t \geq \tau\},$$

where $\mathbf{u}_t$ denotes the random noise realization at time $t \geq \tau$.

3. In the case of a DoS attack, meter measurements can be partially unavailable to the system controller. The measurement model can then be written as

$$\mathbf{y}_t = \mathbf{D}_t(\mathbf{H}\mathbf{x}_t + \mathbf{w}_t),$$

where $\mathbf{D}_t = \mathrm{diag}(d_{1,t}, \ldots, d_{K,t})$ is a diagonal matrix consisting of 0s and 1s. Particularly, if $y_{k,t}$ is available, then $d_{k,t} = 1$, otherwise $d_{k,t} = 0$. Note that $\mathbf{D}_t = \mathbf{I}_K$ for $t < \tau$.

8.2.2 State Estimation

Since the smart grid is regulated based on estimated system states, state estimation is a fundamental task in the smart grid, that is conventionally performed using the static *least square* (LS) estimators [93, 18, 41]. However, in practice, the smart grid is a highly dynamic system due to time-varying load and power generation [162]. Furthermore, time-varying cyber-attacks can be designed and performed by adversaries. Hence, dynamic system modeling as in (8.1) and (8.2) and correspondingly using a dynamic state estimator can be quite useful for real-time operation and security of the smart grid.

For a discrete-time linear dynamic system, if the noise terms are Gaussian, the Kalman filter is the optimal linear estimator in minimizing the mean squared state estimation error [68]. Note that for the Kalman filter to work correctly, the system needs to be observable. The Kalman filter is an online estimator consisting of prediction and measurement update steps at each iteration. Denoting the state estimates at time t with $\hat{\mathbf{x}}_{t|t'}$ where $t' = t-1$ and $t' = t$ for the prediction and measurement update steps, respectively, the Kalman filter equations at time t can be written as follows:

Prediction:

$$\hat{\mathbf{x}}_{t|t-1} = \mathbf{A}\hat{\mathbf{x}}_{t-1|t-1},$$
$$\mathbf{F}_{t|t-1} = \mathbf{A}\mathbf{F}_{t-1|t-1}\mathbf{A}^{\mathrm{T}} + \sigma_v^2 \mathbf{I}_N.$$

Measurement update:

$$\mathbf{G}_t = \mathbf{F}_{t|t-1}\mathbf{H}^{\mathrm{T}}(\mathbf{H}\mathbf{F}_{t|t-1}\mathbf{H}^{\mathrm{T}} + \sigma_w^2 \mathbf{I}_K)^{-1},$$
$$\hat{\mathbf{x}}_{t|t} = \hat{\mathbf{x}}_{t|t-1} + \mathbf{G}_t(\mathbf{y}_t - \mathbf{H}\hat{\mathbf{x}}_{t|t-1}),$$
$$\mathbf{F}_{t|t} = \mathbf{F}_{t|t-1} - \mathbf{G}_t\mathbf{H}\mathbf{F}_{t|t-1},$$

where $\mathbf{F}_{t|t-1}$ and $\mathbf{F}_{t|t}$ denote the estimates of the state covariance matrix based on the measurements up to $t-1$ and t, respectively. Moreover, $\mathbf{G}_t$ is the Kalman gain matrix at time t.

8.3 PROBLEM FORMULATION

Before we introduce our problem formulation, we briefly explain a POMDP setting as follows. Given an agent and an environment, a discrete-time POMDP is defined by the seven-tuple $(\mathcal{S}, \mathcal{A}, \mathcal{T}, \mathcal{R}, \mathcal{O}, \mathcal{G}, \gamma)$ where $\mathcal{S}$ denotes the set of (hidden) states of the environment, $\mathcal{A}$ denotes the set of actions of the agent, $\mathcal{T}$ denotes the set of conditional transition probabilities between the states, $\mathcal{R} : \mathcal{S} \times \mathcal{A} \to \mathbb{R}$ denotes the reward function that maps the state-action pairs to rewards, $\mathcal{O}$ denotes the set of observations of the agent, $\mathcal{G}$ denotes the set of conditional observation probabilities, and $\gamma \in [0, 1]$ denotes a discount factor that indicates how much present rewards are preferred over the future rewards.

At each time t, the environment is in a particular hidden state $s_t \in \mathcal{S}$. Obtaining an observation $o_t \in \mathcal{O}$ depending on the current state of the environment with the probability $\mathcal{G}(o_t|s_t)$, the agent takes an action $a_t \in \mathcal{A}$ and receives a reward $r_t = \mathcal{R}(s_t, a_t)$ from the environment based on its action and the current state of the environment. At the same time, the environment makes a transition to the next state s_{t+1} with the probability $\mathcal{T}(s_{t+1}|s_t, a_t)$. The process is repeated until a terminal state is reached. In this process, the goal of the agent is to determine an optimal policy $\pi : \mathcal{O} \to \mathcal{A}$ that maps observations to actions and maximizes the agent's expected total discounted reward, i.e., $\mathrm{E}\left[\sum_{t=0}^{\infty} \gamma^t r_t\right]$. Equivalently, if an agent receives costs instead of rewards from the environment, then the goal is to minimize the expected total discounted cost. Considering the latter, the POMDP problem can be written as follows:

$$\min_{\pi:\,\mathcal{O}\to\mathcal{A}} \mathrm{E}\left[\sum_{t=0}^{\infty} \gamma^t r_t\right]. \tag{8.2}$$

Next, we explain the online cyber-attack detection problem in a POMDP setting. We assume that at an unknown time τ, a cyber-attack is launched to the system and our aim is to detect the attack as quickly as possible after it occurs, where the attacker's capabilities/strategies are completely unknown. This defines a quickest change detection problem where the aim is to minimize the average detection delay as well as the false alarm rate. This problem can, in fact, be expressed as a POMDP problem (see Fig. 8.1). In particular, due to the unknown attack launch time τ, there are two hidden states: *pre-attack* and *post-attack*. At each time t, after obtaining the measurement vector $\mathbf{y}_t$, two actions are available for the agent (defender): *stop* and declare an attack or *continue* to have further measurements. We assume that whenever the action *stop* is chosen, the system moves into a *terminal* state, and always stays there afterwards.

Furthermore, although the conditional observation probability for

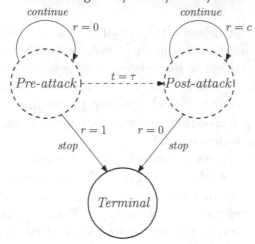

Figure 8.1: State-machine diagram for the considered POMDP setting. The hidden states and the (hidden) transition between them happening at time $t = \tau$ are illustrated with the dashed circles and the dashed line, respectively. The defender receives costs (r) depending on its actions and the underlying state of the environment. Whenever the defender chooses the action *stop*, the system moves into a *terminal* state and the defender receives no further cost.

the *pre-attack* state can be inferred based on the system model under normal operating conditions, since the attacking strategies are unknown, the conditional observation probability for the *post-attack* state is assumed to be totally unknown. Moreover, due to the unknown attack launch time τ, state transition probability between the *pre-attack* and the *post-attack* states is unknown.

Since our aim is to minimize the detection delays and the false alarm rate, both the false alarm and the detection delay events should be associated with some costs. Let the relative cost of a detection delay compared to a false alarm event be $c > 0$. Then, if the true underlying state is *pre-attack* and the action *stop* is chosen, a false alarm occurs and the defender receives a cost of 1. On the other hand, if the underlying state is *post-attack* and the action *continue* is chosen, then the defender receives a cost of c due to the detection delay. For all other (hidden) state-action pairs, the cost is assumed to be zero. Also, once the action *stop* is chosen, the defender does not receive any further costs while staying in the *terminal* state. The objective of the defender is to minimize its expected total cost by properly choosing its actions.

Particularly, based on its observations, the defender needs to determine the stopping time at which an attack is declared.

Let Γ denote the stopping time chosen by the defender. Moreover, let P_k denote the probability measure if the attack is launched at time k, i.e., $\tau = k$, and let E_k denote the corresponding expectation. Note that since the attacking strategies are unknown, P_k is assumed to be unknown. For the considered online attack detection problem, we can derive the expected total discounted cost as follows:

$$E\left[\sum_{t=0}^{\infty} \gamma^t r_t\right] = E_\tau\left[\mathbb{1}\{\Gamma < \tau\} + \sum_{t=\tau}^{\Gamma} c\right]$$
$$= E_\tau\left[\mathbb{1}\{\Gamma < \tau\} + c\left(\Gamma - \tau\right)^+\right]$$
$$= P_\tau(\{\Gamma < \tau\}) + c E_\tau\left[(\Gamma - \tau)^+\right], \qquad (8.3)$$

where $\gamma = 1$ is chosen since the present and future costs are equally weighted in our problem, $\{\Gamma < \tau\}$ is a false alarm event that is penalized with a cost of 1, and $E_\tau\left[(\Gamma - \tau)^+\right]$ is the average detection delay where each detection delay is penalized with a cost of c and $(\cdot)^+ = \max(\cdot, 0)$.

Based on (8.2) and (8.3), the online attack detection problem can be written as follows:

$$\min_{\Gamma} \, P_\tau(\{\Gamma < \tau\}) + c E_\tau\left[(\Gamma - \tau)^+\right]. \qquad (8.4)$$

Since c corresponds to the relative cost between the false alarm and the detection delay events, by varying c and solving the corresponding problem in (8.4), a tradeoff curve between average detection delay and false alarm rate can be obtained. Moreover, $c < 1$ can be chosen to prevent frequent false alarms.

Since the exact POMDP model is unknown due to an unknown attack launch time τ and the unknown attacking strategies and since the RL algorithms are known to be effective over uncertain environments, we follow a model-free RL approach to obtain a solution to (8.4). Then, a direct mapping from observations to the actions, i.e., the stopping time Γ, needs to be learned. Note that the optimal action is *continue* if the underlying state is *pre-attack* and *stop* if the underlying state is *post-attack*. Then, to determine the optimal actions, the underlying state needs to be inferred using observations and the observation signal should be very informative to reduce the uncertainty about the underlying state. As described in Sec. 8.2, the defender observes the measurements $\mathbf{y}_t$ at each time t. The simplest approach can be forming the observation space directly with the measurement vector $\mathbf{y}_t$ but we would like to process the measurements and form the observation space with a signal related to the deviation of the system from its normal operation.

Furthermore, it is, in general, possible to obtain identical observations in the *pre-attack* and the *post-attack* states. This is called perceptual aliasing and prevents us from making a good inference about the underlying state by only looking at the observation at a single time. We further note that in our problem, deciding on an attack solely based on a single observation corresponds to an outlier detection scheme for which more practical detectors are available not requiring a learning phase, see e.g., [98, 134]. However, we are particularly interested in detecting sudden and persistent attacks/anomalies that more likely happen due to an unfriendly intervention to the system rather than random disturbances due to high-level noise realizations.

Since different states require different optimal actions, the ambiguity on the underlying state should be further reduced with additional information derived from the history of observations. In fact, there may be cases where the entire history of observations is needed to determine the optimal solution in a POMDP problem [101]. However, due to computational limitations, only a finite memory can be used in practice and an approximately optimal solution can be obtained. A simple approach is to use a finite-size sliding window of observations as a memory and map the most recent history window to an action, as described in [94]. This approach is particularly suitable for our problem as well, since we assume persistent attacks/anomalies that happen at an unknown point of time and continue thereafter. That is, only the observations obtained after an attack are significant from the attack detection perspective.

Let the function that processes a finite history of measurements and produces the observation signal be denoted with $f(\cdot)$ so that the observation signal at time t is $o_t = f(\{\mathbf{y}_t\})$. Then, at each time, the defender observes $f(\{\mathbf{y}_t\})$ and decides on the stopping time Γ, as illustrated in Fig. 8.2. The aim of the defender is to obtain a solution to (8.4) by using an RL algorithm, as detailed in the subsequent section.

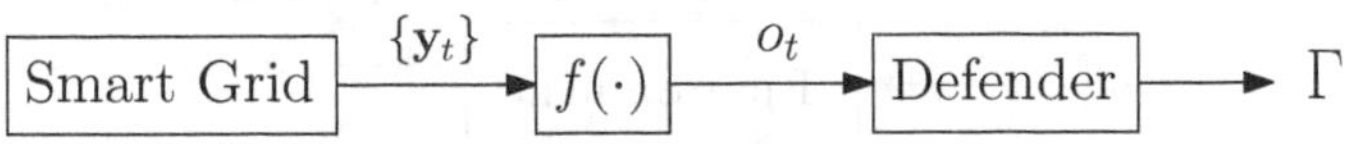

Figure 8.2: A graphical description of the online attack detection problem in the smart grid. The measurements $\{\mathbf{y}_t\}$ are collected through smart meters and processed to obtain $o_t = f(\{\mathbf{y}_t\})$. The defender observes $f(\{\mathbf{y}_t\})$ at each time t and decides on the attack declaration time Γ.

8.4   SOLUTION APPROACH

Firstly, we explain our methodology to obtain the observation signal $o_t = f(\{\mathbf{y}_t\})$. Note that the pdf of meter measurements in the *pre-attack* state can be inferred using the baseline measurement model in (8.2) and the state estimates provided by the Kalman filter. In particular, the pdf of the measurements under normal operating conditions can be estimated as follows:

$$\mathbf{y}_t \sim \mathcal{N}(\mathbf{H}\hat{\mathbf{x}}_{t|t}, \sigma_w^2 \mathbf{I}_K).$$

The likelihood of measurements based on the baseline density estimate, denoted with $L(\mathbf{y}_t)$, can then be computed as follows:

$$L(\mathbf{y}_t) = (2\pi\sigma_w^2)^{-\frac{K}{2}} \exp\left(\frac{-1}{2\sigma_w^2}(\mathbf{y}_t - \mathbf{H}\hat{\mathbf{x}}_{t|t})^\mathrm{T}(\mathbf{y}_t - \mathbf{H}\hat{\mathbf{x}}_{t|t})\right)$$

$$= (2\pi\sigma_w^2)^{-\frac{K}{2}} \exp\left(\frac{-1}{2\sigma_w^2}\eta_t\right),$$

where

$$\eta_t \triangleq (\mathbf{y}_t - \mathbf{H}\hat{\mathbf{x}}_{t|t})^\mathrm{T}(\mathbf{y}_t - \mathbf{H}\hat{\mathbf{x}}_{t|t}) \tag{8.5}$$

is the estimate of the negative log-scaled likelihood.

In case the system is operated under normal conditions, the likelihood $L(\mathbf{y}_t)$ is expected to be high. Equivalently, small (close to zero) values of η_t may indicate normal system operation. On the other hand, in the case of an attack/anomaly, the system deviates from normal operating conditions and hence the likelihood $L(\mathbf{y}_t)$ is expected to decrease in such cases. Then, persistent high values of η_t over a time period may indicate an attack/anomaly. Hence, η_t may help to reduce the uncertainty about the underlying state to some extent.

However, since η_t can take any nonnegative value, the observation space is continuous and hence learning a mapping from each

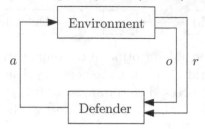

Figure 8.3: An illustration of the interaction between the defender and the simulation environment during the learning procedure. The environment provides an observation o based on its internal state s, and the agent chooses an action a based on its observation and receives a cost r from the environment in return of its action. Based on this experience, the defender updates $Q(o, a)$. This process is repeated many times during the learning procedure.

possible observation to an action is computationally infeasible. To reduce the computational complexity in such continuous spaces, we can quantize the observations. We then partition the observation space into I mutually exclusive and disjoint intervals using the quantization thresholds $\beta_0 = 0 < \beta_1 < \cdots < \beta_{I-1} < \beta_I = \infty$ so that if $\beta_{i-1} \leq \eta_t < \beta_i, i \in 1, \ldots, I$, the observation at time t is represented with θ_i. Then, possible observations at any given time are $\theta_1, \ldots, \theta_I$. Since θ_i's are representations of the quantization levels, each θ_i needs to be assigned to a different value.

Furthermore, as explained before, although η_t may be useful to infer the underlying state at time t, it is possible to obtain identical observations in the *pre-attack* and *post-attack* states. For this reason, we use a finite history of observations. Let the size of the sliding observation window be M so that there are I^M possible observation windows and the sliding window at time t consist of the quantized versions of $\{\eta_j : t - M + 1 \leq j \leq t\}$. Henceforth, by an observation o, we refer to an observation window so that the observation space $\mathcal{O}$ consists of all possible observation windows. For instance, if $I = M = 2$, then $\mathcal{O} = \{[\theta_1, \theta_1], [\theta_1, \theta_2], [\theta_2, \theta_1], [\theta_2, \theta_2]\}$.

For each possible observation-action pair (o, a), we learn a $Q(o, a)$ value, i.e., the expected future cost, using an RL algorithm where all $Q(o, a)$ values are stored in a Q-table of size $I^M \times 2$. After learning the Q-table, the policy of the defender will be choosing the action a with the minimum $Q(o, a)$ for each observation o. In general, increasing I and M improves the learning performance but at the same time results in a

---

Algorithm 22 Learning Phase – SARSA Algorithm

1: Initialize $Q(o, a)$ arbitrarily, $\forall o \in \mathcal{O}$ and $\forall a \in \mathcal{A}$.
2: **for all** training episodes **do**
3:    $t \leftarrow 0$
4:    $s \leftarrow pre\text{-}attack$
5:    Choose an initial o based on the *pre-attack* state and choose the initial $a = continue$.
6:    **while** $s \neq terminal$ and $t < T$ **do**
7:       $t \leftarrow t + 1$
8:       **if** $a = stop$ **then**
9:          $s \leftarrow terminal$
10:         $r \leftarrow \mathbb{1}\{t < \tau\}$
11:         $Q(o, a) \leftarrow Q(o, a) + \alpha\,(r - Q(o, a))$
12:       **else if** $a = continue$ **then**
13:         **if** $t \geq \tau$ **then**
14:            $r \leftarrow c$
15:            $s \leftarrow post\text{-}attack$
16:         **else**
17:            $r \leftarrow 0$
18:         **end if**
19:         Collect the measurements $\mathbf{y}_t$.
20:         Employ the Kalman filter using (8.3) and (8.3).
21:         Compute η_t using (8.5) and quantize it to obtain θ_i if $\beta_{i-1} \leq \eta_t < \beta_i, i \in 1, \dots, I$.
22:         Update the sliding observation window o with the most recent entry θ_i and obtain o'.
23:         Choose action a' from o' using the ϵ-greedy policy based on the Q-table (that is being learned).
24:         $Q(o, a) \leftarrow Q(o, a) + \alpha\,(r + Q(o', a') - Q(o, a))$
25:         $o \leftarrow o', a \leftarrow a'$
26:       **end if**
27:    **end while**
28: **end for**
29: Output: Q-table, i.e., $Q(o, a), \forall o \in \mathcal{O}$ and $\forall a \in \mathcal{A}$.

---

larger Q table, that would require an increase in the number of training episodes and hence the computational complexity of the learning phase. Hence, I and M should be chosen considering the expected tradeoff between performance and computational complexity.

The considered RL-based detection scheme consists of learning and online detection phases. In the literature, SARSA, a model-free RL control algorithm, was numerically shown to perform well over the model-free POMDP settings [127]. Hence, in the learning phase, the defender is trained with many episodes of experience using the SARSA algorithm and a Q-table is learned by the defender. For training, a simulation environment is created and during the training procedure,

---

Algorithm 23 Online Attack Detection

1: Input: Q-table learned in Algorithm 22.
2: Choose an initial o based on the *pre-attack* state and choose the initial
   $a = continue$.
3: $t \leftarrow 0$
4: **while** $a \neq stop$ **do**
5:   $t \leftarrow t + 1$
6:   Collect the measurements $\mathbf{y}_t$.
7:   Determine the new o as in the lines 20–22 of Algorithm 1.
8:   Choose the action $a = \arg\min_a Q(o, a)$.
9: **end while**
10: Declare an attack and terminate the procedure.

---

at each time, the defender takes an action based on its observation and receives a cost in return of its action from the simulation environment, as illustrated in Fig. 8.3. Based on this experience, the defender updates and learns a Q-table. Then, in the online detection phase, based on the observations, the action with the lowest expected future cost (Q value) is chosen at each time using the previously learned Q-table. The online detection phase continues until the action *stop* is chosen by the defender. Whenever *stop* is chosen, an attack is declared and the process is terminated.

Note that after declaring an attack, whenever the system is recovered and returned back to the normal operating conditions, the online detection phase can be restarted. That is, once a defender is trained, no further training is needed. We summarize the learning and the online detection stages in Algorithms 22 and 23, respectively. In Algorithm 22, T denotes the length of a training episode, α is the learning rate, and ϵ is the exploration rate.

8.5 SIMULATION RESULTS

8.5.1 Simulation Setup and Parameters

Simulations are performed on an IEEE-14 bus power system that consists of $N + 1 = 14$ buses and $K = 23$ smart meters. The initial state variables (phase angles) are determined using the DC optimal power flow algorithm for case-14 in MATPOWER [209]. The system matrix $\mathbf{A}$ is chosen to be an identity matrix and the measurement matrix $\mathbf{H}$ is determined based on the IEEE-14 power system. The noise variances for the normal system operation are chosen as $\sigma_v^2 = 10^{-4}$ and $\sigma_w^2 = 2 \times 10^{-4}$.

For the presented RL-based online attack detection scheme, the number of quantization levels is chosen as $I = 4$ and the quantization thresholds are chosen as $\beta_1 = 0.95 \times 10^{-2}$, $\beta_2 = 1.05 \times 10^{-2}$, and $\beta_3 = 1.15 \times 10^{-2}$ via an offline simulation by monitoring $\{\eta_t\}$ during the normal system operation. Further, $M = 4$ is chosen, i.e., the sliding observation window consists of 4 entries. Moreover, the learning parameters are chosen as $\alpha = 0.1$ and $\epsilon = 0.1$, and the episode length is chosen to be $T = 200$. In the learning phase, the defender is firstly trained over 4×10^5 episodes where the attack launch time is $\tau = 100$ and then trained further over 4×10^5 episodes where $\tau = 1$ to ensure that the defender sufficiently explores the observation space under normal operating conditions as well as the attacking conditions. More specifically, since a learning episode is terminated whenever the action *stop* is chosen and observations under an attack become available to the defender only for $t \geq \tau$, we choose $\tau = 1$ in half of the learning episodes to make sure that the defender is sufficiently trained under the post-attack regime.

To illustrate the tradeoff between the average detection delay and the false alarm probability, the presented algorithm is trained for both $c = 0.02$ and $c = 0.2$. Moreover, to obtain a detector that is robust and effective against even small deviations of measurements from the normal system operation, the defender needs to be trained with very low-magnitude attacks that correspond to slight deviations from the baseline. For this purpose, some known attack types with low magnitudes are used. In particular, in one half of the learning episodes, FDI attacks are used with attack magnitudes being realizations of the uniform random variable $\pm\mathcal{U}[0.02, 0.06]$, i.e., $b_{k,t} \sim \mathcal{U}[0.02, 0.06]$ is the injected false datum to the kth meter at time $t \geq \tau$ where $\mathbf{b}_t \triangleq [b_{1,t}, \ldots, b_{K,t}]$. In the other half of the learning episodes, the FDI and jamming attacks are simultaneously used with FDI attack magnitudes being realizations of $\pm\mathcal{U}[0.02, 0.06]$ whereas the jamming noise is chosen as zero-mean *additive white Gaussian noise* (AWGN) with variances being realizations of $\mathcal{U}[2 \times 10^{-4}, 4 \times 10^{-4}]$, i.e., $\mathbf{u}_t = [u_{1,t}, \ldots, u_{K,t}]$, $u_{k,t} \sim \mathcal{N}(0, \sigma_{k,t})$, and $\sigma_{k,t} \sim \mathcal{U}[2 \times 10^{-4}, 4 \times 10^{-4}]$, $\forall k \in \{1, \ldots, K\}$ and $\forall t \geq \tau$.

8.5.2 Performance Evaluation

The performance of the presented RL-based attack detection scheme is evaluated and compared with some existing detectors in the literature. Based on the optimization problem in (8.4), our performance metrics

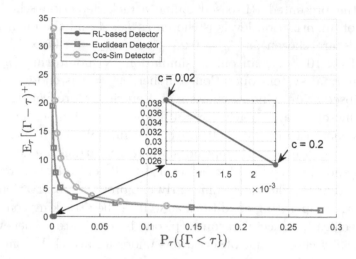

Figure 8.4: Average detection delay vs. probability of a false alarm curves for the presented algorithm and the benchmark tests in the case of an FDI attack.

are the probability of a false alarm, i.e., $P_\tau(\{\Gamma < \tau\})$, and the average detection delay, i.e., $E_\tau[(\Gamma - \tau)^+]$. Notice that both performance metrics depend on the unknown attack launch time τ. Hence, in general, the performance metrics need to be computed for each possible τ. For a representative performance illustration, we choose τ as a geometric random variable with parameter ρ such that $P(\tau = k) = \rho(1 - \rho)^{k-1}, k = 1, 2, 3, \ldots$ where $\rho \sim \mathcal{U}[10^{-4}, 10^{-3}]$ is a uniform random variable.

With Monte Carlo simulations over 10000 trials, we compute the probability of false alarm and the average detection delay for the presented algorithm, the Euclidean detector [98], and the cosine-similarity metric based detector [134]. To obtain the tradeoff curves, we vary the thresholds of the benchmark tests and vary c for the presented algorithm. To evaluate the presented algorithm, we use Algorithm 23 that makes use of the Q-tables learned in Algorithm 22 for $c = 0.02$ and $c = 0.2$.

We evaluate the presented and the benchmark detectors under several different attack scenarios:

1. Firstly, we evaluate the detectors where the system is under an FDI attack with attack magnitudes being realizations of

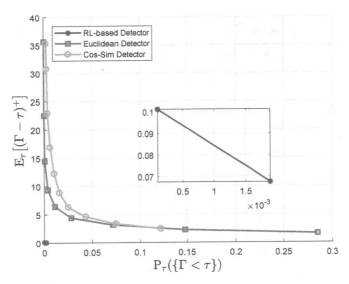

Figure 8.5: Performance curves for the presented algorithm and the benchmark tests in the case of a jamming attack with AWGN.

$\mathcal{U}[-0.07, 0.07]$. The corresponding tradeoff curve is presented in Fig. 8.4.

2. Then, we evaluate the detectors in the case of a jamming attack with zero-mean AWGN where the jamming noise variances are realizations of $\mathcal{U}[10^{-3}, 2 \times 10^{-3}]$. The corresponding performance curve is presented in Fig. 8.5.

3. Next, we evaluate the detectors in the case of a jamming attack with jamming noise correlated over the meters where $\mathbf{u}_t \sim \mathcal{N}(\mathbf{0}, \mathbf{U}_t)$, $\mathbf{U}_t = \mathbf{\Sigma}_t \mathbf{\Sigma}_t^{\mathrm{T}}$, and $\mathbf{\Sigma}_t$ is a random Gaussian matrix with its entry at the ith row and the jth column is $\mathbf{\Sigma}_{t,i,j} \sim \mathcal{N}(0, 8 \times 10^{-5})$. The corresponding performance curve is given in Fig. 8.6.

4. Further, we evaluate the detectors under a hybrid FDI/jamming attack where both attacks are simultaneously launched to the system and the FDI attack magnitudes are realizations of $\mathcal{U}[-0.05, 0.05]$ and the zero-mean AWGN jamming noise variances are realizations of $\mathcal{U}[5 \times 10^{-4}, 10^{-3}]$. The corresponding tradeoff curve is presented in Fig. 8.7.

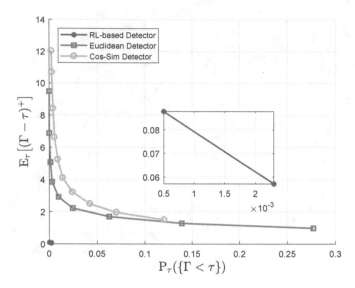

Figure 8.6: Performance curves for the presented algorithm and the benchmark tests in the case of a jamming attack with jamming noise correlated over the space.

5. Finally, we evaluate the detectors in the case of a random DoS attack where the measurement of each smart meter becomes unavailable to the system controller at each time with probability 0.2. That is, for each meter k, $d_{k,t}$ is 0 with probability 0.2 and 1 with probability 0.8 at each time $t \geq \tau$. The performance curve for the random DoS attack is presented in Fig. 8.8.

For almost all cases, we observe that the presented RL-based detection scheme significantly outperforms the benchmark tests. This is because through the training process, the defender learns to differentiate the instantaneous high-level noise realizations from persistent attacks launched to the system. Then, the trained defender is able to significantly reduce its false alarm rate. Moreover, since the defender is trained with significantly low attack magnitudes, it becomes sensitive to detect even small deviations of the system from its normal operation. On the other hand, the benchmark tests are essentially outlier detection schemes making sample-by-sample decisions and hence they are unable to distinguish high-level noise realizations from low-magnitude attacks that make such schemes more vulnerable to false alarms. We note that the performance and the sensitivity of the presented RL-

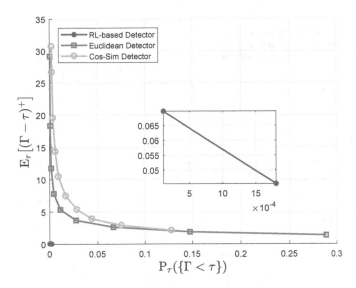

Figure 8.7: Performance curves for the presented algorithm and the benchmark tests in the case of a hybrid FDI/jamming attack.

based detection scheme can be further improved by increasing I and M albeit with a higher computational complexity. Finally, in the case of DoS attacks, since the meter measurements become partially unavailable so that the system greatly deviates from its normal operation, all detectors are able to detect the DoS attacks with almost zero average detection delays, as shown in Fig. 8.8.

8.6 REMARKS

In this chapter, an online cyber-attack detection problem has been formulated as a POMDP problem and a solution based on the model-free RL for POMDPs has been presented. The numerical studies have illustrated the advantages of the presented detection scheme in fast and reliable detection of cyber-attacks targeting the smart grid. The results have also demonstrated the high potential of RL algorithms in solving complex cyber-security problems. In fact, the algorithm presented in this chapter can be further improved using more advanced methods. Particularly, compared to the finite-size sliding window approach, more sophisticated memory techniques can be developed; compared to discretizing the continuous observation space and using a tabular

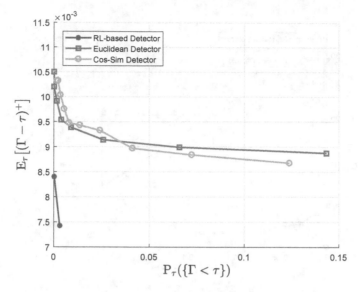

Figure 8.8: Performance curves for the presented algorithm and the benchmark tests in the case of a DoS attack.

approach to compute the Q values, linear/nonlinear function approximation techniques, e.g., neural networks, can be used to compute the Q values.

Finally, we note that the presented online detection method is widely applicable to any quickest change detection problem where the pre-change model can be derived with some accuracy but the post-change model is unknown. This is, in fact, commonly encountered in many practical applications where the normal system operation can be modeled sufficiently accurately and the objective is the online detection of anomalies/attacks that are difficult to model. Moreover, depending on specific applications, if real post-change, e.g., attack/anomaly, data can be obtained, the real data can be further enhanced with simulated data and the training can be performed accordingly, which would potentially improve the detection performance.

CHAPTER 9

Case Study: Defeat Man-in-the-Middle Attack

CONTENTS

9.1　INTRODUCTION

The man-in-the-middle (MITM) [23] attack is an attack where an adversarial computer secretly relays and possibly alters the communication between two computers that believe they are directly talking to each other via a private connection. The conventional approaches to defeat an MITM attack are quite specific to the techniques the hacker uses, a fact that makes the entire system more complicated and vulnerable to new hacking strategies. However, the network flow generated under the attack always follows some detectable patterns, such as abnormal traffic latency or routes. Typically, these abnormal features can be utilized by the designed probes to detect all kinds of attacks at one time. There are a set of probes detecting the distorted network traffic and periodically reporting the results to an analyzing program/device, which can provide a safe data forwarding path and notify the switches to transfer the packet over the new safe route. By doing so, we can ideally bypass the intruded network nodes and defeat the MITM attack.

This model becomes feasible with the *software defined network* (SDN), an approach to facilitate a programmatically efficient network by decoupling the network control from the forwarding functions and then assigning it to a central controller. The controller maintains a global view of the entire network and chooses forwarding paths based on the software it is running. The switches communicate to the controller in a special *language*, usually OpenFlow protocol, to actually forward, discard or process a packet based on the controller's commands.

For example, the probes scattering over OpenFlow switches will periodically tell the controller their detection status as 0 or 1, in which 1 refers to a node intruded by the attackers and 0 refers to a safe node. The controller will synthesize all information and decide to either remain on the current route or switch to another or even discard the packet if there is no safe route. As a consequence, the controller will notify the OpenFlow switch to accordingly change the routes, discard the packet or take no action. Fig. 9.1 illustrates the MITM-attack defending system, which will be discussed in detail in the end of this chapter.

Based on the aforementioned discussions, one can notice that the accuracy of the probe is a key to our whole system. According to the suggestion given in [20], which compares a set of machine learning methods for intrusion detection, the Support Vector Machine (SVM) [113] algorithm could be a fairly good approach considering the requirement of online processing the network traffic and detecting the misuse actions. The detection accuracy of using SVM varies from 66.6% to 97.27%, depending on the attacking technique. Synthesizing the detection accuracy of other methods (Bayes network 75%, artificial neural network (ANN) on anomaly 80%, clustering 70% to 80%, ensemble learning 87% to 93%), without loss of generality, we herein assume the probe detection accuracy as 75%, which means one false in every 4 detections. Definitely, this level of detection accuracy is not always satisfactory. In what follows, we present a scheme of using reinforcement learning to handle this kind of detection uncertainty. Besides, the

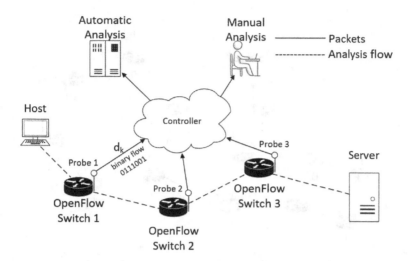

Figure 9.1: Each OpenFlow switch has a probe installed. These switches all connect to a controller, which runs software to analyze the state of the entire network and changes the forwarding path (if necessary) by signifying the OpenFlow switches.

fundamental idea of reinforcement learning, that the agent learns from *trial and error*, will guide the client in our system to appropriately drop the packet or deliver it over an alternative safe route.

Let's make our RL idea concrete by an example. As shown in Fig. 9.2, for instance, node 2 and node 9 connect to the client and the server, respectively. Nodes marked by exclamation denote the intruded nodes controlled by the hacker. All probes, each installed on a node in the network, periodically generate binary status to claim whether its corresponding node is under attack or not. Then the status of all nodes will be aggregated to the controller in the form of a binary sequence over time. According to the sequence, the controller can compute the maximum intrusion likelihood of a monitored node in the next time instance. With all probe likelihoods in hand, a status space can be generated, leading to a safe packet-forwarding path for a client-server pair in the network. If all paths are blocked, the controller will inform the switch to drop the packet and receive a penalty for such an action. Otherwise, if the packets successfully arrive at the destination, the controller will receive a reward. However, if the packet suffers from the

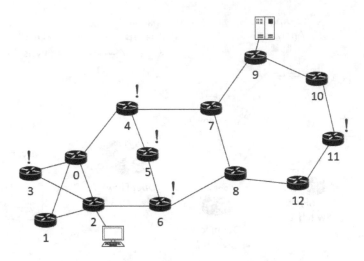

Figure 9.2: The exclamation mark indicates an intrusion on the corresponding node.

MITM attack during the forwarding process, i.e., passing through an intruded node, the controller will receive a relatively large penalty.

9.2 RL APPROACH

We next use the DQN algorithm to handle the problem of an MITM attack. First of all, we define the states, actions and rewards as follows.

9.2.1 State Space

As discussed above, the detection status of all probes at a time instance can be collected at the controller, and forms a binary sequence. In order to make an appropriate decision, the controller can also use the historical detection status from the probes. But the complexity and the computing latency could be substantial if using all historical data. Thus motivated, we introduce a sampling window with length $t_0 > 0$, from which the controller uses the probe samples to make decisions. Further, since the dynamic behavior of a hacker is unknown, one can assume that samples in the sampling window are independent in the time domain.

Specifically, at time instant t we consider a historical sampling window $[t-t_0, t-t_0+1, \cdots, t]$. A node k in the network has been detected sample by sample in such a time window by the corresponding probe, which generates a sequence of detection results,

$$d_k(t - t_0 : t) = [d_k(t - t_0), d_k(t - t_0 + 1), \ldots, d_k(t)],$$

where $d_k(i) = 1$ or 0. Recall that 1 denotes that the node is detected to be intruded while 0 denotes that the node is safe. Next, we use the positive predictive value (PPV) to denote the accuracy of the probe, the probability that the probe reports 1 when the node is actually intruded. Correspondingly, we use the false omission rate (FOR) to denote the probability that the probe returns 1 when the node is actually free from intrusion. [1] Then, the likelihood of a sequence $d_k(t - t_0 : t)$ given that the node k is intruded is:

$$Pr_k^{PPV}[t - t_0 : t] = \prod_{i=t-t_0}^{t} Pr(d_k(i)|\text{intruded}), \qquad (9.1)$$

where

$$Pr(d_k(i)|\text{intruded}) = \begin{cases} PVV, & d_k(i) = 1 \\ 1 - PVV, & d_k(i) = 0. \end{cases} \qquad (9.2)$$

Similarly, the likelihood of a sequence $d_k(t - t_0 : t)$ given that the node k is not intruded is:

$$Pr_k^{FOR}[t - t_0, t] = \prod_{i=t-t_0}^{t} Pr(d_k(i)|\text{not intruded}), \qquad (9.3)$$

where

$$Pr(d_k(i)|\text{not intruded}) = \begin{cases} FOR, & d_k(i) = 1 \\ 1 - FOR, & d_k(i) = 0. \end{cases} \qquad (9.4)$$

Therefore, for a node, the statistic used in the maximum likelihood ratio test on two hypotheses—under attack or not—at time instant t is given as follows,

$$\begin{aligned} r_k(t) &= Pr_k^{PPV}[t - t_0 : t]/Pr_k^{FOR}[t - t_0, t] \\ &= \prod_{i=t-t_0}^{t} \frac{Pr(d_k(i)|\text{intruded})}{Pr(d_k(i)|\text{not intruded})}. \end{aligned} \qquad (9.5)$$

---

[1]The notion PPV and FOR are widely used in statistics and diagnostic tests. The definition of PPV and FOR can be directly derived using Bayes' theorem.

Fig. 9.3 shows the likelihood ratio swinging during the testing. The likelihood ratio, indicating the possibility that a particular node is intruded, keeps changing due to dynamic attack pattern.

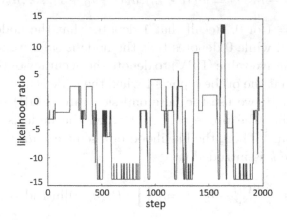

Figure 9.3: Time-varying likelihood ratio of one node: this node is attacked for several times. When the node is safe, the detection sequence of full of 0's leads to a low likelihood ratio value (around -15) with some turbulence caused by the probe detection error. When intrusion occurs, the probe generates a detection sequence of full of 1's, leading to a high likelihood ratio within a few time steps.

Finally, we assume that for a given pair of client and server there are M available client-server routing paths. The current path, denoted as $Path(t) \in \{1, 2, \cdots, M\}$, is known by the controller and can be used to make a next-step decision. Putting the above together, for a given network with N nodes (each with a probe) and a client-server pair, at time t the RL state is modeled as follows,

$$s_t = [r_1(t), r_2(t), r_3(t), \cdots, r_N(t), Path(t)]. \tag{9.6}$$

Note that we set the likelihood r_i to 0 if the current flow does not pass through node i.

9.2.2 Action Space

For a client-server pair, we assume that there are M possible forwarding routes. The controller can decide to either send or drop the data packet on each path. This leads to $2M$ different actions in total. Define the action space as $a = 1, 2, 3, \ldots, 2M$, where taking a from 1 to M indicates that the controller decides to drop the packet on the corresponding path a while taking a from $M + 1$ to $2M$ indicates that the controller decide to transfer the packet on route $(a - M)$.

9.2.3 Reward

As a key element of RL framework, a reward needs to be well defined for the controller to perform *"trial-and-learn."* In particular, the reward is denoted by r. A penalty $(r < 0)$ is given to the action of dropping packets, i.e., $a = 1 \ldots M$. If a packet is successfully forwarded via a selected path, a positive reward $(r > 0)$ is given to the controller. If a packet is forwarded via an eavesdropped path, however, a large penalty $(r << 0)$ will be given for such an action.

9.3 EXPERIMENTS AND RESULTS

In this section, we implement the DQN algorithm in Section 6.3 and provide numerical results to verify the algorithm. In the experiments, the defense algorithm is implemented on a 13-node network shown in Fig. 9.2. This means that the MDP state s has 14 elements, i.e., 13 likelihood ratios plus one path index. To define a routing protocol for a given client-server pair, which should be designed based on the set of available paths, we consider the following:

1. If the network is large, the size of the set of available paths could be exponentially increasing with the number of nodes. As a result, there may exist a scalability issue;

2. If only using the shortest paths, the set could be small. But the capability of avoiding attacks could be substantially degraded since it is very likely that no safe packet-forwarding path can be found when under attack.

As motivated by the above two extreme cases, we construct the set of available paths by balancing the extremes. In particular, for a given client-server pair we first list all available paths and then remove one path from the set if the path can be shortened by directly linking two nodes on the path. Take Fig. 9.4 and Fig. 9.5 as an illustration.

After testing the proposed routing protocol with arbitrary 13-node network topology, we find the average available paths between a client-server pair is 4. Thus in the experiment we use this number as the

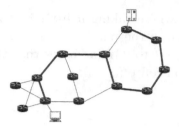

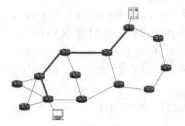

Figure 9.4: Forwarding path (bold).

Figure 9.5: Shortened forwarding path (bold).

largest size of the set of the available routes for a given client-server pair. This indicates that each state has at most 8 actions, i.e., drop packets or transfer packets on paths 1 to 4. The reward function is set as follows:

$$r = \begin{cases} -5 & \text{if a packet is forwarded via an eavesdropped path} \\ -1 & \text{if a packet is dropped} \\ 4 & \text{if a packet is successfully forwarded to the client.} \end{cases}$$

The DQN takes state vectors as inputs and outputs the approximated Q-value for each action. Furthermore, we select a network of 6 layers, consisting of 14, 135, 270, 108, 52 and 8 nodes on each layer. The algorithm was trained for 30,000 steps. To obtain an optimal policy, the network has been exposed to all the attack patterns for enough time in the training phase. In our experiment, we assume the number of intrusion nodes is less than 5. This is because if 5 or more nodes are intruded in our network, the safe routing path hardly exists. In this case, maybe it's better to just suspend all communications. In addition, we maintain a list of intruded nodes which gets updated every 50 frames. In each frame, probes send back a binary detection result of 0 or 1. As the features of the controller, PPV (detection accuracy) and FOR (false omission rate) are set to be 0.8 and 0.05, respectively.

9.3.1 Model Training

The training follows the proposed DQN algorithm. One issue is that with a relatively large fixed learning rate, the deep neural network sometimes converges to a local optima. As a result, the model is trained in a two-stage scheme: at the first stage, we use a large learning rate $\gamma = 10^{-3}$ and check whether the output is trapped in a local optima;

if not trapped, we proceed to the second stage by training the model with a smaller learning rate $\gamma = 10^{-5}$ to refine the network, otherwise, we restart from the first stage. In each stage, the agent runs 6×10^4 steps. As shown in Figs. 9.6(a) and 9.6(b), the loss falls rapidly at the beginning of training and then varies in a small range. The average rewards received by the controller under different attack configurations are plotted in Fig. 9.7.

9.3.2 Online Experiments

After the training phase, we test the controller in several attack patterns of interest. We consider 4 attack configurations on the combinations of the number of intruded nodes and the attack frequency (in frames):

$$(\text{number of intruded nodes, attack frequency})$$

$$\in \left\{ (3, 50), (3, 100), (5, 50), (5, 100) \right\}. \tag{9.7}$$

In the experiments, the intruded nodes are uniform randomly selected in each episode and the agent ran 3×10^3 steps with greedy policy for each configuration. From the online experiments, we found that the controller presents the desired behaviors: it avoids intruded nodes to find a safe path, and keeps dropping packets when all paths are under attack. Moreover, in the experiments, the agent is found to display the ability to ignore the falsely positive detection and falsely negative detection. In other words, the falsely negative detection that ignores the intrusion when the intrusion occurs does not confuse the controller from realizing the risky path. Also, the falsely positive detection that mistakes the normal nodes as intruded nodes does not scare the controller into immediately discarding such a path. The average rewards received by the controller under different attack configurations are plotted in Fig. 9.8.

Some observations can be summarized as follows: On the one hand, the number of intruded nodes negatively influences the performance. The more routers/nodes that are under attack, the less possible safe paths remain. When the attack pattern blocking all paths occurs, the controller drops packets and receives a negative reward -1. Hence, the controller achieves better average reward in the case of 3 intruded nodes. On the other hand, high frequency change of attack patterns impairs the performance. This is because the controller always needs several steps to find the safe routes and ensure that it is trustworthy via constant testing. Also, we evaluated the performance of using probes with different detection abilities. Fig. 9.8(b) depicts the average reward when the positive predictive values (PPVs) are 0.9 and 0.7, respectively. It shows that using probes with higher PPV (PPV = 0.9) achieves higher average reward in the steady state. In addition, the early phase of the average reward curve with PPV = 0.9 implies the occurrence of consecutive detection mistakes, a situation that makes the controller send packets in the intruded path or only stay on the safe path for a short time.

9.4   DISCUSSIONS

We end this chapter with a brief review on the detection systems and a discussion on how to make our model practical with SDN/OpenFlow.

9.4.1   Probe-Based Detection System

To successfully bypass the infected routers while forwarding the packet, a proper MITM attack detection system is crucial. Generally, the detection system has two prongs: probes and an analysis engine.

- **Probe**: As its name would suggest, a probe captures packets in the network and extracts certain information like the packets' source and destination IP addresses. Normally, these probes are network cards in promiscuous mode scattered on the switches/routers (hosts), like NetFlow in [58]. However, the probes may have a severe impact on the performance of the conventional host, so only a small number of hosts will be installed with the probe. Overall, to successfully monitor the behavior of all nodes in a network, a sufficient number of probes should be installed and the probes need to be properly distributed in the network.

- **Analysis Engine**: In this context, the analysis engine aims to discern intrusion nodes after aggregating data from all distributed probes. According to [10], the flow duration will increase if traffic encounters an MITM attack. And considering the attacker has to connect to the local area network (LAN) before the attack, some features, like protocol type, service, src bytes, destination bytes, flag, etc., in intrusion traffic also suits MITM attack traffic. Based on these features, we can manually label a training set with $\{1, 0\}$ to indicate whether a node has been intruded or not. After training a classification model with the labeled training set, the analysis engine will be able to discern each node's status by fitting the upcoming traffic into the classification model. However, the results of the classification model could be misleading sometimes. Thus motivated, the DQN method has been studied in this chapter.

9.4.2   Make Model Practical with SDN/OpenFlow

As mentioned above, we have used the RL method to give an optimal path which is able to bypass the infected node. Therefore, finding all possible forwarding paths and switching among them whenever necessary is the premise of the method. Since an MITM attack usually happens inside a LAN, the routing can narrow down to the intradomain routing protocols including the Routing Information Protocol (RIP).

But in order to update the routing table as desired, it is necessary to use an SDN, an architecture composed of controllers and three-layer switches which usually supports OpenFlow protocol. The controller will process the demands of user-defined applications into the corresponding behavior of OpenFlow switches.

Under the RL framework, the controller will work as an agent, collecting the data from probes located at OpenFlow switches, running a network flow classification process (via an analysis engine) to choose the optimal path, which gives the highest performance of bypassing the attacker's dynamic attack. The agent training time may scale up with the increase of the network size. But additional training is no longer required after the first time training as long as the number of paths between start and end hosts remains the same.

9.5   REMARKS

In this chapter, we have proposed a mechanism to defend man-in-middle-attack in the wired link. Our mechanism takes advantage of the probe and decides whether or not to drop the forwarding packets based on the intrusion detection from the probe. To compensate for the limitations of the probe, reinforcement learning has been used to derive the policy on sending packets and selecting a path. Since the state space of our MDP model is continuous, we have introduced the neural network to approximate the Q value for each state-action pair. We have done a series of experiments on a practical network. The result shows that the proposed algorithm can efficiently avoid the intruded nodes in the network and choose the safe path to send packets. And our algorithm can also react to the changes in the intruded nodes and, hence, is able to be applied to dynamic attacking scenarios.

Although this algorithm succeeds in avoiding intrusion in most cases, it presents some delay when reacting to the intrusion changes and performs with low-efficiency in path selection. This is because under the current model the agent tests the optional path in an almost random fashion, which leads to unnecessary testing costs. This can be certainly improved by recording the last renew time of the likelihood ratio for each node and then adding these logs into the state vector.

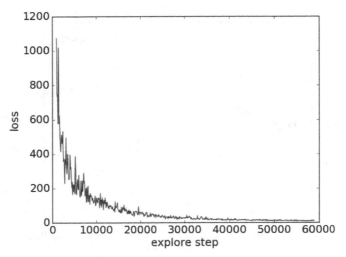

(a) The loss in the first training phase.

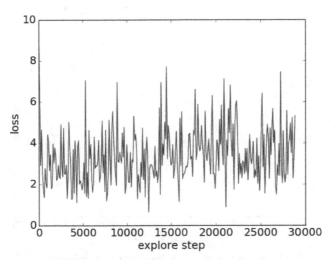

(b) The loss in the second training phase.

Figure 9.6: Learning curves in the training phase.

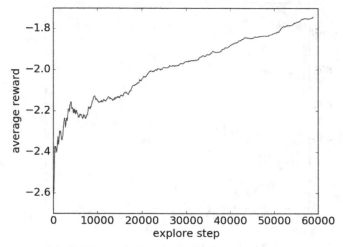

(a) The average reward in the first training phase.

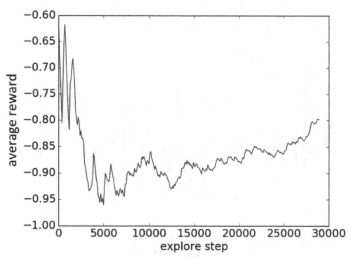

(b) The average reward in the second training phase.

Figure 9.7: Learning curves in the training phase.

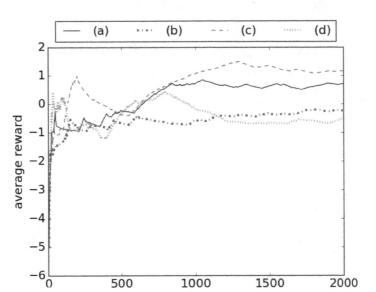

(a) The average rewards under different attack configuration. (a): 3 intruded nodes, attack pattern changes every 50 frames; (b): 5 intruded nodes, attack pattern changes every 50 frames; (c): 3 intruded nodes, attack pattern changes every 100 frames; (d): 5 intruded nodes, attack pattern changes every 100 frames.

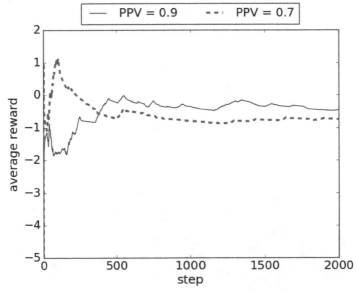

(b) The average rewards using probes with different positive predictive value (PPV).

Figure 9.8: The average rewards under different attack configurations.

Bibliography

[1] A. Abur and A. Gomez-Exposito. *Power System State Estimation: Theory and Implementation*, volume 24. Jan. 2004.

[2] R. Agrawal. Sample mean based index policies with $o(logn)$ regret for the multi-armed bandit problem. *Advances in Applied Probability*, 27(4):1054–1078, 1995.

[3] R. Akella, H. Tang, and B. M. McMillin. Analysis of information flow security in cyber–physical systems. *International Journal of Critical Infrastructure Protection*, 3(3-4):157–173, 2010.

[4] M. H. Ali, B. Mohammed, A. Ismail, and M. F. Zolkipli. A new intrusion detection system based on fast learning network and particle swarm optimization. *IEEE Access*, 6:20255–20261, 2018.

[5] M. A. Aref, S. K. Jayaweera, and S. Machuzak. Multi-agent reinforcement learning based cognitive anti-jamming. In *Proceedings of the Wireless Communications and Networking Conference (WCNC)*, pages 1–6, 2017.

[6] K. Arulkumaran, M. P. Deisenroth, M. Brundage, and A. A. Bharath. Deep reinforcement learning: A brief survey. *IEEE Signal Processing Magazine*, 34(6):26–38, 2017.

[7] C. Asamoah, L. Tao, K. Gai, and N. Jiang. Powering filtration process of cyber security ecosystem using knowledge graph. In *Proceedings of the 2nd IEEE International Conference of Scalable and Smart Cloud*, pages 240–246, 2016.

[8] S. Asri and B. Pranggono. Impact of distributed denial-of-service attack on advanced metering infrastructure. *Wireless Personal Communications*, 83(3):2211–2223, 2015.

[9] P. Auer, N. Cesa-Bianchi, and P. Fischer. Finite-time analysis of the multiarmed bandit problem. machine learning. *Monographs on Statistics and Applied Probability*, 47(2-3):235–256, 2002.

[10] B. Aziz and G. Hamilton. Detecting man-in-the-middle attacks by precise timing. In *Proceedings of the International Conference on Emerging Security Information, Systems and Technologies*, pages 81–86, 2009.

[11] M. Babaeizadeh, I. Frosio, S. Tyree, J. Clemons, and J. Kautz. GA3C: GPU-based A3C for deep reinforcement learning. *ArXiv*, 2016.

[12] L. Baird. Residual algorithms: Reinforcement learning with function approximation. In *Proceedings of Machine Learning*, pages 30–37. Elsevier, 1995.

[13] A. Banino, C. Barry, B. Uria, et al. Vector-based navigation using grid-like representations in artificial agents. *Nature*, 557:429–433, 2018.

[14] A. G. Barto and R. S. Sutton. Simulation of anticipatory responses in classical conditioning by a neuron-like adaptive element. *Behavioural Brain Research*, 4(3):221–235, 1982.

[15] M. Basseville and I. V. Nikiforov. *Detection of Abrupt Changes: Theory and Application*. Prentice-Hall, Inc., Upper Saddle River, NJ, USA, 1993.

[16] D. S. Bernstein, R. Givan, N. Immerman, and S. Zilberstein. The complexity of decentralized control of Markov decision processes. *Mathematics of Operations Research*, 27(4):819–840, 2002.

[17] D. A. Berry and B. Fristedt. Bandit problems: Sequential allocation of experiments. *Monographs on Statistics and Applied Probability*, 1985.

[18] R. B. Bobba, K. M. Rogers, Q. Wang, H. Khurana, K. Nahrstedt, and T. J. Overbye. Detecting false data injection attacks on dc state estimation. In *Preprints of the First Workshop on Secure Control Systems*, 2010.

[19] S. J. Bradtke and M. O. Duff. Reinforcement learning methods for continuous-time Markov decision problems. In *Advances in Neural Information Processing Systems*, pages 393–400, 1995.

[20] A. L. Buczak and E. Guven. A survey of data mining and machine learning methods for cyber security intrusion detection. *IEEE Communications Surveys & Tutorials*, 18(2):1153–1176, 2016.

[21] H. M. Buini, S. Peter, and T. Givargis. Adaptive embedded control of cyber-physical systems using reinforcement learning. *IET Cyber-Physical Systems: Theory & Applications*, 2(3):127–135, 2017.

[22] J. C. Caicedo and S. Lazebnik. Active object localization with deep reinforcement learning. In *Proceedings of the International Conference on Computer Vision (ICCV)*, pages 2488–2496, 2015.

[23] F. Callegati, W. Cerroni, and M. Ramilli. Man-in-the-middle attack to the https protocol. *IEEE Security & Privacy*, 7(1):78–81, 2009.

[24] A. Cardenas, S. Amin, B. Sinopoli, et al. Challenges for securing cyber physical systems. In *Workshop on Future Directions in Cyber-Physical Systems Security*, volume 5, 2009.

[25] A. A. Cardenas, S. Amin, and S. Sastry. Research challenges for the security of control systems. In *HotSec*, 2008.

[26] H. Chae, C. M. Kang, B. D. Kim, J. Kim, C. C. Chung, and J. W. Choi. Autonomous braking system via deep reinforcement learning. *ArXiv*, 2017.

[27] C. S. Chao. A flexible and feasible anomaly diagnosis system for internet firewall rules. In *Proceedings of the 13th Asia-Pacific Network Operations and Management Symposium*, pages 1–8, Sept. 2011.

[28] S. Chattopadhyay, A. Banerjee, and B. Yu. A utility-driven data transmission optimization strategy in large scale cyber-physical systems. In *Design, Automation & Test in Europe Conference & Exhibition (DATE)*, pages 1619–1622, 2017.

[29] F. Chelsea, Y. T. Xin, D. Yan, D. Trevor, L. Sergey, and A. Pieter. Deep Spatial Autoencoders for Visuomotor Learning. In *Proceedings of the International Conference on Robotics and Automation (ICRA)*, 2016.

[30] Y. Chen, S. Huang, F. Liu, Z. Wang, and X. Sun. Evaluation of reinforcement learning based false data injection attack to automatic voltage control. *IEEE Transactions on Smart Grid*, PP(99):1–1, 2018.

[31] T. M. Cover and J. A. Thomas. *Elements of Information Theory*. John Wiley & Sons, Inc., 2006.

[32] H. Cui, H. Zhang, G. R. Ganger, P. B. Gibbons, and E. P. Xing. GeePS: Scalable deep learning on distributed GPUs with a GPU-specialized parameter server. In *Proceedings of the 11th European Conference on Computer Systems*, 2016.

[33] J. Dell, T. Greiner, and W. Rosenstiel. Model-based platform design and evaluation of cloud-based cyber-physical systems. In *Proceedings of the 12th IEEE International Conference on Industrial Informatics (INDIN)*, pages 376–381, 2014.

[34] B. Di, T. Wang, L. Song, and Z. Han. Incentive mechanism for collaborative smartphone sensing using overlapping coalition formation games. In *Proceedings of the IEEE Global Communications Conference (GLOBECOM)*, pages 1705–1710, 2013.

[35] J. S. Dibangoye, C. Amato, O. Buffet, and F. Charpillet. Optimally solving Dec-POMDPs as continuous-state MDPs. *Journal of Artificial Intelligence Research*, 55:443–497, 2016.

[36] C. Diekmann, L. Schwaighofer, and G. Carle. Certifying spoofing-protection of firewalls. In *International Conference on Network and Service Management (CNSM)*, pages 168–172, Nov 2015.

[37] W. Dinkelbach. On nonlinear fractional programming. *Management Science*, 13(7):492–498, 1967.

[38] F. Doshi-Velez, D. Wingate, N. Roy, and J. Tenenbaum. Non-parametric bayesian policy priors for reinforcement learning. In *Proceedings of the 23rd International Conference on Neural Information Processing Systems*, pages 532–540, 2010.

[39] L. Duan, T. Kubo, K. Sugiyama, J. Huang, T. Hasegawa, and J. Walrand. Motivating smartphone collaboration in data acquisition and distributed computing. *IEEE Transactions on Mobile Computing*, 13(10):2320–2333, 2014.

[40] L. Duan, A. W. Min, J. Huang, and K. G. Shin. Attack prevention for collaborative spectrum sensing in cognitive radio networks. *IEEE Journal on Selected Areas in Communications*, 30(9):1685–1665, 2012.

[41] M. Esmalifalak, H. Nguyen, R. Zheng, and Zhu Han. Stealth false data injection using independent component analysis in smart grid. In *IEEE International Conference on Smart Grid Communications (SmartGridComm)*, pages 244–248, Oct 2011.

[42] K. Fang and B. Guo. An efficient data transmission strategy for cyber-physical systems in the complicated environment. In *Proceedings of the 7th International Conference on Intelligent Human-Machine Systems and Cybernetics (IHMSC)*, volume 2, pages 541–545, 2015.

[43] M. Feng and H. Xu. Deep reinforcement learning based optimal defense for cyber-physical system in presence of unknown cyber-attack. In *IEEE Symposium Series on Computational Intelligence (SSCI)*, pages 1–8, 2017.

[44] C. Francois. *Deep Learning with Python*. Manning Publications Co., 2017.

[45] K. Gai, M. Qiu, Y. Li, and X. Y. Liu. Advanced fully homomorphic encryption scheme over real numbers. In *Proceedings of the 4th International Conference on Cyber Security and Cloud Computing (CSCloud)*, pages 64–69, June 2017.

[46] K. Gai, M. Qiu, X. Sun, and H. Zhao. Security and privacy issues: A survey on FinTech. In *Proceedings of International Conference on Smart Computing and Communications*, pages 236–247, Shenzhen, China, 2016.

[47] A. H. Gandomi and A. H. Alavi. Krill herd: A new bio-inspired optimization algorithm. *Communications in Nonlinear Science and Numerical Simulation*, 17(12):4831–4845, 2012.

[48] R. Ganesan, S. Jajodia, A. Shah, and H. Cam. Dynamic scheduling of cybersecurity analysts for minimizing risk using reinforcement learning. *ACM Transactions on Intelligent Systems and Technology (TIST)*, 8(1):4, 2016.

[49] M. Glavic, R. Fonteneau, and D. Ernst. Reinforcement learning for electric power system decision and control: Past considerations and perspectives. *IFAC-PapersOnLine*, 50(1):6918–6927, 2017.

[50] C. D. Green. *Introduction to Animal Intelligence*, Edward Lee Thorndike (1911).

[51] X. Guo and O. Hernandez-Lerma. *Continuous-time Markov Decision Processes*. Springer, 2009.

[52] J. Han, A. Shah, M. Luk, and A. Perrig. Don't sweat your privacy using humidity to detect human presence. *Citeseer*, 2007.

[53] E. A. Hansen and S. Zilberstein. LAO: A heuristic search algorithm that finds solutions with loops. *Artificial Intelligence*, 129(1-2):35–62, 2001.

[54] H. Van Hasselt. Double q-learning. In *Advances in Neural Information Processing Systems*, pages 2613–2621, 2010.

[55] H. Van Hasselt. *Insights in Reinforcement Learning*. Hado Philip van Hasselt, 2011.

[56] I. L. S. Hendarto and Y. Kurniawan. Performance factors of a CUDA GPU parallel program: A case study on a pdf password cracking brute-force algorithm. In *International Conference on Computer, Control, Informatics and Its Applications (IC3INA)*, pages 35–40, Oct 2017.

[57] S. Hochreiter and J. Schmidhuber. Long short-term Memory. *Neural Computation*, 9(8):1735–1780, 1997.

[58] R. Hofstede, P. Celeda, B. Trammell, I. Drago, R. Sadre, A. Sperotto, and A. Pras. Flow monitoring explained: From packet capture to data analysis with NetFlow and IPFIX. *IEEE Communication Surveys & Tutorials*, 16(4):2037–2064, 2014.

[59] D. Horgan, J. Quan, D. Budden, G. Barth-Maron, M. Hessel, H. van Hasselt, and D. Silver. Distributed prioritized experience replay. *ArXiv*, 2018.

[60] R. Houthooft, X. Chen, Y. Duan, J. Schulman, F. De Turck, and Pieter Abbeel. VIME: Variational Information Maximizing Exploration. In *Proceedings of the International Conference on Neural Information Processing Systems (NIPS)*, 2016.

[61] X. Huang and J. Dong. Reliable control policy of cyber-physical systems against a class of frequency-constrained sensor and actuator attacks. *IEEE Transactions on Cybernetics*, 2018.

[62] Y. Bengio I. Goodfellow and A. Courvill. *Deep Learning*. The MIT Press, 2016.

[63] J. Inoue, Y. Yamagata, Y. Chen, C. M. Poskitt, and J. Sun. Anomaly detection for a water treatment system using unsupervised machine learning. *arXiv preprint arXiv:1709.05342*, 2017.

[64] M. R. Islam, M. M. S. Pahalovim, T. Adhikary, M. A. Razzaque, M. M. Hassan, and A. Alsanad. Optimal execution of virtualized network functions for applications in cyber-physical-social-systems. *IEEE Access*, 6:8755–8767, 2018.

[65] S. Levine J. Schulman and P. Abbeel. Trust Region Policy Optimization. In *Proceedings of the 31st International Conference on Machine Learning (ICML)*, pages 1889–1897, 2015.

[66] T. Jaakkola, S. P. Singh, and M. I. Jordan. Reinforcement learning algorithm for partially observable Markov decision problems. In *Proceedings of the 7th International Conference on Neural Information Processing Systems (NIPS)*, pages 345–352, 1994.

[67] M. Kadar, R. Jardim-Goncalves, C. Covaciu, and S. Bullon. Intelligent defect management system for porcelain industry through cyber-physical systems. In *International Conference on Engineering, Technology and Innovation (ICE/ITMC)*, pages 1338–1343, 2017.

[68] R. E. Kalman. A new approach to linear filtering and prediction problems. *Journal of Basic Engineering*, 82(Series D):35–45, 1960.

[69] G. Karatas and O. K. Sahingoz. Neural network based intrusion detection systems with different training functions. In *Proceedings of the 6th International Symposium on Digital Forensic and Security (ISDFS)*, pages 1–6, March 2018.

[70] U. Khurana, H. Samulowitz, and D. Turaga. Feature engineering for predictive modeling using reinforcement learning. *arXiv preprint*, 2017.

[71] H. Koc and P. P. Madupu. Optimizing energy consumption in cyber physical systems using multiple operating modes. In *IEEE Annual Computing and Communication Workshop and Conference (CCWC)*, pages 520–525, 2018.

[72] H. W. Kuhn. The Hungarian method for the assignment problem. *Naval Research Logistics Quarterly*, 2(1–2):83–97, 1955.

[73] M. N. Kurt, O. Ogundijo, C. Li, and X. Wang. Online cyber-attack detection in smart grid: A reinforcement learning approach. *IEEE Transactions on Smart Grid*, 2018.

[74] M. N. Kurt, Y. Yilmaz, and X. Wang. Real-Time Detection of Hybrid and Stealthy Cyber-Attacks in Smart Grid. *ArXiv e-prints*.

[75] M. N. Kurt, Y. Yilmaz, and X. Wang. Distributed quickest detection of cyber-attacks in smart grid. *IEEE Transactions on Information Forensics and Security*, 13(8):2015–2030, 2018.

[76] C. Kwon, W. Liu, and I. Hwang. Security analysis for cyber-physical systems against stealthy deception attacks. In *American Control Conference (ACC)*, pages 3344–3349, 2013.

[77] T. L. Lai and H. Robbins. Finite-time analysis of the multi-armed bandit problem. machine learning. *Advances in Applied Mathematics*, 6(1):4–12, 1985.

[78] S. Lakshminarayana, T. Z. Teng, D. Yau, and R. Tan. Optimal attack against cyber-physical control systems with reactive attack mitigation. In *Proceedings of the International Conference on Future Energy Systems*, pages 179–190, 2017.

[79] P. L. Lanzi. Adaptive agents with reinforcement learning and internal memory. In *Meyer, J.-A. et al., (Eds.), From Animals to Animats 6: Proceedings of the Sixth International Conference on the Simulation of Adaptive Behavior*, pages 333–342. MIT Press, 2000.

[80] Y. LeCun, L. Bottou, Y. Bengio, and P. Haffner. Gradient-based learning applied to document recognition. *Proceedings of the IEEE*, 86(11):2278–2324, 1998.

[81] E. Lee. The past, present and future of cyber-physical systems: A focus on models. *Sensors*, 15(3):4837–4869, Feb 2015.

[82] J. Lee, B. Bagheri, and H. A. Kao. A cyber-physical systems architecture for industry 4.0-based manufacturing systems. *Manufacturing Letters*, 3:18–23, 2015.

[83] S. Levine and V. Koltun. Guided policy search. In *Proceedings of the International Conference on Machine Learning (ICML)*, 2013.

[84] L. Li, W. Chu, J. Langford, and R. E. Schapire. A contextual-bandit approach to personalized news article recommendation. In *Proceedings of the 19th International Conference on World Wide Web*, pages 661–670, 2010.

[85] L. Li and M. L. Littman. Lazy approximation for solving continuous finite-horizon MDPs. In *AAAI*, pages 1175–1180, 2005.

[86] Q. Li, Y. Li, J. Gao, B. Zhao, W. Fan, and J. Han. Resolving conflicts in heterogeneous data by truth discovery and source reliability estimation. In *Proceedings of ACM Special Interest Group Manage. Data (SIGMOD)*, pages 1187–1198, Snowbird, UT, USA, 2014.

[87] S. Li, Q. Ni, Y. Sun, G. Min, and S. Al-Rubaye. Energy-efficient resource allocation for industrial cyber-physical IoT systems in 5G era. *IEEE Transactions on Industrial Informatics*, 14(6):2618–2628, 2018.

[88] S. Li, Y. Yilmaz, and X. Wang. Quickest detection of false data injection attack in wide-area smart grids. *IEEE Transactions on Smart Grid*, 6(6):2725–2735, Nov. 2015.

[89] G. Liang, J. Zhao, F. Luo, S. Weller, and Z. Y. Dong. A review of false data injection attacks against modern power systems. *IEEE Transactions on Smart Grid*, 8(4):1630–1638, 2016.

[90] T. P. Lillicrap, J. J. Hunt, A. Pritzel, N. Heess, T. Erez, Y. Tassa, D. Silver, and D. Wierstra. Continuous control with deep reinforcement learning. In *Proceedings of the International Conference on Learning Representations (ICLR)*, 2016.

[91] M. H. Ling, K. L. A. Yau, J. Qadir, G. S. Poh, and Q. Ni. Application of reinforcement learning for security enhancement in cognitive radio networks. *Applied Soft Computing*, 37(C):809–829, 2015.

[92] P. Liu, Y. Gao, and W. Guo. Improved krill group algorithm based on natural selection and stochastic perturbation. In *Small Microcomputer System (MICO), 38(8)*, pages 1845–1849, 2017.

[93] Y. Liu, P. Ning, and M. K. Reiter. False data injection attacks against state estimation in electric power grids. In *Proceedings of the 16th ACM Conference on Computer and Communications Security*, pages 21–32, New York, NY, USA, 2009.

[94] J. Loch and S. P. Singh. Using eligibility traces to find the best memoryless policy in partially observable Markov decision processes. In *Proceedings of the International Conference on Machine Learning (ICML)*, pages 323–331, San Francisco, CA, USA, 1998.

[95] G. Lorden. Procedures for reacting to a change in distribution. *Ann. Math. Statist.*, 42(6):1897–1908, 1971.

[96] L. Ma, L. Tao, K. Gai, and Y. Zhong. A novel social network access control model using logical authorization language in cloud computing. *Concurrency and Computation: Practice and Experience*, 29(14), 2017.

[97] L. Ma, L. Tao, Y. Zhong, and K. Gai. RuleSN: Research and application of social network access control model. In *Proceedings of International Conference on Intelligent Data and Security*, pages 418–423, New York, USA, 2016.

[98] K. Manandhar, X. Cao, F. Hu, and Y. Liu. Detection of faults and attacks including false data injection attack in smart grid using kalman filter. *IEEE Transactions on Control of Network Systems*, 1(4):370–379, Dec 2014.

[99] W. Manuel, S. Jost, B. Joschka, and R. Martin. Rectified linear units improve restricted boltzmann machines. In *Proceedings of the International Conference on Neural Information Processing Systems (NIPS)*, pages 2746–2754, 2015.

[100] S. Mazumdar, E. Ayguade, N. Bettin, et al. Axiom: A hardware-software platform for cyber physical systems. In *Euromicro Conference on Digital System Design (DSD)*, pages 539–546, 2016.

[101] N. Meuleau, L. Peshkin, K-E. Kim, and L. P. Kaelbling. Learning finite-state controllers for partially observable environments. In *Proceedings of the Fifteenth Conference on Uncertainty in Artificial Intelligence*, pages 427–436, San Francisco, CA, USA, 1999.

[102] R. Meyes, H. Tercan, S. Roggendorf, et al. Motion planning for industrial robots using reinforcement learning. *Procedia CIRP*, 63:107–112, 2017.

[103] D. Michie. Trial and error. *Science Survey*, pages 129–145.

[104] D. Michie. *On Machine Intelligence*. Edinburgh University Press, Edinburgh, 1974.

[105] D. Michie and R. A. Chambers. Boxes: An experiment in adaptive control. *Machine intelligence*, 2(2):137–152, 1968.

[106] M. Minsky. Steps toward artificial intelligence. In *Proceedings of the IRE*, pages 8–30, 1961.

[107] M. L. Minsky. *Theory of neural-analog reinforcement systems and its application to the brain-model problem*. PhD thesis, Princeton University, 1954.

[108] V. Mnih, A. P. Badia, M. Mirza, et al. Asynchronous methods for deep reinforcement learning. In *Proceedings of the International Conference on Learning Representations (ICLR)*, 2016.

[109] V. Mnih, K. Kavukcuoglu, D. Silver, et al. Human-level control through deep reinforcement learning. *Nature*, 518(7540):529–533, 2015.

[110] H. Mo and G. Sansavini. Dynamic defense resource allocation for minimizing unsupplied demand in cyber-physical systems against uncertain attacks. *IEEE Transactions on Reliability*, 66(4):1253–1265, 2017.

[111] S. Mohamed and D. J. Rezende. Variational information maximization for intrinsically motivated reinforcement learning. In *Proceedings of the International Conference on Neural Information Processing Systems (NIPS)*, 2015.

[112] G. V. Moustakides. Optimal stopping times for detecting changes in distributions. *Ann. Statist.*, 14(4):1379–1387, 1986.

[113] S. Mukkamala, G. Janoski, and A. Sung. Intrusion detection using neural networks and support vector machines. In *Proceedings of the International Joint Conference on Neural Networks*, volume 2, pages 1702–1707, 2002.

[114] A. Nair, P. Srinivasan, S. Blackwell, et al. Massively parallel methods for deep reinforcement learning. *ArXiv*, 2015.

[115] V. Nair and G. E. Hinton. Rectified linear units improve restricted Boltzmann machines. In *Proceedings of the International Conference on Machine Learning (ICML)*, pages 807–814, 2010.

[116] V. Navda, A. Bohra, S. Ganguly, and D. Rubenstein. Using channel hopping to increase 802.11 resilience to jamming attacks. *IEEE 26th Conference on Computer Communications (INFOCOM)*, pages 2526–2530, 2007.

[117] Y. Nevmyvaka, Y. Feng, and M. Kearns. Reinforcement learning for optimized trade execution. In *Proceedings of the International Conference on Machine learning (ICML)*, pages 673–680, 2006.

[118] M. Nielsen. *Neural Networks and Deep Learning.* Online ebook: http://neuralnetworksanddeeplearning.com/index.html, 2016.

[119] W. Niklas, B. S. Thomas, and M. P. Deisenroth. Learning deep dynamical models from image pixels. In *Proceedings of IFAC Symposium on System Identification (SYSID)*, 2015.

[120] W. Niklas, B. S. Thomas, and M. P. Deisenroth. Policy learning with deep dynamical models. In *International Conference on Machine Learning Workshop on Deep Learning*, 2015.

[121] J. Oh, X. Guo, H. Lee, R. L. Lewis, and S. Singh. Action-conditional video prediction using deep networks in Atari games. In *Proceedings of the International Conference on Neural Information Processing Systems (NIPS)*, 2015.

[122] X. Pan, Y. You, Z. Wang, and C. Lu. Virtual to real reinforcement learning for autonomous driving. *ArXiv*, 2017.

[123] Y. P. Pane, S. P. Nageshrao, and R. Babuska. Actor-critic reinforcement learning for tracking control in robotics. In *IEEE Conference on Decision and Control (CDC)*, pages 5819–5826, 2016.

[124] R. Pascanu, Y. Li, O. Vinyals, N. Heess, et al. Learning model-based planning from scratch. *arXiv:1707.06170*, 2017.

[125] D. Pathak, P. Agrawal, A. A. Efros, and T. Darrell. Curiosity-driven exploration by self-supervised prediction. In *Proceedings of the International Conference on Machine Learning (ICML)*, 2017.

[126] T. J. Perkins. Reinforcement learning for POMDPs based on action values and stochastic optimization. In *AAAI*, pages 199–204, Menlo Park, CA, USA, 2002.

[127] L. Peshkin, N. Meuleau, and L. P. Kaelbling. Learning policies with external memory. *CoRR*, cs.LG/0103003, 2001.

[128] A. S. Polunchenko and A. G. Tartakovsky. State-of-the-art in sequential change-point detection. *Methodology and Computing in Applied Probability*, 14(3):649–684, Sep 2012.

[129] M. Pontil. Advanced topics in machine learning. *GI13 Course Exam Notes, University College London*, 2005.

[130] H. V. Poor and O. Hadjiliadis. *Quickest Detection*. Cambridge University Press, 2008.

[131] S. Racaniere, T. Weber, D. P. Reichert, L. Buesing, et al. Imagination-augmented agents for deep reinforcement learning. In *Advances in Neural Information Processing Systems*, pages 5690–5701, 2017.

[132] R. R. Rajkumar, I. Lee, L. Sha, and J. Stankovic. Cyber-physical systems: The next computing revolution. In *Proceedings of the 47th Design Automation Conference*, pages 731–736. ACM, 2010.

[133] J. Randlv and P. Alstrm. Learning to drive a bicycle using reinforcement learning and shaping. In *Proceedings of the International Conference on Machine Learning (ICML)*, pages 463–471, 1998.

[134] D. B. Rawat and C. Bajracharya. Detection of false data injection attacks in smart grid communication systems. *IEEE Signal Processing Letters*, 22(10):1652–1656, Oct 2015.

[135] T. C. Reed. *At the Abyss: An Insider's History of the Cold War*. Presidio Press, 2005.

[136] R. L. Rivest, L. Adleman, and M. L. Dertouzos. On data banks and privacy homomorphisms. *Foundations of Secure Computation, Academia Press*, pages 169–179, 1978.

[137] H. Robbins. Some aspects of the sequential design of experiments. *Bulletin of the American Mathematical Society*, 58(5):527–535, 1952.

[138] M. Rosenberg and N. Confessore. Justice department and F.B.I. are investigating Cambridge Analytica. *The New York Times*, May 2018.

[139] S. Ross, J. Pineau, B. Chaib-draa, and P. Kreitmann. A Bayesian approach for learning and planning in partially observable Markov decision processes. *J. Mach. Learn. Res.*, 12:1729–1770, July 2011.

[140] D. E. Rumelhart, G. E. Hinton, and R. J. Williams. Learning representations by back-propagating errors. *Nature*, 323(6088):533, 1986.

[141] S. Shammah S. Shalev-Shwartz and A. Shashua. https://www.dropbox.com/s/136nbndtdyehtgi/, 2016.

[142] B. Satchidanandan and P. R. Kumar. Secure control of networked cyber-physical systems. In *Proceedings of IEEE Conference on Decision and Control (CDC)*, pages 283–289, 2016.

[143] J. Schmidhuber. A possibility for implementing curiosity and boredom in model-building neural controllers. *In SAB*, 1991.

[144] J. Schulman, P. Moritz, S. Levine, M. Jordan, and P. Abbeel. High-dimensional continuous control using generalized advantage estimation. In *Proceedings of the International Conference on Learning Representations (ICLR)*, 2016.

[145] H. Van Seijen, H. Van Hasselt, S. Whiteson, and M. Wiering. A theoretical and empirical analysis of expected sarsa. *IEEE Symposium on Adaptive Dynamic Programming and Reinforcement Learning*, 2009.

[146] B. Shahriari, K. Swersky, Z. Wang, R. P. Adams, and N. Freitas. Taking the human out of the loop: A review of Bayesian optimization. *Proceedings of the IEEE*, 104(1):148–175, 2016.

[147] S. Shalev-Shwartz, S. Shammah, and A. Shashua. Safe, multi-agent, reinforcement learning for autonomous driving. *arXiv preprint arXiv:1610.03295*, 2016.

[148] J. Shin, Y. Baek, Y. Eun, and S. H. Son. Intelligent sensor attack detection and identification for automotive cyber-physical systems. In *IEEE Symposium Series on Computational Intelligence (SSCI)*, pages 1–8, 2017.

[149] J. Silberholz and B. Golden. *Comparison of Metaheuristics*, pages 625–640. Springer US, Boston, MA, 2010.

[150] D. Silver, A. Huang, and *et al.* C. J. Maddison. Mastering the game of go with deep neural networks and tree search. *Nature*, 529(7587):484–489, 2016.

[151] D. Silver, G. Lever, N. Heess, T. Degris, D. Wierstra, and M. Riedmiller. Deterministic policy gradient algorithms. In *Proceedings of the International Conference on Machine learning (ICML)*, 2014.

[152] S. P. Singh and R. S. Sutton. Reinforcement learning with replacing eligibility traces. *Machine Learning*, 22:123–158, 1996.

[153] J. Slay and M. Miller. Lessons learned from the Maroochy water breach. In *International Conference on Critical Infrastructure Protection*, pages 73–82. Springer, 2007.

[154] E. J. Sondik. The optimal control of partially observable Markov processes. Technical report, Stanford, 1971.

[155] B. C. Stadie, S. Levine, and P. Abbeel. Incentivizing Exploration in Reinforcement Learning with Deep Predictive Models. In *Proceedings of the International Conference on Neural Information Processing Systems (NIPS)*, 2015.

[156] W. Stallings. *Cryptography and Network Security: Principles and Practice*. Pearson Education India, 2003.

[157] R. S. Sutton. Single channel theory: A neuronal theory of learning. *Brain Theory Newsletter*, 4:72–75, 1978.

[158] R. S. Sutton and A. G. Barto. Toward a modern theory of adaptive networks: Expectation and prediction. *Psychological Review*, 88(2):135, 1981.

[159] R. S. Sutton and A. G. Barto. *Reinforcement Learning: An Introduction*. MIT press Cambridge, 1998.

[160] R. S. Sutton, D. A. McAllester, S. P. Singh, and Y. Mansour. Policy gradient methods for reinforcement learning with function approximation. In *Proceedings of the International Conference on Neural Information Processing Systems (NIPS)*, volume 12, pages 1057–1063, 1999.

[161] J. Sztipanovits. Cyber physical systems: New challenges for model-based design. 2008. Report.

[162] S. Tan, D. De, W. Z. Song, J. Yang, and S. K. Das. Survey of security advances in smart grid: A data driven approach. *IEEE Communications Surveys Tutorials*, 19(1):397–422, 2017.

[163] H. Tang, S. Feng, X. Zhao, and Y. Jin. Virtav: An agentless antivirus system based on in-memory signature scanning for virtual machine. In *Proceedings of the 18th International Conference on Advanced Communication Technology (ICACT)*, pages 124–133, Jan 2016.

[164] A. Teixeira, S. Amin, H. Sandberg, K. H. Johansson, and S. S. Sastry. Cyber security analysis of state estimators in electric power systems. In *Proceedings of the 49th IEEE Conference on Decision and Control (CDC)*, pages 5991–5998, 2010.

[165] W. R. Thompson. On the likelihood that one unknown probability exceeds another in view of the evidence of two samples. *Biometrika*, 25(3-4):285–294, 1933.

[166] S. Thrun and L. Pratt. *Learning to Learn*. Kluwer Academic Publishers Norwell, MA, USA, 1998.

[167] R. Tkatchuk. Is data the currency of the future? *CIO*, Sep. 2017.

[168] W. T. Uther and M. M. Veloso. Tree based discretization for continuous state space reinforcement learning. In *AAAI/IAAI*, pages 769–774, 1998.

[169] V. V. Veeravalli and T. Banerjee. Quickest change detection. In *Academic Press Library in Signal Processing: Array and Statistical Signal Processing*, volume 3, pages 209–255. Elsevier, 2014.

[170] M. Vilgelm, O. Ayan, S. Zoppi, and W. Kellerer. Control-aware uplink resource allocation for cyber-physical systems in wireless networks. In *Proceedings of 23th European Wireless Conference;*, pages 1–7, 2017.

[171] G. C. Walsh and H. Ye. Scheduling of networked control systems. *IEEE Control Systems*, 21(1):57–65, Feb 2001.

[172] M. Waltz and K. Fu. A heuristic approach to reinforcement learning control systems. *IEEE Transactions on Automatic Control*, 10(4):390–398, 1965.

[173] J. Wan, D. Zhang, Y. Sun, K. Lin, C. Zou, and H. Cai. VCMIA: A novel architecture for integrating vehicular cyber-physical systems and mobile cloud computing. *Mobile Networks and Applications*, 19(2):153–160, 2014.

[174] B. Wang, Y. Wu, K. J. R. Liu, and T. C. Clancy. An anti-jamming stochastic game for cognitive radio networks. *IEEE Journal on Selected Areas in Communications*, 29(4):877–889, 2011.

[175] E. K. Wang, Y. Ye, X. Xu, S-M. Yiu, L. C. K. Hui, and K-P. Chow. Security issues and challenges for cyber physical system. In *Proceedings of the IEEE/ACM Int'l Conference on Green Computing and Communications & Int'l Conference on Cyber, Physical and Social Computing*, pages 733–738, 2010.

[176] H. Wang, J. Li, and H. Gao. Dynamic resource allocation of gateways for packet transmission in cyber-physical systems. In *Proceedings of the 11th International Conference on Mobile Ad-hoc and Sensor Networks (MSN)*, pages 150–157, 2015.

[177] W. Wang, L. Chen, K. G. Shin, and L. Duan. Thwarting intelligent malicious behaviors in cooperative spectrum sensing. *IEEE Journal on Selected Areas in Communications*, 14(11):2392–2405, 2015.

[178] W. Wang and Z. Lu. Cyber security in the smart grid: Survey and challenges. *Computer Networks*, 57(5):1344–1371, 2013.

[179] C. Watkins and J. C. Hellaby. *Learning from delayed rewards*. PhD thesis, King's College, Cambridge, 1989.

[180] J. Wei and G. J. Mendis. A deep learning-based cyber-physical strategy to mitigate false data injection attack in smart grids. In *Joint Workshop on Cyber-Physical Security and Resilience in Smart Grids (CPSR-SG)*, pages 1–6, 2016.

[181] B. Widrow, N. K. Gupta, and S. Maitra. Punish/reward: Learning with a critic in adaptive threshold systems. *IEEE Transactions on Systems, Man, and Cybernetics*, (5):455–465, 1973.

[182] Wikipedia. Sufficient statistic, 2018. [Online; accessed 9-April-2018].

[183] R. J. Williams. Simple statistical gradient-following algorithms for connectionist reinforcement learning. *Machine Learning*, 6:229–256, 1992.

[184] R. J. Williams and L. C. Baird. Tight performance bounds on greedy policies based on imperfect value functions. Technical report, Citeseer, 1993.

[185] I. H. Witten. An adaptive optimal controller for discrete-time Markov environments. *Information and Control*, 34(4):286–295, 1977.

[186] W. Wolf. News briefs. *Computer*, 40(11):104–105, Nov. 2007.

[187] A. Wood and J. Stankovic. Denial of service in sensor networks. *IEEE Computer*, 35(10):54–62, 2002.

[188] D. Work, A. Bayen, and Q. Jacobson. Automotive cyber physical systems in the context of human mobility. In *National Workshop on High-Confidence Automotive Cyber-Physical Systems*, pages 3–4, 2008.

[189] G. Wu, W. Bao, X. Zhu, W. Xiao, and J. Wang. Optimal dynamic reserved bandwidth allocation for cloud-integrated cyber-physical systems. *IEEE Access*, 5:26224–26236, 2017.

[190] L. Xiao, Y. Li, G. Han, H. Dai, and H. V. Poor. A secure mobile crowdsensing game with deep reinforcement learning. *IEEE Transactions on Information Forensics and Security*, 2017.

[191] L. Xiao, Y. Li, G. Han, G. Liu, and W. Zhuang. PHY-layer spoofing detection with reinforcement learning in wireless networks. *IEEE Transactions on Vehicular Technology*, 65(12):10037–10047, 2016.

[192] L. Xiao, Y. Li, X. Huang, and X. Du. Cloud-based malware detection game for mobile device with offloading. *IEEE Transactions on Mobile Computing*, 16(10):2742–2750, 2017.

[193] L. Xiao, X. Wan, C. Dai, X. Du, X. Chen, and M. Guizani. Security in mobile edge caching with reinforcement learning. *arXiv preprint arXiv:1801.05915*, 2018.

[194] C. Xie and L. Xiao. User-centric view of smart attacks in wireless networks. In *IEEE International Conference on Ubiquitous Wireless Broadband*, pages 1–6, 2017.

[195] L. Xie, Y. Mo, and B. Sinopoli. False data injection attacks in electricity markets. In *Proceedings of the 1st IEEE International Conference on Smart Grid Communications*, pages 226–231, Oct. 2010.

[196] W. Xu, T. Wood, W. Trappe, and Y. Zhang. Channel surfing and spatial retreats: Defenses against wireless denial of service. In *Proceedings of the 3rd ACM Workshop on Wireless Security (WiSe)*, pages 80–89, 2004.

[197] Z. Xu and Q. Zhu. Secure and practical output feedback control for cloud-enabled cyber-physical systems. In *IEEE Conference on Communications and Network Security (CNS)*, pages 416–420, 2017.

[198] J. Yan, H. He, X. Zhong, and Y. Tang. Q-learning-based vulnerability analysis of smart grid against sequential topology attacks. *IEEE Transactions on Information Forensics and Security*, 12(1):200–210, Jan 2017.

[199] Y. Yan, Y. Qian, H. Sharif, and D. Tipper. A survey on cyber security for smart grid communications. *IEEE Communications Surveys & Tutorials*, 2012.

[200] K. Yang, D. Blaauw, and D. Sylvester. Hardware designs for security in ultra-low-power IoT systems: An overview and survey. *IEEE Micro*, 37(6):72–89, November 2017.

[201] Y. Yang, Y. Ma, W. Xiang, X. Gu, and H. Zhao. Joint optimization of energy consumption and packet scheduling for mobile edge computing in cyber-physical networks. *IEEE Access*, 6:15576–15586, 2018.

[202] H. Yin, K. Gai, and Z. Wang. A classification algorithm based on ensemble feature selections for imbalanced-class dataset. In *Proceedings of the 2nd IEEE International Conference on High Performance and Smart Computing*, pages 245–249, New York, USA, 2016.

[203] B. Yoshua, L. Jerome, C. Ronan, and W. Jason. Curriculum learning. In *Proceedings of the International Conference on Machine Learning (ICML)*, 2009.

[204] T. Young, D. Hazarika, S. Poria, and E. Cambria. Recent trends in deep learning based natural language processing. *arXiv preprint arXiv:1708.02709*, 2017.

[205] A. Yu, R. Palefsky-Smith, and R. Bedi. Deep reinforcement learning for simulated autonomous vehicle control. *Course Project Reports: Winter*, pages 1–7, 2016.

[206] Y. Zhang, L. Wang, W. Sun, R. C. Green, and M. Alam. Distributed intrusion detection system in a multi-layer network architecture of smart grids. *IEEE Transactions on Smart Grid*, 2(4):796–808, 2011.

[207] Y. Zhang, I-L. Yen, F. B. Bastani, A. T. Tai, and S. Chau. Optimal adaptive system health monitoring and diagnosis for resource constrained cyber-physical systems. In *Proceedings of the*

20th International Symposium on Software Reliability Engineering, pages 51–60, 2009.

[208] Q. Zhu, C. Rieger, and T. Bassar. A hierarchical security architecture for cyber-physical systems. In *Proceedings of the 4th International Symposium on Resilient Control Systems (ISRCS)*, pages 15–20, 2011.

[209] R. D. Zimmerman, C. E. Murillo-Snchez, and R. J. Thomas. Matpower: Steady-state operations, planning, and analysis tools for power systems research and education. *IEEE Transactions on Power Systems*, 26(1):12–19, Feb. 2011.

Index